WAR
WALKS 2

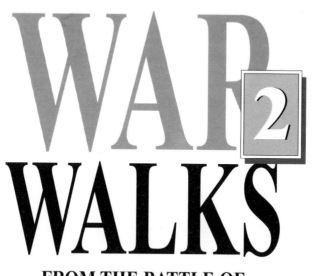

WAR 2 WALKS

FROM THE BATTLE OF
HASTINGS TO THE BLITZ

Richard Holmes

I would like to thank my wife Lizzie and daughters
Jessica and Corinna for showing tolerance beyond the call of
duty while I wrote this book and neglected them. My horse
Thatch carried me over three of these battlefields on his
broad back, and Frances McDonald kept the old
ruffian fed, watered and happy.

This book was published to accompany the second television
series of *War Walks* which was first broadcast in 1997
Executive Producer Grant Mansfield · Series Producer Mark Fielder ·
Producer/Directors Rachel Bell, Steven Clarke, Mark Fielder and Keith Sheather

Published by BBC Worldwide Limited,
Woodlands, 80 Wood Lane, London W12 0TT

First published in Hardback 1997
Reprinted 1997, 1998
This paperback edition was first published in 1998
© Richard Holmes 1997
The moral right of the author has been asserted

ISBN 0 563 38386 0 (hardback)
ISBN 0 563 38481 6 (paperback)

Photographic acknowledgements

BBC Books would like to thank the following for providing photographs and for permission to
reproduce copyright material. While every effort has been made to trace and acknowledge all copyright holders, we would like to apologize should there be any errors or omissions.

Page 13 (above) © Michael Holford (below) © British Museum; p.19 (above) The Royal
Armouries, Leeds (below) Kunsthistorisches Museum, Vienna; p.25 & 38 © Michael Holford;
p.43 Collections/© David Bowie; p.45 (above) The Royal Armouries, Leeds (below) ET Archive;
p.54–55 (above & below) The Royal Armouries, Leeds (centre) ET Archive; p.66 The University of
Ghent; p.70 National Portrait Gallery; p.71 The Bridgeman Art Library; p.78–79 (both)
Collections/© David M Hughes; p 85 (main picture) The Fotomas Index (cut-out) The Royal
Armouries, Leeds; p.90 The Bridgeman Art Library/Alnwick Castle, Northumberland; p.94 The
Bridgeman Art Library/Forbes Magazine Collection, New York; p.95 (both) The Royal Armouries;
p.97 & 98 National Portrait Gallery; p.114–115 The Fotomas Index; p.121(left) The Fotomas Index
(right) Mary Evans Picture Library; p.128–129 (both) The Royal Armouries; p.134 Ulster Museum,
Belfast; p.135 The Bridgeman Art Library/Scottish National Portrait Gallery; p.144 ET
Archive/National Army Museum; p.147 Mary Evans Picture Library; p.151 © Pacemaker Press
International; p.153 (above) Aviation Picture Library/Imperial War Museum © Austin J Brown
(centre) ET Archive/Imperial War Museum (below) Hulton Getty; p.154–155 ET Archive/Imperial
War Museum; p.163 Imperial War Museum; p.169 Dover Museum; p.177 & 179 Imperial War
Museum; p.185 © Times Newspapers Ltd; p.191 (both) Hulton Getty; p.195 (left) Imperial War
Museum (right) Hulton Getty; p.197 (both) Imperial War Museum; p.209 Imperial War Museum;
p.211 ET Archive © Imperial War Museum; p.215 Imperial War Museum.

Maps by Line and Line
Picture research by Deirdre O'Day

Set in Times New Roman
Printed and bound in Great Britain by Butler and Tanner Ltd, Frome and London
Colour separations by Radstock Reproductions, Midsomer Norton
Jacket printed by Lawrence Allen Ltd, Weston-super-Mare
Cover printed by Belmont Press Ltd, Northampton

Contents

Introduction

In a sense this is an unfashionable book, for historiography has long moved away from 'scraps and chaps'. Yet battles and the men who fought them are important: more so than we might wish to admit in an age when war's credibility as a means of pursuing political aims is increasingly questioned. And they are particularly momentous for Britain, a nation and a people whose history has been marked by war.

Britain's experience of conflict has been conditioned by that quirk of geography which placed the English Channel's 'moat defensive' between her and mainland Europe. Triumphant invasion has been rare. If we exclude William of Orange's almost unopposed arrival in 1688, Britain has not been successfully invaded since 1066. There is no livid scar of national capitulation, no plundered capital or lost provinces. There is even less evidence of military preparation: Britain's medieval castles and twentieth-century pill-boxes scarcely compete with a continental landscape littered with ravelins, bastions, casemates, cupolas and all the other paraphernalia of military engineering. And while compulsory military service became the norm in a Europe compelled to have big battalions in waiting, Britain was able to avoid it until the First World War.

When Britons fought they usually did so abroad. Sometimes, like the Scots and Irish adventurers who made such a remarkable contribution to European armies from the sixteenth to the nineteenth century, they soldiered on the basis of private enterprise. Sometimes, profiting by Francis Bacon's maxim that a nation which enjoyed command of the sea could take as much or as little of the war as it wished, Britain used her seapower to send expeditionary forces across the globe. Latterly the two world wars saw millions of Britons fight abroad, most of them in a North-West Europe sprinkled with the cemeteries which testify to the devotion of two generations, and scarcely fewer across the world's continents and oceans.

Choosing the Battles

This book focuses, in contrast, on battles in Britain – or, in one case, on a struggle which straddled the Channel. Choosing six battles from a long list of potential candidates was far from easy, but each has a logic of its own. Hastings (1066) selected itself. The opposing commanders were men on a dramatic scale. Its consequences were far-reaching, for it brought a change of dynasty, ruling class, language and culture. It is particularly well-documented for the battles of the age, and its battlefield remains striking.

Selecting a later medieval battle was more difficult. Bannockburn (1314), Robert Bruce's great victory over Edward II, was a strong possibility: so too was Towton (1461), the bloodiest battle ever fought on English soil. Eventually I decided on Bosworth (1485), partly because of its political consequences – it was midwife to the Tudor dynasty, and in that sense more influential even than Bannockburn – and partly because of the extraordinary conundrum of Richard III, part-hero and part-villain, who died on its field, fighting manfully to the last.

There was less reflection on Naseby (1645). Although Marston Moor, fought the year before, was a much bigger battle, Naseby was the climax of the Civil War, a clash whose result determined the war's outcome, and which brought several of the war's leading protagonists – Charles I, Prince Rupert, Sir Thomas Fairfax and Oliver Cromwell – together. It was a decisive battle, whose loss saw Charles accelerate his slide down the slippery slope which was to end on a scaffold in freezing Whitehall.

The restoration of the monarchy in 1660 might have been followed by lasting peace had it not been for the personality of James II, last of the ruling Stuarts. After his 'abdication' – deposition might be a fairer word – in 1688 there were several attempts to restore him or his successors to the throne. Jacobite victory would have changed Britain's political landscape, and so one of the great Jacobite battles in Ireland in 1690–91 or in Scotland in 1745–6 had to appear in these pages. I shied away from Culloden (1746) because it has already been described so well, in print and on film, that I felt there was nothing new to add, however much the poignancy of the bagpipes shrieking through the sleet captures the imagination.

The Boyne (1690) was different. It is part of the enduring mythology of Irish history, freshly remembered, or bitterly detested, as each summer brings the marching season to Northern Ireland. It saw the personal

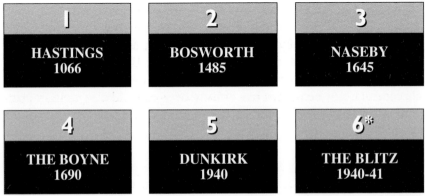

1	2	3
HASTINGS **1066**	**BOSWORTH** **1485**	**NASEBY** **1645**

4	5	6*
THE BOYNE **1690**	**DUNKIRK** **1940**	**THE BLITZ** **1940-41**

* Although London was most heavily bombed, other cities and towns were also attacked.

confrontation of James II and William III on a river which already had enormous cultural significance – the tomb at Newgrange, on the battle-field, is the oldest building known to man. And yet its details are, by comparison with Culloden, poorly catalogued, with much of the relevant research in that admirable journal *The Irish Sword* which, for all its virtues, scarcely enjoys a mass readership.

Napoleon had his invasion schemes, though it is doubtful whether even he took them seriously. His nephew Napoleon III seemed threaten-ing enough for those red-brick forts to be built on Portsdown Hill to defend the naval base of Portsmouth against attack by a French army which had landed on the south coast. But it was not really until the First World War that Britain was again in serious peril, and this time the threat came not from invading armies but from German U-Boats.

The struggle against submarines in both world wars is a story worth retelling, but it would have fitted uncomfortably into a book like this where the relationship of men to the ground on which they they fought is so important. I chose Dunkirk (1940) because the loss of the British Expeditionary Force (the outcome robustly predicted by its commander, Lord Gort) would have made the pressure for a compromise peace extra-ordinarily hard to withstand. The operation was controlled from Dover, from tunnels under a castle built by the Conqueror's son, and although historians are right to warn that the contribution made by the 'little ships' is easily over-rated, it was nonetheless a remarkable flowering of national resolve.

Hastings had been fought by a tiny proportion of England's popula-tion, and many of these who died there were professional warriors. At Dunkirk, though, the professionals were few and the amateurs many, and when the Germans began air attacks on the United Kingdom distinctions between combatants and non-combatants were blurred. The final chapter, therefore, examines the Blitz and the Battle of Britain which led up to it. It is as close as my parents' recollections and my own memories of a London pockmarked by bomb damage. Hitler, as Churchill knew, had to 'break us in this island or lose the war.' The Blitz, in its way, was as decisive as Hastings, nearly nine hundred years before, although many of its combatants were housewives rather than household troops, and its bat-tlefield was not a sandy ridge in Sussex but the streets and squares of the nation's cities.

Using This Book

Each chapter has three parts. The first puts events into political and military context, the second describes campaign and battle, and the third, 'a view of the field', suggests ways in which the battlefield can be visited. Any battlefield tour is greatly improved by a map – the Ordnance Survey Landranger 1:50,000 scale, or the rather better Pathfinder 1:25,000 for England. Ireland is in the process of being re-mapped, and, as this book went to press, Meath (the sheet covering the Boyne battlefield) was still only available in the old 1:126,720 scale, though a more modern edition is imminent. A compass is also a help, for north can sometimes seem elusive without one.

Notable Museums

Although most chapters give specific recommendations for museums, three deserve early mention. A visit to the Royal Armouries, now in its splendid new accommodation at Leeds, will bring helmet and hauberk, matchlock and flintlock, bill and baldric to life, and its painstaking re-enactments give a good idea of the skills required by the men of iron whose footsteps we follow. The National Army Museum, Royal Hospital Road, Chelsea, now includes a gallery whose life-size figures could easily have swaggered or slouched away from Bosworth, Naseby or the Boyne. I am particularly fond of that doughty cavalier, Captain Richard Atkyns of Prince Maurice's Regiment of Horse. The Imperial War Museum, south of the River Thames in Lambeth, is concerned with the two world wars and post-war campaigns: both it and its satellite, on the old airfield at Duxford near Cambridge, richly repay a visit.

The Preservation of Battlefields

Britain has not been good at preserving battlefields or providing visitors with help in their interpretation: the visitors' centre at Bosworth is one of the few honourable exceptions. There may be a Victorian memorial, but it is often in the wrong place and sometimes vandalized. Worse still, new roads dissect haunted acres, and brick and concrete mask vital ground. It is rarely easy to combine progress with preservation, but battlefields have often fared worse than they ought. I applaud the efforts of the Battlefields Trust, which has helped English Heritage to compile a register of battlefields and does its best to ensure that they are not ravaged in the cause of progress. The Trust is always eager for more members, and its co-ordinator is Michael Rayner, Meadow Cottage, 33 High Green, Brooke, Norwich NR15 1HR.

'Every man thinks meanly of himself for not having been a soldier, or not having been at sea,' declared Samuel Johnson.

'Lord Mansfield does not,' replied James Boswell.

'Sir,' retorted Johnson, 'if Lord Mansfield were in a company of generals or admirals who'd seen service he'd wish to creep under the table.'

There is in many of us a desire, not perhaps to trail a pike or shoulder a musket ourselves, but to understand something about those who did. If this book does nothing else, it ought to bring us closer to our forebears who played their part in life's most passionate drama and, all too often, died doing their duty as they saw it.

CHAPTER I

Hastings
1066

Background

Hastings was a clash of Titans. William the Bastard, Duke of Normandy, was at the height of his powers. He was about 38 years old, 5 feet 10 inches (178 cm) tall, with a stockiness that would turn to corpulence in later life, red hair cropped at back and sides in the Norman fashion and fleshy face smooth-shaven. So physically tough that he could carry another man's armour as well as his own, he was harsh to the point of brutality. In 1051 citizens of Alençon had waved cow hides from the walls of their besieged town to remind William of his humble origins (his mother was the daughter of a tanner). William, to retaliate, had some of the citizens skinned when he took the place.

Harold Godwinson, King of England, was about 45. Tall and handsome, with the long hair and moustaches in the Saxon style 'he stood before the people as another Judas Maccabeus'. Like his rival he was an experienced soldier, with a reputation for dash and quick decision. When the two met on a sandy Sussex ridge that bright October day, beneath the leopards of Normandy and the dragon of Wessex, it was a fight to the death.

Yet Hastings was more than an epic struggle between two towering personalities. It was that rare event, an utterly decisive battle. One side defeated the other – and killed its leader into the bargain – in a clash which decided the war. The long-term political, social and economic changes that flowed from it were nothing short of revolutionary. It was the end of the Saxon England of ale-bench and bright mead, folk-moot, earl and churl, of monarchs who were sometimes little more, and occasionally rather less, than first amongst equals. In their place came a king who

The Bayeux Tapestry shows how, at
the height of the battle, William pushed
back his helmet to show his shaken troops
that he was still alive. Count Eustace
of Boulogne, who has seized the papal
banner, points to the Duke, helping him
rally the army. William carries a wooden
club, a symbol of his authority rather
than a practical weapon. The knight on
the left wields a cruciform-hilted sword,
similar to that in the centre photograph.
At the bottom right is a great axe, swung
two-handed, with deadly effect, by many
of Harold's men.

affirmed that he ruled the land, and that his nobles, no matter how mighty, held territory as his tenants and owed him counsel and support.

One of the Conqueror's biographers summed him up as 'admirable; unlovable; dominant; distinct'. He may have been a hero to the Normans, but the English and their Scandinavian kinsmen lamented that:

Cold heart and bloody hand
Now rule the English land.

It is small wonder that the echoes of 1066 reverberated for centuries. Nearly six hundred years later, at the time of the Civil War, the Levellers complained of the 'Norman Yoke' and looked back to an imagined Eden when every man was as good as his fellow. Sir Walter Scott's *Ivanhoe,* pitting cruel Normans against brave if sometimes muddle-headed Saxons, was part of a wider perception which cast the Norman as part-villain, part fall-guy. And when W. J. Sellar and R. J. Yeatman wrote their wonderful spoof history almost seventy years ago they fastened on one of the only two dates they thought every schoolboy would know, and called it *1066 and All That.*

Hastings is extraordinarily well-documented for a battle of the period. History has a tendency to be written by the victors, and Hastings is, by and large, no exception. William of Poitiers and William of Jumièges wrote contemporary accounts from the Norman point of view, and Guy, Bishop of Amiens, probable author of the *Carmen de Hastingae Proelio,* identified with William's French–Flemish allies. Ordericus Vitalis and Robert Wace, wrote, slightly later, from the Norman standpoint. Three versions of *The Anglo-Saxon Chronicle*, together with the monks William of Malmesbury and Florence of Worcester, tell the Saxon side of the story. All vary in style and reliability. William of Poitiers, for instance, cast Duke William as a classical hero for an audience who expected as much entertainment as history, while *The Anglo-Saxon Chronicle* simply catalogued those events which seemed, to its monkish authors, to be important.

Finally, the Bayeux tapestry provides another invaluable source. It is an embroidered scroll 20 inches (51 cm) high and 230 feet (70 m) long, and was made, possibly at the instigation of William's half-brother Odo of Bayeux, shortly after the battle. Its cartoon-style combination of pictures and captions is extraordinarily detailed, but its interpretation is steadfastly pro-Norman, and there are areas where it is tantalizingly ambivalent. In studying the battle we must pick our way with care through this litter of source material, much of it incomplete and sometimes conflicting. But enough of scrolls and chronicles: let us move on to the events leading to the battle itself.

The Causes of the Norman Invasion

The Norman invasion of England in 1066 was the immediate result of the death of King Edward the Confessor. The King was childless, and it had seemed for some time that a disputed succession would follow his death. The rules governing succession were flexible: being designated as heir by the reigning monarch, coming from the royal family and being acclaimed by the leading nobles all counted for much.

England had not been a kingdom for long. After the departure of the Romans, waves of Germanic Anglo-Saxon invaders had pushed the native Celts into Cornwall, Wales and Scotland. There were Viking raids in the ninth and tenth centuries, and Scandinavians had settled in the area north of the Wash, known as the Danelaw. Until the ninth century Britain was divided into several kingdoms, although those south of the Humber came under the unified authority of the *Bretwalda*, 'ruler of Britain'. In the tenth century the Saxon kings of Wessex recaptured the Danelaw, establishing a united kingdom.

Edward the Confessor came from the old Saxon line of kings. He was the son of Ethelred II – known as Ethelread the Unready, though this sobriquet is a corruption of 'Unraed', or 'Bad counsel'. A new wave of Viking attacks encouraged Ethelred to send Edward and his brother Alfred to safety in Normandy, whose ruler, Duke Richard, was the brother of Ethelred's wife Emma. Edward's half-brother Edmund Ironside ruled England briefly, but was followed by the Dane Cnut (Canute to the English), who married Ethelred's widow Emma and was succeeded by his sons Harold and Harthacnut.

Edward accepted the crown in 1042, but it brought him little pleasure. Some Scandinavian princes had a strong claim to the throne, so trouble from the Vikings could be expected. His realm was divided between earls who enjoyed enormous power. Chief among them was Earl Godwin of Wessex, who held southern England from Cornwall to Kent. One of his sons, Sweyn, held part of the West Midlands, and another son, Harold, held East Anglia. Edward's brother Alfred had been blinded, probably at Godwin's behest, on a visit to England in 1036 and had died as a result. Nevertheless the King was forced to marry Godwin's daughter Edith.

Though Edward did his best to build up his own party, encouraging Normans to settle in England, he could do little against Godwin. Yet when, in 1051, Godwin broke into open revolt, the King was supported by

Earl Siward of Northumbria and Earl Leofric of the Midland earldom of Mercia: Godwin was exiled, Edith was repudiated as Edward's queen, and William, Duke of Normandy, was nominated Edward's heir.

William had been born in Falaise in 1027 or 1028, the illegitimate son of Robert, sixth Duke of Normandy, and Herleve, a tanner's daughter. Herleve was soon married off to Herluin of Conteville, and bore him Odo, later Bishop of Bayeux, and Robert of Mortain, who became one of the largest landowners in eleventh-century England. William was never legitimized, nor initially had he much reason to think of himself as heir to the dukedom. But when Duke Robert died on pilgrimage to the Holy Land in 1035 William was his natural successor, though it took him till 1060 to make his position secure.

The duchy of Normandy had been settled in the early tenth century by Vikings, mainly of Norwegian stock, and their leader Rollo had come to an agreement with Charles the Simple of France which gave him possession of the duchy. There were close links between England and Normandy. Both were Christian, through both retained strong threads of Scandinavian culture interwoven with elements of old religions.

By the time of William's birth Normandy was, as the Conqueror's biographer David C. Douglas writes, 'French in its speech, in its culture, and in its political ideas.' The duchy was thickly populated and well-cultivated, and its ports, especially Caen, enjoyed rich trade, much of it with Scandinavia. William strengthened the Duke's authority, dispossessing awkward noblemen: in 1055 Werlenc, Count of Mortain, was replaced by William's half-brother Robert. 'The Norman conquest of England,' declares Douglas, 'was made possible by the growth of Norman power during the earlier half of the eleventh century, and by the consolidation of the Duchy under the rule of Duke William.'

Edward's links with Normandy made William a perfectly proper choice for his heir. Yet no sooner had the decision been made than it was overturned. In 1052 Godwin and his sons re-established themselves by force of arms. King Edward's Norman allies were expelled – the Norman archbishop of Canterbury was replaced by the Saxon Stigand, a cleric of doubtful reputation who was promptly excommunicated by the Pope – and the King was compelled to reinstate Godwin's daughter Edith as his Queen. Godwin died in 1053, and his sons prospered. Tostig had already become Earl of Northumbria, and Harold, Godwin's eldest surviving son, succeeded his father as Earl of Wessex. Another brother, Gyrth, ruled East Anglia, and a fourth, Leofwine, had an earldom stretching from Buckinghamshire to Kent. In 1064 a chronicler called Harold 'subregulus' – under-king – and well he might.

Harold was by no means certain to succeed Edward. William had a claim to the throne, and so too, in their ways, did Walter of the Vexin, Ethelred's grandson; Eustace of Boulogne, Edward's brother-in-law; and Harald Hardrada, King of Norway. In 1064 Edward sent Harold to Normandy, possibly to confirm William's succession. His ship was blown off course and landed near the mouth of the Somme: the local count threw him into prison but released him at William's request. According to both William of Poitiers and the Bayeux tapestry, Harold swore an oath of fealty to William, undertaking to represent him at Edward's court and support his succession. We cannot be sure if Harold took the oath under duress, was tricked, or hoped that he might gain from the arrangement. He went campaigning with William in Brittany, and then returned to England laden with gifts. On his return the family's position deteriorated further. Tostig's subjects rebelled against him: Tostig fled abroad, as yet another claimant to the throne, and his earldom was given to Morcar, bother of Earl Edwin of Mercia.

Edward died on 5 January 1066, having, on his death-bed, nominated Harold as his successor, though whether the King was aware of his actions in his last moments with Harold and his supporters at the bedside must remain doubtful. Harold was immediately accepted as king by the *witanagemot*, the council of magnates, and the next day he was crowned in Westminster Abbey.

As soon as he heard the news, William took counsel with his own magnates. Encouraged, notably by William fitzOsbern, to believe that an invasion of England was practicable, he took pains to foster support in Normandy and beyond. Emissaries were sent to the Pope, who supported his claim: the Duke was to fight at Hastings beneath a papal banner. While William's diplomatic activity helped secure his position in Europe, his military preparations went on apace and he began to assemble an invasion fleet at the mouth of the River Dives.

Changes in Fighting Tactics
William's assault came at a time when military institutions were in the process of far-reaching change. Some military historians have seen Hastings as the classic example of a clash between infantry and cavalry armies: as those last long-haired axemen crumpled around the corpse of their king, they suggested, there dawned an age in which the armoured knight rode supreme over his opponents. The Saxons, Sir Charles Oman declared, simply applied 'the stationary tactics of a phalanx of axemen', and Major-General J. F. C. Fuller saw Hastings as 'the final great infantry fight'.

It was not that simple. That the armoured horseman was gaining steadily in importance there can be little doubt. But the process which legally linked land tenure to an obligation to provide a set number of knights for a given period, usually 40 days – known in historical short-hand as feudalism – was far less advanced in eleventh-century Normandy than historians used to believe. Indeed, it is possible that only after such feudal obligations had been imposed on conquered England was the system generally applied in Normandy. Nevertheless, if it was rare for great landowners, lay and ecclesiastical, to be expected to produce a fixed quota of knights, most of William's Norman troops were raised by his magnates, many of them his own relatives. Some knights lived in their lord's hall at his expense; others had holdings on his estates; and wealth-ier knights would themselves maintain warriors who lived with them or were settled on their land.

William's knights fought on horseback at Hastings. But this was not inevitable: at the battles of Tinchebray (1106) and the Standard (1138) Norman knights fought on foot. Their weapons and equipment were not notably different from those of the well-equipped foot-soldier.

Armour and Weaponry

In the Bayeux tapestry Norman knights and Harold's thegns and house-carls are almost identically clad and armed. A mail shirt (hauberk), made from interlocked iron rings hammered or riveted together, was the main defensive garment. The short mail corselet, reaching just below the waist, was old-fashioned by 1066, though some were worn in both armies. Knights wore knee-length hauberks, split front and rear for riding, often provided with an integral mail hood.

Some figures on the Bayeux tapestry have long mail sleeves, while others have short sleeves with leather strapping to protect their forearms. The hauberk, worn over a thick tunic, was heavy and uncomfortable, and was donned only when battle was imminent. Hauberks were expensive, and there were never enough to go round: the tapestry suggests that while fighting was in progress the dead were stripped of their hauberks so that the unarmoured living could put them to good use.

The conical iron helmet, with a nasal to protect the nose, was the common form of Viking military headdress in both England and Normandy. Some helmets were hammered from a single piece of iron, but most were made of segments riveted together. A lining of leather or padded cloth helped cushion the head against blows. A helmeted warrior had a grim, impersonal appearance: when it was rumoured that William had been killed he pushed his helmet back so that his face was clearly identifiable.

This mail shirt post-dates Hastings but is similar to those worn there. Mail, which offered reasonable protection against cuts and stabs, but less against crushing blows, was too expensive for fyrdmen, though thegns and housecarls, like Norman knights and heavy infantry, wore it. Research on skeletons found on battlefields suggests that many fatal wounds were inflicted on the head, often after the warrior had been brought down by a blow to the legs. A helmet greatly increased a man's chances of survival. This helmet is conical, inducing blows to glance off, and the nasal offers protection against a stroke to the face.

Norman knights carried both sword and spear. Their swords were long, straight, double-edged weapons with a cruciform hilt. While a sword's edge would be defeated by mail, a heavy blow could break bones beneath the mail, and the garments of humbler foot-soldiers offered little protection against the sword. Spears were of two distinct types. Javelins, which usually had slender heads, were thrown; and other spears, often fitted with broader heads, were used for thrusting.

The Bayeux tapestry suggests that these stabbing-spears were used for over-arm thrusts, or couched beneath the arm so that the weapon would strike with the full impetus of man and horse. This was a new tactic, of which knights in succeeding centuries were to make much use. Saddles had high pommels and cantles to front and rear, and stirrups – a relatively recent arrival from the East – were worn on long leathers, so that the knight, legs straight, was almost standing in them.

Horsemen and most foot-soldiers carried a shield. All of those being carried by knights in the tapestry are kite-shaped, though some infantry had the older round or oblong version. Shields were made of wood, often lime, the 'war-linden' of Norse sagas, sometimes with metal rims to prevent them being split by a blow to the edge. Circular shields had a central metal boss which covered the hole in which the warrior's hand grasped an iron grip, and probably had a leather strap through which the forearm passed. Another strap enabled the shield to be slung from the warrior's shoulder on the march or allowed him to use a weapon with both hands.

Kite-shaped shields were more convenient than round shields for a mounted man, and offered protection to the side of his body and his upper leg. They too had straps for hand and forearm, and a longer strap to permit the use of both hands. Shields bore a variety of symbols: these were not, as they would later become, heraldic devices.

A few knights carried maces, metal clubs with flanged or knobbed heads. These delivered lethal blows to unprotected skulls and could even defeat a helmet. Both William and his half-brother Odo are shown in the tapestry carrying smaller wooden clubs. These are symbols of command, rather like the vine-staff of Roman centurions and the batons carried by senior officers in later centuries.

The majority of William's men were infantry. Most of his heavy infantry wore mail hauberks and conical helmets, protected themselves with shields, and bore spears and swords. He also had archers, some of whom carried bows and others crossbows. The bow was shorter and less powerful than the longbow which was to become a characteristic weapon of English armies during the Hundred Years War (1337–1453). The tapestry shows it being drawn to the chest, but it is more likely that it was drawn to the face. Arrows were carried in quivers slung from shoulder or waist-belt, or in larger containers which stood on the ground. Recent evidence suggests that at least some arrow-heads resembled the bodkin point used by English and Welsh archers in the Hundred Years War. These narrow heads were effective against mail at close range. However they could not penetrate shields, and the tapestry depicts English shields bristling with arrows.

Although the tapestry shows no crossbows, it is likely that William had crossbowmen, for both William of Poitiers and the *Carmen* refer to them. Crossbows shot stubby bolts with iron heads and parchment quills which could penetrate mail at close range. The crossbows themselves were less powerful than later types, which required a winch or lever to draw the string back: William's crossbowmen simply placed their feet on the bow and drew the string with their hands. One hauberked archer appears in the tapestry, but the great majority of Norman archers wore little protective clothing: a fortunate few might have had helmets or padded coats.

The Fighting Man

Robert Wace affirms that William had little difficulty in obtaining promises of more men than he required for the campaign. Magnates were induced to take part by more than loyalty or obligation, for there was every prospect that there would be rich pickings in a conquered kingdom. The Norman contingent numbered about 4000 men under William himself, and included not only leading noblemen, like his half-brothers Odo of Bayeux and Robert of Mortain, but also a sprinkling of younger sons who had everything to gain from a successful campaign. Robert, son of Roger of Beaumont, for instance, fought well in command of a detachment on William's right during the battle, and was created Earl of Leicester.

There were two substantial allied contingents. Count Eustace of Boulogne led a Franco-Flemish contingent of about 1500 men, and there were perhaps 2000 Bretons, probably under Alan Fergant, cousin of their ruling count and William's son-in-law. Once again the prospect of profit was a major attraction, and the fact that the Pope had blessed the enterprise must have helped. It is difficult to be precise about numbers, but William had about 2000 cavalry, 4000 heavy infantry and 1500 archers under his command.

Harold's army reflected the administrative and social structure of Saxon England. The earls were effectively viceroys in their earldoms. These were made up of shires, which were themselves divided into hundreds. The sheriff (shire-reeve) administered the king's estates within his shire and had a host of other legal and administrative functions, summoning and commanding the fyrd, the military levy of the shire, amongst them.

Saxon society had three tiers: thegns, churls and slaves. Men might rise and fall: a merchant who made three successful voyages became a thegn, and a thegn who failed in his duty to the king might become a slave. Social status was bound up with land – at this time a thegn had to hold at least five hides of land, a hide (between 60 and 120 acres, depending on locality) being assessed on the land's worth.

The Danish kings of England had adopted the practice of retaining household troops called housecarls, and the earls followed suit, keeping warriors at their own expense or settling them on estates. Harold was to be handicapped in 1066 by fighting two campaigns in rapid succession, the first against his brother Tostig and Harald Hardrada in the north, and the second against William in the south. When the losses of the northern campaign are taken into account, Harold and his brothers Gyrth and Leofwine may have brought 1000 housecarls to Hastings.

While housecarls were, as Warren Hollister called them, 'a unique, closely-knit organization of professional warriors who served the kings of England from Canute to Harold Godwineson [sic] and became the spearhead of the English army,' they were more than mere mercenaries. They were paid by their lords, but, as Richard Abels has suggested, 'their obligation to fight did not arise from the cash nexus but from the bonds of lordship.' The Anglo-Saxon vernacular poem *The Battle of Maldon*, describing the unsuccessful struggle of Earl Byrthnoth and the East Anglian fyrd against Vikings in 991, makes much of the housecarl's duty not to leave the field if his lord has fallen. After the Earl's death, one of his men declares:

Steadfast warriors around Sturmere will have no cause
to taunt me with words, now my beloved one is dead,
that I travelled home lordless,
turned away from the fight, but a weapon must take me...

We cannot assume that poetic imagination is historical fact, but *The Battle of Maldon* described a heroic ideal and, as we shall see at Hastings, it was a code the housecarls lived and died by: they were not men who intended to journey home lordless.

If housecarls were professional warriors, the members of the fyrd were not. We cannot be sure of the precise relationship between land tenure and military service across the whole of Saxon England, but in Berkshire, whose record survives, one man was required to serve for every five hides of land. King's thegns, landowners on a large scale, were required to produce one man for each of their five hides, and towns were assessed on a similar basis.

Fines were imposed for failing to appear at muster when summoned, and a king's thegn could lose his land if he declined to do service. If the king was present in person with the army desertion was punishable by death. But if a warrior fell in battle at his lord's side, his heirs could succeed to his land without paying the customary heriot (death duty). Similar obligations, increasingly commuted for monetary payment, applied to provide men for service at sea. Regional groupings called 'ship-sokes', usually three hundreds, were each responsible for paying for a vessel. The sea ports of Kent and Sussex supplied ships and warriors of their own, financing them from the profits of their courts, which would otherwise have been paid to the king.

The fyrd could be called up for a period of two months, and this summons could be repeated if required, though morale, agriculture and trade would suffer. Fyrdmen were liable for service anywhere within the realm, or even overseas. In an acute emergency the king could summon the general fyrd – every able-bodied freeman – to serve within the borders of his shire. The militia thus raised was little use in open field, but it could garrison towns or watch the coasts.

In many respects Harold's army looked like William's. Housecarls and thegns wore byrnies – hauberks – and conical helmets, protected themselves with shields, and fought with sword and spear. Fyrdmen were less well-equipped. Robert Wace described them as 'a great gathering of *vilainaille*, of men in everyday clothes', but this is an over-simplification. In 1108 *The Anglo-Saxon Chronicle* notes that the King ordered that a helmet and byrnie should be produced from every eight hides of land in England. Many fyrdmen would have worn iron helmets or leather caps, and some would have followed the Viking practice of wearing tough hide coats, almost as good as mail for warding off point or edge.

The axe was widely used by Harold's men. Small axes could be swung or thrown single-handed. But the broad or bearded axe was the Saxon warrior's most formidable weapon. Its massive head was mounted on an ash shaft about 3 feet long (1 m) long; swung two-handed, with the force of battle-frenzy behind it, it could split a horse's skull.

The tapestry shows only one Saxon archer, and the small size of the figure implies that he might be a boy. The apparent absence of archers in Harold's army has caused historians some difficulties. It is clear that a missile exchange, in which arrows were shot, stones slung or cast, and javelins thrown, was the usual preliminary to battle: *The Battle of Maldon* describes an early stage of the fight when 'bows were busy'. In the saga *Heimskringla* Snorri Sturluson describes the English making good use of archers at Stamford Bridge. However, Snorri is so clearly wrong on so many matters that his evidence is generally regarded as untrustworthy.

There is, though, abundant evidence of archery in England in the immediate aftermath of the Conquest, leading Richard Glover to deduce that 'bows were as common as dogs in the England ruled by the Conqueror's son.' He goes on to point out that Harold took the fyrd of southern and central England to Stamford Bridge with him. Having won the battle, he heard of William's landing on 1 October: he lay dead on the field of Hastings, 250 miles (400 km) away, on 14 October. The infantry of the day would have had no chance of covering this distance in a dozen days: the only men to fight in both battles would have been housecarls and thegns who made the journey on horseback. Glover concludes that there were indeed archers in the English army in 1066, but they had gone to Stamford Bridge with Harold and were not available to him at Hastings. In this respect, as in many others, the Duke should perhaps be known, as John Gillingham has suggested, as William the Lucky Bastard.

Glover also argues that the *Heimskringla*'s suggestion that the English fought on horseback at Stamford Bridge may not be as absurd as is usually thought. Anglo-Saxons and Vikings alike had used horses for transport off the battlefield. The question of whether or not the Anglo-Saxons of this period fought mounted is too complex to resolve here, but the weight of evidence suggests that they sometimes did so. In her study of the medieval warhorse, Ann Hyland points out that horses frequently formed part of the heriot paid by Anglo-Saxon noblemen. From their description these are no shaggy ponies or ambling palfreys, but warhorses. This said, there is no doubt that Harold's men fought on foot at Hastings, as their ancestors had at Ashdown in 871: 'Shield to shield, and shoulder to shoulder.'

'The cohesion of the shield-wall,' writes Nicholas Brooks, 'was the fundamental principle of Anglo-Saxon battle tactics.' Poets wrote of the 'battle-hedge' and the 'shield-fort'; and breaking the line, through cowardice, to plunder, or in misplaced zeal, could be fatal. Men formed up so that their shields presented an unbroken front: William of Poitiers tells us that at Hastings the English were packed together so densely that the dead could not fall and the wounded could not leave the ranks. There was probably one man for every 2 feet (60 cm) of the front rank, with another ten ranks behind. It was not simply a matter of jamming warriors

The Bayeux Tapestry shows the English shield-wall under attack. These warriors are well-equipped thegns or housecarls, whose overlapping shields offer good protection. Some of them are using stabbing-spears, and others have bundles of javelins. There is an archer; a mace (top left) is amongst the missiles hurled at the oncoming knights. The small pennants (gonfanons) may designate individual contingents.

together, for a man needed room to use his weapons. The broad axe demanded space, because its user swung it back across his shoulder, leaving himself, so Wace assures us, vulnerable to a frontal thrust.

Both armies had distinctive banners and war-cries. Harold's men fought beneath the dragon of Wessex, rather like a wind-sock, and the king's own banner, an embroidered figure of a fighting man. The Norman banner bore the leopards of Normandy, and, in addition, William had been given a consecrated banner by the Pope. Many warriors on both sides had small pennants, gonfanons, fluttering from their spears: these may have denoted the leaders of small units. The Norman war-cry was '*Dex Aie*' –'God's Aid'. Wace describes the English war-cries as 'Olicrosse' and 'Godemite' – his rendering of 'Holy Cross' and 'God Almighty'. The fyrd barked its defiance in an older, simpler form: 'Out, out'. Harold had about 7000 men at Hastings, and the sight of their phalanx, bristling with spears and axes and reverberating to the roar of 'Out, out' and the clatter of weapons striking shields, must have been formidable.

Campaign and Battle

Harold spent Easter 1066 at Westminster, where he would have marvelled at what *The Anglo-Saxon Chronicle* calls 'the long-haired star' (in fact Halley's comet, widely regarded as a portent of great trouble). As if on cue, his brother Tostig, who had wintered in Flanders, raided the south coast with a fleet of 60 ships. Harold assembled what the *Chronicle* calls 'a naval force and a land force larger than any king had assembled before in this country', and Tostig sailed off northwards, rebuffed by Earls Edwin and Morcar when he tried to land. Many of his sailors deserted, and he eventually reached Scotland with only 12 small ships. Tostig seems to have contacted William, with a view to forming some sort of alliance, without success. By the summer, however, he had come to terms with Harald Hardrada, another claimant to the throne.

William Prepares to Invade
While Harold was preparing to deal with his recalcitrant brother, William's preparations went on. His fleet assembled in the Dives estuary, north-east of Caen. The coastline has changed, but the marshes east of Dives-sur-Mer – which helped form a hard shoulder on the British left when the Allies landed in Normandy in 1944 – mark what was once a substantial estuary.

Wace declared that William had 696 ships, for his father had told him so, but he admits that nobody was really sure of the number. In a study of the naval logistics of the campaign, C. M. Gillmor concludes that, while it is impossible to be certain, Wace's is a fair estimate. Both the limited time available and the amount of timber required – 74 trees were needed to build a Viking ship of the period – suggest that some vessels must already have existed. There was a small Norman navy, and some ships were hired from Flanders: Flemish mercenaries had manned most of Tostig's ships. Even so, the work required, and its impact on the forests of Normandy, must have been prodigious. Most of William's ships were clinker-built transports, broader in the beam than fighting vessels, relying upon a single square-rigged sail and using auxiliary oars to get out into open sea or to move when becalmed.

The activity inland was scarcely less intense. Adding non-combatants, like armourers, butchers, cooks and servants to soldiers and sailors, William would have had more than 10,000 men encamped around Dives-sur-Mer. It speaks volumes for his abilities as both disciplinarian and logistician that this concentration of personnel was sustained without the starvation, disease or indiscipline which frequently attended such ventures.

Some of the time was spent training. Medieval armies, with their complex cross-currents of loyalty, were often no better than armed mobs. Individual knights, bred to the use of arms, were usually skilled and courageous. Small groups of mounted warriors, known as conroys, organised in multiples of five men and following the gonfanon – banner – of their leader, were accustomed to working together. Combining disparate conroys from different lordships – Norman, Breton and Flemish – was another matter altogether. We cannot be sure of the state of collective training in William's army, and this uncertainty lies behind one of the central questions at Hastings: was the retreat of the Norman army, which drew the English down in pursuit, real or feigned?

That summer Harold kept the southern fyrd assembled to face an invasion, first by Tostig and then by William, and he eventually gathered together a fleet of 700 ships. He himself embarked and lay off the Isle of Wight: *The Anglo-Saxon Chronicle* says that he then considered setting out in search of the Norman fleet. In early September his army ran out of supplies and had to be disbanded. 'When the Nativity of St Mary came, the men's provisions were finished,' laments the *Chronicle*, 'and no one could keep them there any longer.' Harold sent his fleet to London – some vessels foundered en route – and he set off for his capital on horseback.

With the English fleet out of his way, William was able to move his own armada along the coast to St-Valéry-sur-Somme. He too lost some ships, and the bodies of passengers and crew were buried at night so as not to dishearten the rest of the force. The horses were probably sent overland, following a similar route to that used by Henry V in the early stages of the Agincourt campaign in 1415. Once at St Valéry William was much closer to the coast of southern England, clear of the difficult currents in the Bay of the Seine, and better able to profit from the southerly wind for which he waited impatiently.

The Battle of Stamford Bridge

Having lost the first round of the campaign, Harold found himself facing a new peril. In the first week of September Harald Hardrada unfurled his raven banner 'Land-Ravager' and crossed the North Sea with perhaps 300 ships. He was joined in the Tyne by Tostig and his own little fleet, and together they moved down the coast, raiding as they went. In mid-September they entered the Ouse and reached Riccal, 10 miles (16 km) from York. On 20 September Earls Edwin and Morcar met them at Gate Fulford, just outside the city, and after a hard-fought battle the earls were beaten: York surrendered at once.

HASTINGS
1066: The Two Campaigns

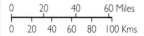 Harold, King of England's movements

→ Harold Hardrada's and Tostig's movements

→ William of Normandy's movements

```
0      20      40      60 Miles
0   20  40  60  80  100 Kms
```

The Sussex Coast in 1066

Andredsweald

⚔

•Hastings

•*Pevensey
Castle*

Harold heard of the Norwegian invasion shortly after disbanding his army. He summoned the fyrd, spent a fortnight gathering troops, and set off north up the old Roman road. As Denis Butler observes, the march was 'without parallel or precedent in its own time.' Harold covered 190 miles (306 km) in five days – an astonishing achievement for the fyrdmen – to reach Tadcaster on 24 September. Troops from the Midland shires joined the King on his march, and he was also met by some of the survivors from Gate Fulford. On 25 September he reached York, discovered that his enemies seemed to have no idea of his presence, and marched on towards them at Stamford Bridge on the River Derwent, 8 miles (13 km) away.

About two-thirds of the invaders were at Stamford Bridge, awaiting the arrival of local leaders who were to formally assent to Hardrada's rule. Although they had helmets, shields and personal weapons with them, most had left their byrnies with the ships at Riccal, guarded by the remainder of the force, under the nominal command of Hardrada's son Olaf with his brother-in-law Eystein Orre, known as the gorcock (red grouse) and other experienced warriors to advise him.

The sudden arrival of Harold's army was a tremendous shock: Snorri wrote that, as it appeared through a dust cloud on the York road, the flash of armour and weapons looked like the glint of sunlight on broken ice. Hardrada asked Tostig for advice, and the Earl recommended falling back to the ships. This would have been difficult, for, although the armies were separated by the Derwent, the invaders would have had to cross at Kexby to reach their ships, and the English were likely to reach the crossing first. Hardrada decided to accept battle, sent gallopers to Riccal ordering the remainder of his army to join him, and set up Land-Ravager on what are now called Battle Flats.

The Norsemen had been dispersed when Harold appeared: some had wandered down to the river or begun to round up cattle on the water-meadows. Those caught on the east bank sold their lives dearly, buying time for their comrades to form their shield-wall around Land-Ravager. One axeman, who had worn his byrnie on the march up from Riccal, held the narrow bridge, hewing down more than forty assailants, until an Englishman in a small boat or swill-tub manoeuvred himself under the bridge and thrust his spear through a gap in the planks and up, under the man's armour.

Hardrada rode round his army on a black horse. It stumbled on the uneven ground, throwing him, but he quipped that a fall was luck for a traveller. Snorri says that a group of horsemen approached the Vikings and hailed Tostig, offering him his old earldom and a third of the kingdom if he submitted. When Tostig asked what Hardrada would receive, he was told: 'Seven feet of English ground, or as much more as he may be taller than other men.'

This may be more poetic imagination than fact, for Snorri goes on to say that the English then charged on horseback, which is improbable if for no other reason than the state of the horses after the long march. It is more likely that this was like Maldon writ large: first an exchange of arrows, javelins and stones, and then a brutal hand-to-hand fight as shield-wall met shield-wall. It was an unequal contest, for the Norsemen were unarmoured. Hardrada was mortally wounded in the neck by an arrow, and the battle flowed fast against his men. Harold may have sent messengers to offer his brother quarter, but the surviving Norsemen 'called out all of them together that they would rather fall, one across the other, than accept quarter from the Englishmen.' Tostig died soon afterwards, hit by an arrow as he stood beside Land-Ravager.

The black raven banner still fluttered over the carnage when Eystein Orre and his men arrived from Riccal. Although they were tired after their march in armour, the impact of their assault was so fierce that 'ever since in England "gorcock's storm" is used to mean great peril of men', and they cut their way through to Land-Ravager. Many threw off their armour to fight unencumbered, and offered easy targets. At last the gorcock was killed and Land-Ravager was taken: 'darkness fell before the slaughter was altogether ended.' Harold allowed Olaf Haraldson and the survivors to sail home, taking Hardrada's body with them. The slaughter had been so great that they needed only 24 of their 300 ships.

Stamford Bridge would be better-remembered were it not obscured by Hastings. It ended the last of the great Viking invasions, and was the ultimate revenge for years of burnt farmsteads and butchered peasants. The battle, and the campaign which led up to it had shown Harold Godwinson at his best: whatever the twists and turns on his path to the throne, he had proved himself a decisive leader. But he had little time for self-congratulation, he may even have been enjoying his victory feast when, on or just after 1 October, a messenger brought word that William had landed.

The Arrival of the Normans

William had grown so frustrated waiting for a southerly wind at St Valéry that he had had the saint's relics paraded around the town. The wind obediently changed direction, and it was probably on the afternoon of 27 September that the Normans embarked, sailing before dusk. William led the way in his own ship, the *Mora*, a gift from his wife. A lantern at the masthead was intended to help the fleet keep direction, but dawn found *Mora* on her own. Mindful of his men's morale, William enjoyed an ostentatiously good breakfast while he waited for the rest of his fleet. Soon there was 'a forest of masts' with *Mora*: two ships lost their way and probably landed at Old Romney, where their crews were killed.

It was about 9 a.m. on 28 September that the first of William's ships entered Pevensey Bay, 56 miles (90 km) from St Valéry. The coastline of the area was markedly different then. Pevensey Bay was larger, with a tidal lagoon behind it, protected by a narrow spit of land, with the ruined Roman fort of Anderida at its tip. To the east was the Hastings peninsula, all but cut off by the Brede to the east and Bulverhythe lagoon to the west. Inland, the brooding forest of the Andredsweald stretched away northwards.

The fleet approached land prepared for resistance, but it was soon clear that the coastline was undefended. As William landed he slipped on the shingle, threw out his hands to protect himself as he fell, and scratched his face. There was a flicker of alarm, but William fitzOsbern shouted that the omen was good: the Duke had grasped England with both hands, and meant to guarantee it to his successors with his blood. Pioneers protected the landing place by adding a ditch and some timber to the Roman fort – William had brought wood for prefabricated forts with him – and patrols scouted inland.

William moved army and fleet to Hastings either later on the same day or the following day, erecting his remaining prefabricated forts, probably in the old Roman castle, and camping on Baldslow Ridge above the town. The peninsular was large enough to form a secure base for his army, and was easily defended. The move to Hastings suggests that William intended taking the road to Dover and thence to London, rather than the single road through the Andredsweald to London, where his horsemen would have been at a disadvantage in close country.

William's initial caution stemmed, at least in part, from the fact that he had no recent news of Harold's whereabouts. Indeed, it was only when a messenger from Robert fitzWymarc, a kinsman who held land in England, brought news of Stamford Bridge that he knew just how fortuitous that south wind had been. Time was not on his side. Harold might hold the neck of the peninsula and, at the same time, blockade Hastings with his fleet, forcing William to starve or fight. There was everything to be gained by provoking Harold into attacking, and William's patrols ravaged the surrounding villages, gathering supplies which would be useful if Hastings was blockaded and deliberately insulting Harold, in whose old earldom Sussex lay.

Preparing for Battle

Harold himself had taken only five days to reach London, where he once again summoned troops (no easy task in view of the demands already placed upon the fyrd). A monk was sent with a formal message to William, a Norman monk returned, rejecting Edward's nomination of Harold, and offering to resolve the dispute in court or by single combat. Wace suggests that Gyrth, Harold's brother, advised the King not to risk battle but to devastate the countryside round Hastings, starve the Normans out, and to allow him to command the army. Harold refused: he did not wish to ravage his own territory, and was determined to lead his army himself. It is clear that Harold left London before his army was complete.

William of Jumièges wrote that the king 'rejected caution', and Florence of Worcester believed that 'one half of his army had not arrived'. Harold set off on 11 October and marched through the Andredsweald, reaching Caldbec Hill, a mile from the forest edge, on the evening of 13 October. The hill was crowned by a prominent hoar-apple tree which served as a rallying-point, and the nearby forest road met the roads to Chichester and Dover: Hastings itself was 7 miles (11 km) south.

It is likely that Harold hoped to catch the Normans unawares and attack at once, as he had at Stamford Bridge, though suggestions of a night attack are fanciful. It is possible that he simply hoped to confine his enemies in Hastings while his own army grew stronger. But the initiative was no longer his. William's scouts reported the arrival of the English, and the Duke called in his foragers and kept his men under arms all night. Wace maintains, with some wonderfully misspelt Saxon toasts, that the English spent the night drinking and dancing: '*Bublie*, they cried and *weissel*, and *laticome* and *dricheheil*…' The Normans, in contrast 'made confession of their sins…'

Communal drinking was certainly part of the process of male bonding in Anglo-Saxon society – as in so many others. A warrior in *The Battle of Maldon* had exhorted his comrades to 'remember the times that we often made speeches over mead…about fierce encounters.' However, we may doubt whether Harold's men were much inclined to carouse after an exhausting march and with the prospect of imminent battle.

William heard mass and took the sacrament before dawn on Saturday 14 October. At some stage he addressed his troops, perhaps haranguing their leaders so that his exhortation could be passed on, or simply speaking to those around him. His message was clear. 'You fight not merely for victory but also for survival,' according to William of Poitiers. He hung round his neck the sacred relics on which Harold had sworn his oath in

1064, and at about 6 a.m. moved off northwards along the Roman road. The Bretons, with detachments from Anjou, Maine and Poitou, led the way, followed by the Franco-Flemings under William fitzOsbern and Eustace of Boulogne. The Normans, led by William on his black charger, brought up the rear. Each contingent had both infantry and cavalry, and at this stage the horsemen were probably on foot, their hauberks laid across their saddles.

About an hour later the head of the column reached Blackhorse Hill, the highest point of the long ridge of Telham Hill. Here William's men prepared for action, donning their hauberks. About 1000 yards (900 m) away the English army had formed up on Senlac Hill, a ridge running squarely east-east across the road. Small streams with marshy banks flowed away from both its ends, and the ground immediately to the south-west was boggy. Both flanks were steep (about 1 in 12) and covered with trees and undergrowth. The southern face of the ridge had a gentler gradient, 1 in 15 near the road and 1 in 33 at the ridge's western end. South-west of Senlac the road crossed a saddle, with two more brooks running off to the west.

Harold's standards flew from the highest point of the ridge, and his army extended for about 400 yards (365 m) on either side. It is impossible to be certain of its exact disposition, but it is possible that the King's brothers, Gyrth and Leofwine, were on either flank, and that the first few ranks of the array consisted of housecarls and thegns, with the less well-armed fyrdmen behind them. A bodyguard protected Harold and the standards. The Bayeux tapestry shows a fyrdman arriving at the last moment, yet more evidence that Harold's army was incomplete.

Its arming finished, William's army probably continued along the road and crossed the saddle, only then shaking out into battle order, with the Bretons on the left, the Franco-Flemish on the right and the Normans in the centre. To have deployed earlier would have presented difficulties because of the brooks and boggy ground, and although William was now very close to the English, he probably calculated that they would not come down from their commanding position to attack him.

Each division formed up with its archers and slingers to the front. Then came the heavy infantry with spears, and lastly the cavalry. William planned to disorganize the English phalanx with missile weapons, then use heavy infantry to make gaps in the shield-wall, and finally unleash the knights to shatter the defence and pursue any survivors. The Duke himself was probably on the high ground behind the centre of his line, with a bodyguard and the leopard standard carried by Turstin, son of Rollo.

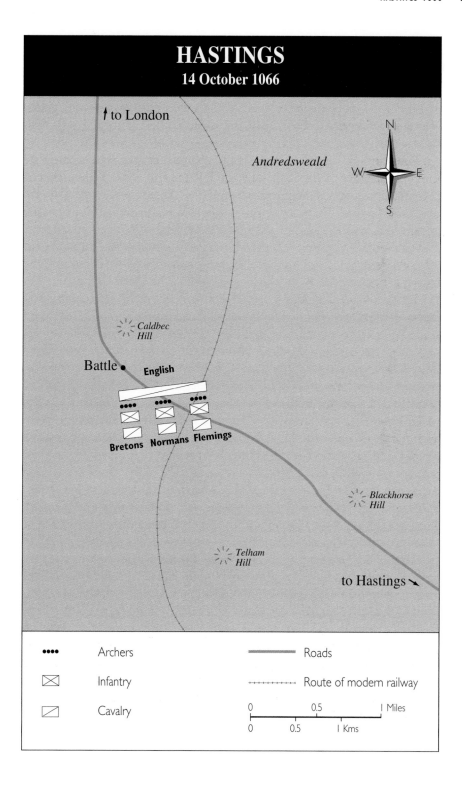

HASTINGS
14 October 1066

↑ to London

Andredsweald

N
W — E
S

Caldbec Hill

Battle ●   English

Bretons Normans Flemings

Blackhorse Hill

Telham Hill

to Hastings ↘

●●●●	Archers	▬▬▬	Roads
⊠	Infantry	··············	Route of modern railway
⊠	Cavalry		

0   0.5   1 Miles
0   0.5   1 Kms

The Battle Begins

Guy of Amiens tells how the minstrel Taillefer, who had ridden forward singing the epic *Song of Roland* and juggling with his sword, asked William for permission to strike the first blow. He rode forward, attacked a group of Englishmen and killed two, but was soon cut down. The battle proper began at about 9 a.m. with a terrible braying of trumpets on both sides. William's archers and crossbowmen moved forward and engaged the English line. They were shooting uphill, and their arrows were either caught on the shield-wall or passed over the English altogether. As Harold had few archers there were almost no arrows to pick up and re-use, and ammunition would soon have run short. The missile attack had been a failure, and the English line was scarcely touched.

William now committed his heavy infantry, who toiled up the slope to be met first by a few arrows, javelins, stones, throwing-axes – even, if the tapestry is to be believed, maces – and then the great expanse of the shield-wall. This was the sort of fighting with which housecarls and thegns were grimly familiar, and the attackers made little progress. Even when William sent in his cavalry they were unable to break the shield-wall. The English profited from the slope, their close cohesion and the effectiveness of their weapons. Horsemen were felled by spear or axe as they sought an opportunity to thrust where the shield-wall wavered or where an axeman left his chest uncovered as he drew his weapon back to strike; and knights throwing javelins were themselves hit by missiles.

It may be that the Breton horsemen, who attacked where the slope was most gentle, collided with the shield-wall before their allies to the right and bore the strain of fighting longer. In any event they were the first to break, and poured down the slope, their panic infecting other contingents. 'Almost the whole of the Duke's army yielded,' admits William of Poitiers. Even the Normans began to fall back, in their case not in 'shameful flight, but a sorrowful withdrawal' because they believed William had fallen.

William rose to meet the crisis. He galloped in front of the fugitives, striking some and threatening others with his lance, pushing his helmet back so that his features could be seen and shouting; 'Look at me! I am alive, and will be the victor, with God's help! What madness induces you to flee? What avenue of retreat is open to you?' He rallied enough knights to turn on a party of Englishmen who had followed the Bretons down the hill, and cut them to pieces as they made a stand on a hillock at the foot of the ridge. The tapestry, which shows unarmoured figures falling to Norman swords, suggests that they were probably ill-disciplined fyrdmen, but some scholars have suggested that the counter-attack was led by Harold's brothers, both of whom were killed at about this time.

This reverse weakened Harold's right – he would probably have thinned the rest of his line in order to make good the losses – but it left his overall position intact. William's men renewed the attack, and William of Poitiers pays particular tribute to the Normans, who fought 'with a courage beyond compare'. However, 'realising that they could not overcome an enemy so numerous and standing so firm without great loss to themselves, [they] retreated, deliberately feigning flight.' All the contemporary sources refer to this stratagem, which Poitiers suggests was repeated three times, and William of Malmesbury makes it the chief reason for the Norman victory. Every time the Normans retreated the English pursued, and, in doing so, were cut down as the knights spurred back into battle.

The flight, real or feigned, has spilt scarcely less ink over the past nine centuries than it did blood that October day. Weighty authorities, Sir Charles Oman prominent amongst them, have suggested that medieval cavalry was so inherently poorly disciplined that a manoeuvre of this subtlety would have been beyond it, and Colonel Charles Lemmon pointed out that it was difficult for well-trained modern troops to carry out such a manoeuvre in a military tournament. On the other hand, both Bernard Bachrach and R. Allen Brown point out that the feigned retreat was described in contemporary histories and military textbooks, and had been used by the Normans at Arques in 1053 and Messina in 1060.

The truth is that there are too many ifs and buts to be certain. We know neither how much collective training had gone on at Dives and St Valéry, nor how well-disciplined William's knights, and, no less to the point, their chargers, really were. On the one hand it is improbable that the whole of William's cavalry would have pretended to flee. Given the primitive arrangements for command and control, it would have been impossible to tell all the riders when, where and how far to retreat. On the other, it is likely that individual detachments, conroys or their multiples, could have wheeled to follow their leader's gonfanon down the slope and then rallied on it, drawing some battle-maddened defenders down in unwise pursuit. During this phase of the battle, grinding on into the short October afternoon, we should perhaps see the solidarity of the shield-wall being eroded all along its length by local feigned retreats and counter-charges.

Whether as a result of feigned retreats or simply hours of savage fighting, the English army was much-reduced by early afternoon, though it remained, as Poitiers tells us, 'a formidable force and difficult to surround'. His use of the word 'surround' suggests that the Normans had still not established themselves on the ridge, and even if casualties had thinned its ranks, with fyrdmen stepping forward to replace fallen house-carls and thegns, Harold's battle-line retained its original length.

The Bayeux Tapestry tells its story like a comic strip. *Above:* On the left we see the Bretons, their horses in difficulties on the boggy ground near the hillock to the right front of Harold's line. The unarmoured fyrdmen, plying shield and spear, who had followed up the fleeing Bretons are shown making their stand on a hillock. All of them were killed when William's men rallied and returned to the attack. *Left:* Although it is not possible to be absolutely sure how Harold died, most scholars now agree that he was wounded by an arrow in the eye and then cut down by a Norman knight. William of Malmesbury's version of his death, which accords with what we see in the tapestry, is that Harold's thigh was hacked after he had fallen: the knight who struck the blow was expelled from the army for his ignoble deed.

The Last Hours of the Battle

It was about 3 p.m., with daylight beginning to fade, when William again threw his army up the trampled and slippery slope, littered with the debris of earlier attacks. There would have been little momentum to this final assault, for men were exhausted and horses blown. The three divisions had become one: many knights had lost their horses and were fighting on foot, and William himself, Poitiers assures us, had had three horses killed under him.

It is often assumed that William paved the way for this last attack by ordering his archers to shoot into the air so that their arrows fell behind the shield-wall. Robert Wace makes much of this, but contemporary accounts do not mention it, and, although the tapestry shows some archers with their bows at a higher than usual angle, it is inconclusive evidence. What is certain is that, by this late stage in the battle, the shield-wall would have been far less cohesive than it had been in the morning, and many of the men in its front rank would by now have been poorly armed, so archery was more likely to be effective.

Harold has traditionally been regarded as the most illustrious victim of the Norman bowmen, though the section of tapestry that seems to show him hit in the eye by an arrow is enigmatic and there are several different accounts of his death. Beneath the caption 'here King Harold is killed' we see one figure, equipped with shield and spear, struggling to pull an arrow from its eye, and another, with axe and banded leggings, falling to a horseman's sword-cut. The weight of scholarly opinion now tends to favour the old interpretation: Harold, wounded by an arrow in or above the eye, was killed by a knight.

The English position was already crumbling badly when Harold fell, and his death no doubt encouraged numerous fyrdmen to slip away. Retreat was not an honourable option for surviving members of his body-guard, who, with most of the housecarls and thegns, formed a shrinking circle around the banners of the dragon and the fighting man, and the body of their king. Eventually the dragon was beaten down and the fighting man taken, to be sent to the Pope in return for his own gift of a banner. Then the last of the English on the field, 'few in number', says William of Malmesbury, 'but brave in the extreme,' – died fighting.

The Aftermath

By this time many fyrdmen and, no doubt, a few housecarls and thegns too, had left the field. Some took horses tethered in the rear and made off on them. 'Many died in the depth of the forest:' wrote Poitiers, 'their pursuers found corpses all along the roads.' He goes on to say that the pursuit was hampered by poor light and difficult ground, and that some of those escaping made a stand near 'a deep valley and numerous ditches'. There is even less unanimity amongst the chroniclers about this, the so-called Malfosse (evil ditch) incident, than about most other aspects of the battle. Inconclusive though the sources are, it is not unlikely that some of the survivors did indeed turn on their pursuers in the half-light of that dreadful day, for the Saxons, as Poitiers acknowledges, 'were always ready to cross swords'.

William returned to the battlefield from the pursuit, and 'could not gaze without pity on the carnage'. The next morning the victors began the enormous task of separating friend from foe amongst the corpses, perhaps as many as 4000 in all. The Normans were buried, and the families or friends of dead Englishmen were allowed to take them away for inter-ment. The remainder were probably left where they fell, like the Norsemen who died at Stamford Bridge: Ordericus Vitalis saw their whitened bones there 70 years later. Although the bodies of Gyrth and Leofwine were found, Harold himself could not be recognized. His mis-tress Edith Swan-Neck is said to have waited near the battlefield and was able to identify the King's mutilated body. William of Malmesbury claims that a knight was expelled from the army for having cut Harold's hands off after death. Harold's mother Gytha offered William her son's weight in gold for his body. William, unwilling to grant burial in hallowed ground to a man whose ambition had caused so much grief, refused. The body was probably buried beneath a pile of stones on unconsecrated ground but, according to a strong tradition, was later moved to Waltham Abbey in Essex.

William Seals His Victory

Complete though William's victory at Hastings was, it did not end the war at a stroke. After waiting five days in his camp above Hastings, resting his army and hoping in vain that the English would send a delegation, William marched, via Tenterden and Lympne, to Dover, where his army was afflicted by an outbreak of dysentery. William himself pushed on to accept the surrender of Canterbury, where he too was overtaken by sickness. A strong detachment made for London, fired Southwark, but found London Bridge firmly defended and was unable to take the city by surprise.

William's main force continued westwards, through Guildford, and on to Winchester, the ancient capital of Wessex, which surrendered. Parties of mounted men fanned out across Hampshire and Berkshire, laying waste to the countryside to obtain food and intimidate the Londoners. Archbishop Stigand submitted at Wallingford, and other English leaders came in to surrender at Little Berkhamsted in Hertfordshire. Encouraged by his own army and by these magnates, who believed that William's assumption of the throne would bring the stability they desired, the Duke advanced on London. Recent evidence suggests that there was a sharp battle with hostile Londoners near St Paul's, but the army that had won Hastings was not to be thwarted by this sort of resistance, and William was crowned king in Westminster Abbey on Christmas Day 1066.

A View of the Field

Despite a shifting coastline and over nine centuries of building, the key events of October 1066 are easy to trace on the ground. Pevensey Castle is a good starting-point, though it is important to remember my caution-ary words about the changed outline of the coast in this part of Sussex. The low-lying Pevensey Levels, north of the town, are in fact the silted-up lagoon, and the A259 to Bexhill runs across the narrow neck which once joined it to the sea.

The Romans built Anderida, one of the Saxon shore forts, on a spit of land then open to the sea on three sides. In 491 it was besieged and taken by Aelle, King of the South Saxons, who massacred every man, woman and child in it: 'there was not even one Briton left there,' laments *The Anglo-Saxon Chronicle*. When William landed there he made prepara-tions for hasty defence, and later the site was strengthened by his half-brother Robert of Mortain, who built a keep in the south-east corner of the Roman fort. The castle was besieged several times, notably by Simon de Montfort's son in 1264-5, but was never taken by assault. As the sea receded it gradually lost importance, though it was briefly fortified during the Spanish invasion scare of 1587-8, and during the Second World War machine-gun positions were built into its ancient walls. Pevensey Castle is open daily from 10 a.m. to 6 p.m.

Hastings
We cannot be sure whether, after his first landing at Pevensey, William moved to Hastings by land, or accompanied his fleet. Local tradition suggests the latter, for the massive Conqueror's Stone, on the seafront near the pier, is said to have served as table for his first meal in England. The castle on the hill above the old town was begun in 1067 or 1078 to replace the wooden structure put up immediately after the landing. There are substantial remains, including parts of the north and east walls, a gatehouse and a tower, although the steady advance of the cliff-edge has claimed the southern part of the castle. It is open daily between 10 a.m.

and 4.30 p.m., and the Battle of Hastings Experience is repeated every half-hour. The Town Hall contains the Hastings embroidery, a 243 foot (74 m) long tapestry depicting events in British history since 1066, made by the Royal School of Needlework to commemorate the nine hundredth anniversary of the Conquest.

Battle

The town of Battle, where the battle of Hastings took place, is 7 miles (11 km) from Hastings on the A2100. This partly follows the route of the old road, and, approaching the battlefield as the Conqueror would have done, the traveller crosses Blackhorse Hill, where William's men halted to don their hauberks. Then, further north, the track to Telham Court leads to a spot on the old road from which William might first have caught sight of his opponents on Senlac Hill, although trees now obscure his view.

William crossed the saddle in the area between the lodge of Battle Abbey Park and Battle station, and deployed for battle on both sides of the road. The site of Harold's position is now dominated by the ruins of Battle Abbey. William ordered that a church should be build on Senlac Hill to commemorate his victory, and its high altar was traditionally placed on the spot where Harold fell. Bendictine monks later built St Martin's Abbey nearby, and its fourteenth-century gatehouse, dormitory and refectory survive. The building of the abbey and subsequent work in the sixteenth century altered the slope of the hill, which is gentler now than it was in 1066.

Much of the battlefield is now sensitively administered by English Heritage, and is entered from a car park at the bottom of Battle High Street. A public car park stands directly in front of the gatehouse, now the entrance to Battle Abbey School, and the battlefield car park is a little further on, to the right. There is an introductory video, and vistors can then use hand-held audio wands to take a 30- or 45-minute battlefield tour. Route maps are provided for those who prefer not to take the audio tour.

Although the west range of abbey buildings forms part of Battle Abbey School and can only be visited during the school's summer holiday, the greater part of the abbey, including church, cloister, common room and novice's room, is open to the public. The position of the high altar of the Norman church is marked by a stone, erected in 1903 to mark the place where Harold fell, and there is a smaller stone nearby giving a more modern suggestion for the spot. The site is still very atmospheric, and there are open grassy slopes south-east of the abbey, where much of the fighting took place.

Harold's battle-line ran to east and west across ground which later bore the abbey buildings. With the twin towers of Princess Elizabeth's Lodging

The twin towers of Princess Elizabeth's Lodging, part of the complex of buildings, Battle Abbey and Battle Abbey School, which are now on the site of Harold's position. Here they are seen from the slope up which the Normans attacked. In 1066 this ground was open and the slope was steeper. The English shield-wall ran along the ridge, its front roughly following the line of this fence.

behind us we can see, off to our right front, the hillock where the English who pursued the fleeing Bretons made their last stand. Beyond it the stream, which helped make the ground so boggy in 1066, was later dammed to make fish ponds for the abbey. Harold's right probably stretched some 250 yards (230 m) beyond Princess Elizabeth's Lodgings. A broad track along the ridge-top, past the children's activity area, leads to a wooded area where the ground falls away sharply and marks the right end of Harold's line. His left probably ended about 50 yards (45 m) south of the primary school in Battle itself.

Harold's army approached the position along the line of the modern High Street, and Whatlington Road which swings right at its northern end. About 500 yards (460 m) along it, a white windmill, now a private house, stands on the position of the hoar-apple tree on Caldbec Hill. Kingsmead Open Space, just behind the mill, is probably where Harold and so many of his men spent their last night on earth.

CHAPTER 2

Bosworth
1485

Background

It was the last hurrah of English chivalry. Richard III, in full armour, gold crown around his helmet, led a handful of his closest adherents down the hill. He had already declined a captain's suggestion that he should flee, replying: 'This day I will die as a king or win.' His target was the knot of knights surrounding his rival, Henry Tudor, and so great was his impact that he killed Henry's standard-bearer, William Brandon, and knocked down John Cheney, a man 'of surpassing bravery'.

It could not last. Some of Richard's supposed supporters turned against him, and his little band was encircled and outnumbered. However gallant his last charge, there was nothing romantic about his last moments. His horse stuck fast in a swamp, and he was dragged from its back by foot-soldiers and finished off as he writhed on the ground. Then his mangled body was stripped and thrown across a horse, 'hair hanging as one would bear a sheep.'

Bosworth marked a change of direction for the monarchy which had been initiated, nearly four centuries before, after another English king had died in battle. William the Conqueror's coronation on Christmas Day 1066 had not secured Norman rule. William faced repeated uprisings, and his stern response culminated in his systematic ravaging of the North in 1069: he could not bend the Saxons, so broke them instead.

The Conquest was much more than a change of dynasties. As John Gillingham has observed: 'England received not just a new royal family but also a new ruling class, a new culture and language.' In 1066 there were some 4000 thegns. When the *Domesday Book* completed its survey 20 years later only two significant English lords remained: fewer than 200 Norman barons now

Gothic armour *(top)* was popular at the time of Bosworth. Well-fitting armour was less cumbersome than it appears, and a man-at-arms could mount and dismount in armour. Although horses could be partly protected, and would bite and kick in self-defence, they were vulnerable to an infantryman who ducked beneath them. The halberd *(bottom)* was a popular infantry weapon: it could be used for cutting and stabbing, and sometimes had a hook to pull a horseman from his charger.

held the land. The castles which are still a feature of our landscape bear witness to the fact that the Conqueror's was a garrison state.

The extent to which Norman rule permeated English society has divided historians, though most agree that if the Conquest brought profound change, it did not sever strong threads of continuity. At one level, French language and culture were dominant: at another, as D. M. Stenton observed, 'the slow routines of the agricultural year remained the basic facts of life, and Englishmen pursued them as they had done for centuries before Hastings was fought and lost'.

The Plantaganets

William's sons, William Rufus (reigned 1087–1100) and Henry I (reigned 1100–1135), clashed with their elder brother Robert, who had inherited Normandy. With Robert's defeat at Tinchebray in 1106 kingdom and duchy were again united. Henry's heir was his daughter Matilda, married to Geoffrey Plantaganet, son of Count Fulk of Anjou. But Henry's nephew Stephen also laid claim to the throne, and in 1153, after a bitter civil war, it was agreed that Stephen would reign for life, and that on his death Matilda's son Henry Plantaganet would succeed. The name Plantaganet derives from the Angevin emblem of *planta genista* – broom plant – and the memorial marking the spot where Richard III is believed to have fallen at Bosworth observes that he was the last of the Plantaganet kings.

Henry II (reigned 1154–1189) inherited an empire running from the Pyrenees to the Scottish border. He spent two-thirds of his reign on the Continent, holding his possessions together, and determined to partition them between his three eldest sons. In the event, Richard I (reigned 1189–1199) inherited most of his father's domains and spent little time in England. He died childless, and although his brother John (reigned 1199–1216) took over most of the Angevin Empire he could not hold it.

In England, a baronial revolt forced John to accept limitations on royal power embodied in Magna Carta (1215). Attempts to implement it led to more clashes, and the barons offered the throne to the French Prince Louis. The supporters of John's son Henry III (reigned 1216–1272) defeated Louis, but Henry proved less successful on the Continent, giving up most of the Angevin Empire and doing homage to the French king for Gascony. He too found himself in difficulties with his barons, but the defeat of Simon de Montfort at Evesham in 1265 enabled him to pass on a stable kingdom to his son Edward.

Edward I (reigned 1272–1307) spent much of his rule at war. Between 1276 and 1284 he subdued Wales, though, despite his nickname 'the hammer of the Scots', he was less successful in Scotland. His son Edward II (reigned 1307–27) was defeated by Robert Bruce at Bannockburn in 1314, a victory which helped Scotland win recognition as an independent nation.

Edward was no more successful at home, and was imprisoned and murdered in 1327. His son Edward III (reigned 1327–1377) continued to fight the Scots but was never able to make his victories conclusive. He campaigned in France on an even greater scale, claiming the French throne by right of his mother, Isabella, a princess of the French royal house. Although he won Crécy (1346), the first land battle of the Hundred Years War, and his son the Black Prince went on to win Poitiers (1356), decisive victory eluded him in France as it had in Scotland.

The War of the Roses
Edward's death saw the first stirrings of another conflict. Its title, 'The Wars of the Roses', has irritated some historians, who have pointed out that red and white roses were only two of the many badges used by the Houses of Lancaster and York. Instead of a long-running dynastic struggle, John Gillingham identifies three distinct wars. The first was caused by Henry VI's failure as king, the second by the discontent of the Earl of Warwick and the third by Richard III's seizure of the throne. These conflicts all occurred within a single society and the space of one generation. They were largely wars within the political nation, and much of the country's social, economic and religious life went on around them.

Edward III's fourth son, John of Gaunt, Duke of Lancaster, an enormously wealthy man, dominated the government under the last years of Edward. He was opposed by his elder brother the Black Prince, and by Edmund Mortimer, Earl of March, who enjoyed wide influence in Wales and the Marches and was married to Edward's grand-daughter. In as much as the Wars of the Roses were about dynastic rivalry, the warring dynasties were founded by John of Gaunt and Edmund Mortimer.

King Edward outlived the Black Prince, whose ten-year-old son Richard II succeeded to the throne in 1377. During his minority, war went badly in France, Spain and the Scottish Borders, and in 1381 the growing burden of taxes sparked off the Peasants' Revolt. The young king behaved with great courage, and the rebels dispersed, encouraged by charters abolishing serfdom and trade restrictions. After the rising the ruling class reasserted itself. 'Villeins ye are still,' Richard told a delegation of peasants, 'and villeins ye shall remain.'

The King was less fortunate with his noble opponents, who resented his attempts to bring the Continental war to an end. In 1397 their

'Merciless' Parliament executed, imprisoned or exiled most of his supporters. Richard took pains to rebuild his own authority, and in 1398 served his opponents the same way. Determined to snuff out all sources of resistance, he exiled John of Gaunt's son, Henry Bolingbroke, Duke of Lancaster.

It was a fatal mistake. Richard misjudged his own power and alienated much of the political nation, for if a duke could be exiled without reason, whose property was safe? Bolingbroke speedily returned with an army at his back: Richard was captured and 'agreed' to abdicate. Bolingbroke claimed the throne by descent, conquest and the need for better rule, and became Henry IV.

'The consequences of the usurpation of 1399,' wrote A. R. Myers, 'dogged the Lancastrian dynasty like a Nemesis which in the long run it could not escape.' Henry's rule depended on might, not right, and the men who had helped him to the throne had to be rewarded. There was a conspiracy in early 1400, which narrowly failed to kill Henry but sealed the fate of Richard II, who died in Pontefract Castle soon afterwards. Owain Glyndwr led a rising in Wales, and in the North the powerful Percys allied themselves to the Scots and marched south to join him. Henry defeated them at Shrewsbury, but it was not until 1408 that the Earl of Northumberland, head of the Percys, was killed. Although the last five years of Henry's reign were relatively peaceful, the country was prey to tensions which the crown's dependence on the magnates prevented it from checking.

Henry V, who came to the throne in 1413, was a pious, self-confident young man who had gained experience in his father's wars. He asserted his claim to the throne of a France weakened by factional strife. Though Henry was sincere, his claim also made good political sense, for the war offered noblemen and humble soldiers alike the prospect of personal profit, and success would demonstrate that his father's seizure of the throne had divine approval. His victory at Agincourt that October eclipsed even Crécy and Poitiers, but it was not until 1420 that Henry was able to conclude a treaty which would give him the French throne on the death of its holder.

Henry died early, however, in 1422, and was succeeded by his two-year-old son, Henry VI. During the first years of the new king's minority power was in the hands of a council, its factions led by Henry's uncle Humphrey, Duke of Gloucester and Henry Beaufort, Bishop of Winchester. Another uncle, John, Duke of Bedford, was Regent of France, and it was thanks to his skill that England retained a tenuous grasp on her continental possessions. The war went badly, and its cost promoted resentment in Parliament and encouraged the Beaufort faction to seek terms with France. The young king's marriage to a French princess, Margaret of Anjou, brought a two-year truce. When the war flared up again in 1449 the French over-ran the whole of Normandy and went on, in 1453, to destroy the last English army at Castillon in Gascony, leaving only Calais in English hands.

The loss of Normandy provoked violent reaction. The King's chief minister, the Duke of Suffolk, was impeached in Parliament and fled, only to be captured by mutinous sailors and summarily beheaded, and Jack Cade led a Kentish rising which briefly occupied London. The gentle and devout Henry VI was never robust and now suffered a complete collapse. Richard, Duke of York, Edmund Mortimer's great-grandson and, since Duke Humphrey's death in 1447, leader of the opposition to the Beauforts, was declared Protector of the Realm during the King's illness. Queen Margaret bore a son in October 1453, and although York was swift to recognize him as heir to the throne, the Queen's fears for the child's safety made her an implacable enemy of York's. The scene was set for the first round of open war.

In May 1455 the Yorkists advanced on London, and at the first Battle of St Albans, Edmund Beaufort, Duke of Somerset, was killed and King Henry captured. Fighting broke out afresh in 1459, and in December 1460 York, who had now claimed the throne, was defeated and killed at Wakefield. Margaret then marched south and beat the Yorkist Richard Neville, Earl of Warwick, at the second Battle of St Albans, but her husband dissuaded her from taking London. Instead, it was York's eldest son Edward, a youth of 19, who entered the capital, where he was proclaimed Edward IV.

Edward and Warwick marched north against the Lancastrians, and on Palm Sunday 1461 the armies met at Towton, 6 miles (10 km) north of Ferrybridge in Yorkshire. The battle was fought in a driving snowstorm, and Lord Fauconberg, commanding the Yorkist vanguard, ordered his archers to shoot a volley of arrows which, with the gale behind them, hit the Lancastrians. The Lancastrians shot back, but to little effect as their arrows fell short. When the armies came to hand-strokes the battle was pursued with unusual ferocity. The turning-point came when the Duke of Norfolk arrived on the Lancastrian left flank with Yorkist reinforcements, and as night fell the Lancastrians broke. The survivors had to cross the River Cock as they made for Tadcaster, and many died under the swords of the pursuing cavalry. Contemporary estimates of 28,000 killed are probably too high, but Towton was the largest battle of the Wars of the Roses and the bloodiest ever fought on English soil.

Many leading Lancastrians were slain in the battle, and other notable captives were killed shortly afterwards. The Bishop of Exeter was among the many who hoped that this carnage signalled the end of the blood-letting. 'After so much sorrow and tribulation,' he mused, 'I hope that grateful tranquillity and quiet will ensue, and that after so many clouds we shall have a clear sky.'

The good bishop was to be disappointed, and the reason for this lay in the characters of two of the architects of Yorkist victory, Edward IV and his cousin Richard, Earl of Warwick. The young king was affable and pleasure-loving, and left the affairs of the kingdom to Warwick. In 1464, after a long campaign in the north, the Earl defeated Queen Margaret, and captured her hapless spouse the following year. Warwick was in the process of negotiating a peace with France, which would have been sealed by a marriage between Edward and a French princess, when he was told that the King had already wed a pretty Lancastrian widow, Elizabeth Woodville. Royal favours were showered upon the Woodvilles, and Warwick, stung to the quick, began to shift his allegiance, coming to an agreement with the King's brother, George, Duke of Clarence, to whom he married his daughter.

In the spring of 1469 there were risings in Yorkshire in which Robin of Redesdale – probably Sir William Conyers, a Neville supporter – played a leading part. But Warwick first pretended to be an honest intermediary, pressing the King to meet the rebels' demands for reform, but on 26 July 1469 he beat the royal army at Edgecote, executing its captured leaders. Edward himself was taken shortly afterwards and kept in honourable cap-tivity. But Warwick could not exploit his success. He did not wish to restore Henry VI, and could not govern through Edward IV, who was soon released and swiftly reasserted his authority.

Early in 1470 Warwick and Clarence began another rising, but it was nipped in the bud by Edward's victory at Lose-cote Field near Stamford in Lincolnshire, so called because of the speed with which the rebels jettisoned their armour. Edward declared Warwick and Clarence traitors, and they fled to France where, under pressure from Louis XI, they were reconciled with the exiled Queen Margaret.

In September 1470 England was invaded by Warwick and Clarence with Lancastrian support. King Edward fled to Burgundy, and Henry IV, wits quite gone, was removed from the Tower of London and reinstalled on the throne. The Duke of Burgundy supported his royal guest, and in March 1471 Edward landed at Ravenspur on the Humber. Most Yorkists rallied to him, and even Clarence changed sides, realizing that the associ-ation between Margaret and Warwick would be fatal to his own ambitions.

Edward entered London unopposed, and on 13 April moved north to meet Warwick who was approaching with a larger army.

The battle of Barnet was fought on Easter Sunday, 14 April 1471, in a fog so thick that the armies were not quite aligned, and the right wing of each overlapped the other's left. The Lancastrian right beat the Yorkist left and vice versa, but when the victorious Lancastrians returned to the field they were fired on by their own side and fled in panic. Although both sides suffered heavy losses, the battle was a Yorkist victory, for Warwick himself perished.

Queen Margaret had not accompanied Warwick to England, depriving him of the aid of Lancastrians who might have risen against Edward IV. She landed at Weymouth, with her son Edward, Prince of Wales, the day Warwick died at Barnet, and found much support in the West Country. King Edward left Windsor with a hastily assembled force on 24 April, and on 3 May he caught up with the Lancastrians at Tewkesbury. The Duke of Somerset, the Lancastrian commander, took up a strong natural position south of Tewkesbury Abbey, but appears to have been provoked into attacking by the superior firepower of the leading Yorkist division, under Edward IV's brother Richard, Duke of Gloucester. The armies were locked in battle when a small force of Yorkist spearmen, posted in Tewkesbury Park on Edward's left, swung in and crumpled Somerset's right flank. The Lancastrian army broke, and its casualties were heavy: Queen Margaret's son, young Prince Edward, was amongst the slain. Somerset and other surviving nobles took refuge in Tewkesbury Abbey but were hauled out and beheaded the following day.

There were risings elsewhere, only one of them serious. Thomas Fauconberg, an illegitimate son of William Neville, Lord Fauconberg, and a cousin of Warwick's, led a force of seamen, soldiers from the Calais garrison, and disaffected men from Kent and Essex in an assault on London. It had been dealt with by citizens and loyal noblemen before King Edward returned to the capital on 21 May.

He quickly set the seal on his victories. Margaret, captured after Tewkesbury, was imprisoned and then exiled to France. The captive Henry VI died 'of pure displeasure and melancholy', though it would not be unfair to see Edward's hand behind his demise. The Lancastrian nobility had been decimated by death in battle and execution after it, although modern research has shown that the damage done to the nobility by the Wars of the Roses was not as great as contemporaries opined. One of the two remaining Lancastrian peers, John de Vere, Earl of Oxford, was captured in 1474 after a siege in St Michael's Mount off the Cornish coast. He was packed off to prison at Hammes Castle, near Calais.

The dynasty seemed secure. Edward IV had two sons, Edward, born in 1470, and Richard, born three years later. The crown's chronic financial weakness was being remedied by the enormous wealth of the house of York, confiscations from defeated Lancastrians, and a subsidy paid by the French as the price of ending a brief war in 1475. The troublesome North was in the capable hands of the King's brother, Richard of Gloucester. Clarence, forgiven for his earlier lapse, took to intriguing again and was killed – he may, as legend suggests, have been drowned in a tub of Malmsey wine. There was some bickering at court, but when was there not? Whatever the failings of Shakespeare's *Richard III* as history, its opening lines (a pun on the family's *rose-en-soleil* badge) deftly captures this apotheosis of the royal house:

> Now is the winter of our discontent
> Made glorious summer by this sun of York
> And all the clouds that lour'd upon our house
> In the deep bosom of the ocean buried.

Changes in Weaponry and Armour

While combat in the Wars of the Roses would not have shocked the men who fought at Hastings, war had moved on. The bad-egg stink of black powder was now laced into the familiar battlefield stench of blood, sweat and ordure, human and equine. Gunpowder had been known in China in the eleventh century, and primitive cannon were in use in Europe early in the fourteenth, but it was another century before they were widespread. Iron cannon tended to be fragile, so most guns were cast in brass.

Though standardization of calibres was still more than a century away, cannon came in several general types. At the lower end of the scale were close-range weapons like the orgue, a group of gun-barrels fastened to a frame so that all could be fired at once (the ancestor, in its clumsy way, of the machine-gun). Larger cannon, like the serpentine, provided the armies of the period with the closest they came to field artillery. Although these might throw iron or stone balls 1000 yards (900 m), their crews would be fortunate to get off ten shots an hour and more fortunate still to hit what they aimed at. Many battles began with a cannonade, but few rounds were fired before the opposing armies were at work with sword and axe.

If cannon had a limited effect on battles in open field, they were devastating against castle walls. Sieges, which might once have lasted for months as engineers tried to undermine fortifications, or cost many lives as infantry assaulted up scaling-ladders or from siege towers, could now be over in days: in 1405 Berwick surrendered after a single shot had been fired.

Engineers responded by building fortifications lower and putting sloping earth, not rising stonework, in the way of the cannon ball. At the very end of the fifteenth century the bastion, an arrow-head gun-platform thrust forward from the walls of a fortress, made its first appearance, and soon became the quintessential item of artillery fortification. Although there are some examples in the British Isles, artillery fortification never speckled the British landscape as it did the continental.

Gunpowder also contributed to infantry firepower. By 1485 primitive 'hand-gonnes' had been replaced by weapons which were beginning to resemble the musket of later generations. These had a wooden butt and, in some cases, a mechanism which brought a smouldering cord down to the touch-hole when the firer pressed its trigger.

Hand-guns could kill men and terrify horses, but for range, accuracy and rate of fire they were eclipsed by the longbow: in 1549 insurgents under the Norfolk landowner Robert Kett outshot German mercenary hand-gunners sent against them. The longbow's origins remain disputed, though the Welsh were certainly making good use of it as early as 1150, when Gerald de Barri observed that Welsh archers sent arrows through an oak door four fingers thick. In 1252 the royal Assize of Arms decreed that all Englishmen who owned land worth more than 40 shillings or chattels worth 9 marks were to provide themselves with sword, dagger, bow and arrows.

The bow's use had been developed during Edward I's Scottish and Welsh wars, and it was the characteristic English infantry weapon of the Hundred Years War. In the Wars of the Roses the archers on both sides often cancelled one another out. It was only when one side gained a clear advantage – like the Yorkists at Towton – or was unable to bring its bowmen into play – like the Yorkists at Edgecote – that the bow proved a battle-winner. Plate armour was now so well developed as to keep out most arrows save at close range, though areas protected only by mail were always vulnerable.

It is almost true to say that archers were born, not made, for it took years of practice for a man to achieve the upper body strength to use a war-bow with a draw-weight of over 100lb (45 kg). Dominic Mancini, an Italian priest who visited England in 1482–3 told his bishop:

Their bows and arrows are thicker and longer than those used by other nations just as their arms are stronger than other people's, for they seem to have hands and arms of iron. As a result their bows have as long a range as our crossbows.

Battlefield losses made inroads into the stock of trained archers. Sixteenth-century complaints that the bow was falling into disuse doubtless

had much to do, as contemporaries suspected, with the rise of
football and other 'lewd games',
but the casualties of the century's bloodier
battles also played their part.

If the longbow had developed since
Hastings, so too had its cousin the crossbow.
Many fifteenth-century crossbows had steel or composite
staves, and their increased power meant that they had to be
drawn by a windlass or pulley. Their stubby
bolts could crack plate armour if they struck it
squarely, and a well-trained crossbowman could
shoot four or five times a minute.

Some infantrymen bore staff weapons. The long-bladed English bill
was popular throughout the period. The halberd, with an axe-blade one
side and a point on the other, was equally effective. Mercenaries from the
Low Countries served on both sides, and often used the pike, with a shaft
up to 18 feet (5.5 m) long.

The pike had an awesome reputation on the Continent, and Swiss pikemen inflicted catastrophic defeats on feudal cavalry. In Flemish hands,
too, it was a weapon to be reckoned with, but in the Wars of the Roses it
never assumed the same importance, possibly because wedges of pikemen
were vulnerable to bowmen at a distance and to billmen once their shorter
weapon was inside the pike's reach. Much of the conflict between Scots
and English centred around the interplay between tough Scottish spearmen, who drew up in masses called *schiltroms,* and English archers and
billmen.

The man-at-arms was still king of the battlefield. He was the descendant of William's horsemen, though his appearance had changed since the
days of the conical helmet and mail hauberk. Plate armour arrived to rein-
force mail in the thirteenth century, full plate was in use at the beginning
of the fifteenth, and over the next hundred years it reached a peak of
sophistication. Armour was subject to the vagaries of fashion and the
impact of technology. Curved surfaces induced blows to glance off, and
articulated joints assisted movement. Surfaces might be gilded or
engraved, or blued, browned or painted to protect them from rust.

Some armour was English-made, but much came from Flanders, South
Germany and North Italy. A wealthy man could afford a suit in the latest
fashion – the flamboyant Gothic style was popular at the time of
Bosworth – but there was mixing and matching as old but serviceable
armour was retained in use. The term man-at-arms includes any warrior

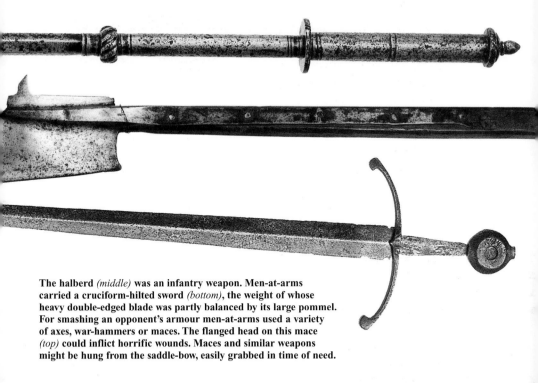

The halberd *(middle)* was an infantry weapon. Men-at-arms
carried a cruciform-hilted sword *(bottom)*, the weight of whose
heavy double-edged blade was partly balanced by its large pommel.
For smashing an opponent's armour men-at-arms used a variety
of axes, war-hammers or maces. The flanged head on this mace
(top) could inflict horrific wounds. Maces and similar weapons
might be hung from the saddle-bow, easily grabbed in time of need.

fighting in full armour – knight, esquire, gentleman or mounted sergeant.
The latter, derived from the Latin *serviens*, servant, denoted a warrior
below the rank of gentleman but above that of common soldier.

Not all men-at-arms wore full armour. Some could not afford it, and
others, especially if fighting on foot, abandoned breast- and back-plate in
favour of a brigandine, a jerkin made of several layers of cloth or leather
with small iron plates sandwiched between. A knight's brigandine might
be covered in rich material and finished with gilded rivets, while a lower-
ranking man-at-arms or infantryman would have been content with something less decorative. Simpler still was the jack, a quilted canvas jacket or
jerkin stuffed with padding, worn by many infantrymen. Brigandines and
jacks were worn over mail, if the soldier had it, and might be reinforced
by plate armour, for instance in the form of arm or leg defences.

The straight cruciform-hilted sword was the classic knightly weapon,
but other arms were often more appropriate. The lance was invaluable in
the first impact of a charge. War-hammers and maces could combine
blades, spikes and hammerheads to pierce or smash armour. The pole-axe,
with a spiked or bladed head on a shaft 3–4 feet (90–120 cm) long, was a
favourite weapon for men-at-arms on foot. At Edgecote the Yorkist Sir

William Herbert 'valiantly acquitted himself in that, on foot and with his pole-axe in his hand, he twice by main force passed through the battle of his adversaries and without any mortal wound returned.' Soldiers carried a knife of some sort, from the knightly misericorde (so called because it slipped between plates of armour to ease the life out of a crippled opponent) to the 'ballock' dagger, with its distinctive two-globed guard, favoured by foot-soldiers.

Although some foot-soldiers plied a small one-handed buckler, shields went out of general use in the middle of the fifteenth century. They had been a convenient way of displaying heraldic devices which aided recognition in battle, but these could still be shown on tabards worn over armour. Contingents raised by individuals or towns usually wore coloured livery tunics, with a badge on chest or shoulder, over their jacks or brigandines: Warwick's men wore red jackets with his badge of bear and ragged staff in white. Badges like this were simpler than coats of arms. Richard III used his white boar, Henry Tudor a red dragon, and the Earl of Oxford a white star: Lord Welles, with a rather weak pun, favoured a bucket and chain.

Military Organization

Liveries and badges reflected military organization. The Norman conquest saw the establishment of feudalism in England: great noblemen, the king's tenants-in-chief, held their land in return for providing agreed numbers of knights for a set period; and they in turn granted land to knights who would serve when required. Other knights might form part of their lord's household, or simply be hired.

The process was never entirely satisfactory for the monarch, who risked seeing knights melt away as their term of service expired, or who might simply find them inappropriate for the task in hand. Magnates and retainers, who faced the disruption arising from a call to arms, found the arrangement no more appealing. Increasingly, feudal service was commuted into payment called scutage – from the Latin *scutum* (shield) which offered greater flexibility. Infantry were often recruited by means of a commission of array, which appointed commissioners – usually men of military experience – to supervise levies raised by local communities.

Edward III tried to revive feudal obligations, insisting that a man worth £40 in land was obliged to provide two men-at-arms. Successes in the Scots War restrained the outcry caused by such demands, but in 1352 he conceded that they would be made only with Parliament's agreement. Thereafter he developed the practice of contracting with leaders, who, in return for pay, agreed to provide a force of a specified size at a given date.

These contractors tended to be noblemen, who used the bonds of loyalty which already existed around their estates as the basis for their contingents. Great landowners maintained knights and squires who were paid annuities or given land-holdings to retain their loyalty, and who acted as sub-contractors by turning out with retinues of their own. Some archers served full-time in the household of a nobleman, but others were recruited only in time of war.

The contract system worked well enough during the Hundred Years War, when soldiers might expect rich pickings in France. After the war England was awash with unemployed soldiers, many of whom found employment in the retinues of great nobles. When royal authority was weak, noblemen with armed bands grew increasingly powerful, encouraging lesser men to put themselves under their protection and, in return, to provide military service, wearing the lord's badge and livery.

Though there was no standing army in the late Middle Ages, the royal household provided the kernel for raising an army. Kings maintained bodyguards of knights and men-at-arms: Edward IV had his own archers, and soon after his accession Henry VII founded the Yeomen of the Guard. Calais was an English-held enclave in France, with castles like Hammes and Guines protecting it. Its garrison was composed of professional soldiers, and the post of Captain of Calais was a powerful one. English kings had frequently recruited foreign mercenaries, who were often more reliable than Englishmen in civil wars, provided their wages were paid. Finally, most monarchs had a regional power base and family affiliations which made it easier for them to raise troops on home ground.

Yet the fact remains that, to raise a large army, a king relied heavily on the support of great nobles, and much of the manoeuvring of the age was intended to encourage loyalty by means of dynastic links, and grants of money, land or titles. Disloyalty was punished not simply by death – beheading for noblemen and hanging, drawing and quartering for lesser men – but by attainder, which deprived the condemned man of lands, title and possessions, leaving his family paupers.

Campaign and Battle

'Between 1483 and 1485,' writes Michael Bennett, 'it is tempting to see all roads leading to Bosworth. This quiet market centre, in the heart of *champion* England, seems almost to have exercised a gravitational pull on the actors in the tragedy of Richard III.' And tragedy it was, for in two short years the sun of York burned out for ever, scorching many who came close to it.

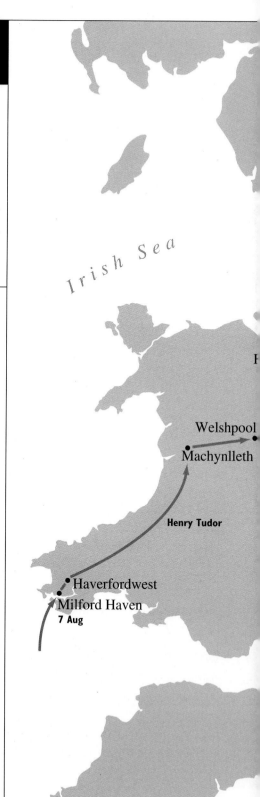

BOSWORTH
1485: The Campaign

→ Henry Tudor's
troop movements

→ Richard III's
troop movements

0   20   40 Miles

0   20   40   60   80 Kms

Irish Sea

H

Welshpool
Machynlleth

Henry Tudor

Haverfordwest
Milford Haven
7 Aug

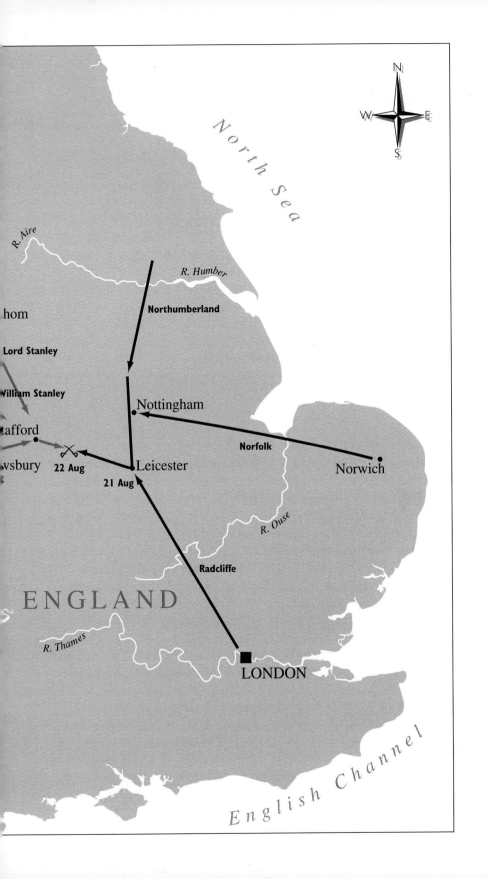

hom

Lord Stanley

William Stanley

afford

wsbury

22 Aug

21 Aug

Leicester

Nottingham

Northumberland

Norfolk

Norwich

Radcliffe

■
LONDON

ENGLAND

North Sea

R. Aire

R. Humber

R. Ouse

R. Thames

English Channel

N
W E
S

The Protectorate

Edward IV unexpectedly fell ill at Easter 1483 and died on 9 April. On his
death-bed he exhorted his counsellors to make peace with one another, and
nominated his brother Richard as Protector, chairman of the council which
would govern in his son's minority. No sooner was the King dead than
Queen Elizabeth and her relatives, notably her brother Earl Rivers and
Thomas Grey, Marquess of Dorset, her son by her first marriage, sought
to bring the thirteen-year-old young King Edward down from Ludlow with
a Woodville escort and have him crowned as soon as possible. Richard
was away in the North, probably at his castle at Middleham, but saw the
risks he ran. Not only would his influence count for little in a Woodville-
dominated court, but his personal safety could hardly be guaranteed.

Others found the Queen's faction equally threatening. Edward IV's
chief counsellor Lord Hastings feared that 'if power slipped into the grasp
of the Queen's relatives they would avenge the injuries they claimed he
had done them – for between him and them there was a feud of long
standing.' Hastings was Captain of Calais, and warned the Queen's kinsmen that if they made Edward V's escort too large he would flee to Calais
– whence, in collaboration with the French or Burgundian courts, he
could make their lives difficult. They agreed that the escort should not
exceed 2000 men. The powerful Henry Stafford, Duke of Buckingham,
had been married off at the age of 11 to one of the Queen's sisters, but
resented the match and regarded his in-laws as arrivistes: he too was not
anxious to see the Woodvilles triumphant.

On 29 April Gloucester met Buckingham at Northampton, and the
Dukes were not pleased to find that the young King Edward and his
escort had already passed on their way to London. When Earl Rivers and
his nephew Sir Richard Grey rode back to welcome the Dukes they were
arrested. Gloucester and Buckingham then rode on to Stony Stratford
where they took charge of the King, seizing more of his entourage and
sending them off to castles in the North. The Queen took sanctuary in
Westminster Abbey when she heard the news, taking with her Richard,
Duke of York, her younger son and the Marquess of Dorset.

The Dukes entered London on 4 May, announcing that they had
rescued the King from evil counsellors and parading cartloads of
weapons bearing the Woodville badge as proof that the Queen's kinsmen
had intended to rule by force. The Queen's brother Sir Edward Woodville
was in command of the fleet, but it was persuaded to rally to the
Protector. Richard's government seemed evenly balanced. The Queen's
relatives were ousted, but Hastings remained Lord Chamberlain and
Captain of Calais, and even Archbishop Rotherham and Bishop Morton,

who had supported the Woodvilles, were allowed to remain on the council.

Thus far Richard's behaviour had not been unreasonable, and it is easy to argue, as his supporters still do, that he was simply acting in self-defence and seeking to promote stability. The events of the weeks that followed make that justification harder to uphold but, with so little evidence at our disposal, it is difficult to be sure of his real motives. Certainly, Shakespeare's characterization of Richard as a man bent on securing the crown at all costs cannot be sustained. He had been conspicuously loyal to Edward IV, and immediately after the King's death threw his weight behind Edward V, though he pressed his claim to be Protector.

This may well have been the full extent of his ambition until the first week of June 1483, but thereafter it is clear that he was indeed determined to pluck down the crown. We cannot be sure whether he was spurred on by personal ambition, had come to the conclusion that only decisive action on his part could end the risk of anarchy, or, as seems most likely, had allowed these motives to become blurred.

There were risks in inaction. Richard's powers as Protector were limited and would eventually end. The council was unwilling to arraign the Queen's relatives for treason. Some historians have argued that Hastings, Morton and other council members were conducting secret negotiations with the Queen through Jane Shore, an ex-mistress of Edward IV who had also been involved with Hastings and Dorset.

Richard Claims the Crown

Early in June Richard began to order his supporters in the North to assemble soldiers, who were to muster at Pontefract on 18 June and then march south under the Earl of Northumberland. In the event he struck without their aid. On 13 June hostile members of the council were arrested while sitting at the Tower of London: Hastings was dragged outside and beheaded on the spot. It is possible that he had been sounded out on Richard's next proposed step, and death was his penalty for demurring. On 16 June soldiers surrounded Westminster Abbey, and the Archbishop of Canterbury persuaded the Queen to hand over the Duke of York, who was lodged with his brother in the state apartments in the Tower.

The coup was pressed ruthlessly. On 22 June the Lord Mayor's brother, Dr Ralph Shaa, preached a sermon in St Paul's, suggesting that Edward IV and Elizabeth Woodville had not been properly married. As the princes in the Tower were illegitimate they could not succeed to the throne, and the Duke of Gloucester was invited to do so instead. The Woodvilles seized in April were executed, while Thomas Howard and Thomas Berkeley (who had backed Richard) became Duke of Norfolk and Earl of

Nottingham. The Earl of Northumberland duly entered London with his army and Richard was crowned on 6 July.

Richard continued to reward his followers, many of them northerners. Viscount Lovell became Lord Chamberlain and Sir Robert Brackenbury Constable of the Tower. Both were appointed to the king's council, as were Lord Scrope, Sir Richard Radcliffe, Sir James Tyrell and Sir Richard FitzHugh. These new appointments, which reflected a shift towards the Nevilles – Richard's wife Anne was a Neville – caused some dissatisfaction, not least amongst traditional Yorkist supporters. The fate of the princes in the Tower of London also tweaked tender sensibilities. The surviving evidence would not convict Richard of complicity in their death, and there is some reason to suspect that they were murdered on Buckingham's orders in late July, but it was obvious that Richard stood to gain from the demise of his nephews.

Shortly after his coronation Richard travelled slowly to his old stamping ground in the North, received a warm welcome in York, and went on to see his son Edward invested as Prince of Wales. On 11 September he was passing through Lincoln on his way back to London when he heard that rebellion had broken out across the South, and that no less a man than Buckingham was implicated in it.

The autumn rising included not only Woodville supporters – Dorset had escaped from Westminster Abbey – but also close adherents of the late Edward IV and some prominent Lancastrians. Buckingham may have joined the rebellion because he felt that it was bound to succeed, and it certainly attracted widespread support across the South.

The Emergence of Henry Tudor

One of the strengths of the rising was the participation of Henry Tudor. His grandfather Owen, scion of a proud but undistinguished family of Welsh gentry, had been a member of Henry V's household and after the King's death had secretly married his widow, Catherine of Valois, who bore him two sons. When news of the union emerged Owen was imprisoned and Catherine sent off to a nunnery, but Henry VI soon warmed to his half-brothers, creating the elder, Jasper, Earl of Pembroke and the younger, Edmund, Earl of Richmond. Edmund married Margaret Beaufort, daughter and heir of John Beaufort, Duke of Somerset. The Beauforts were the result of an irregular union between Edward III's son John of Gaunt and Catherine Swynford. Although they had subsequently been legitimized, the Beauforts had also been barred from the succession. In 1456 Edmund died young, but not before begetting a son named in honour of Henry VI.

Henry Tudor, Earl of Richmond, had spent his life tossed on the stormy seas of politics. He was looked after by his uncle Jasper until 1461, when the Yorkist Lord Herbert was rewarded with Jasper's earldom of Pembroke and Henry became Lord Herbert's ward. Henry may have been presented at court in 1470 when Jasper helped restore Henry VI, but the following year he and his uncle fled abroad after the Yorkist triumph.

The fugitives were making for France but landed on the coast of Brittany, where they became pawns in the power-play between the Duke of Brittany, the King of France and the King of England. However, in mid-1483 the Duke of Brittany was prepared to give Henry military support. The fact that his formidable mother Margaret had married Lord Stanley, Steward of the King's Household, can have done him no harm. Moreover, Margaret and Elizabeth Woodville were in contact, and discussed the possibility of a marriage between Henry and the former Queen's daughter Elizabeth of York.

Henry's first intervention in English politics failed miserably. The 1483 rising lacked central direction, while Richard and his allies acted with determination. The King summoned troops to Leicester, whence he offered a free pardon to commoners caught up in the rebellion and put a price on their leaders' heads, while Norfolk moved down to protect the capital and deal with rebels in the South-East. Unseasonably bad weather made Buckingham's advance from South Wales particularly dispiriting. The Duke was betrayed and taken in chains to Salisbury, and when Richard arrived on 2 November Buckingham was executed.

Henry Tudor put in briefly at Plymouth, heard that the rebellion had collapsed, and returned to Brittany. Michael Bennett is right to observe that it was in a spirit of defiance rather than optimism that, before a gathering of exiles in Rennes Cathedral on Christmas Day 1483, Henry formally laid claim to the crown of England, though his title to it was weak indeed, and promised to marry Elizabeth of York as soon as he was king.

Richard Loses Support

Richard had reason to believe that the collapse of the rising left him secure, and many foreign observers agreed with him. They were not, on the face of things, wrong to do so, for the new King had many sterling qualities. He had administered the North efficiently, and shown himself a capable commander. He was genuinely pious, and proved a generous patron of the Church. If lack of stature robbed him of his brother's commanding presence, it obscured neither his regal bearing nor his Plantaganet features. He took a well-informed interest in the law, and prized good and equitable government.

But as king he was a failure. There had always been a streak of ruthlessness within him, and as he tried to tighten his grip on power he seemed out of sympathy with the mood of the land and reliant on a small group of advisers, notably Lovell, Radcliffe and Sir William Catesby. A piece of contemporary doggerel linked them to the King's white boar badge:

The Rat, the Cat, and Lovell the Dog
Do rule all England, under the Hog.

The 1484 Parliament, with Catesby as its Speaker, passed an unprecedented 100 acts of attainder in a single session: there had been 140 for the whole of Edward IV's reign.

The death that year of Richard's only legitimate son, Edward of Middleham, was a crushing blow. It is indicative of popular mistrust that, although the King came to an accommodation with Elizabeth Woodville, enabling her to leave sanctuary, it was widely believed that he had done this only in order to marry her daughter Elizabeth of York. Worse, it was said that he poisoned his wife Anne, who died in 1485, to be free to do so. The middle of the year found him at Nottingham, well aware that an invasion was likely, and anxious for it to come, not merely to end the uncertainty but to give him the chance to seek God's judgement in battle.

As Richard's position deteriorated so Henry's improved. In 1485 he left the Breton court and moved to that of Charles VIII of France. He had not been there long when he was joined by the Earl of Oxford, released from Hammes Castle by its disaffected governor. Richard recaptured Hammes and in 1485 appointed his own illegitimate son, John of Gloucester, Captain of Calais, effectively taking it into his own hands. His trusted henchman Sir James Tyrell was installed as Captain of Guines, but in the process lost his grip on Glamorgan, for which he was also responsible. It was not, as events were to show, a fair exchange.

Henry's chances of success hinged on undercutting Richard's support, for, unless he did so, any invasion force would be swamped by a larger royal army. John Howard, Duke of Norfolk, was head of a new noble family, and had gained his dukedom, the earldom of Surrey for his son Thomas, and much confiscated land to boot, as a reward for backing Richard. The Howards had played a notable part in putting down the 1483 rising, and, although they preferred their mighty castle of Framlingham to the royal court, they had much to lose from a change of regime.

In contrast Henry Percy, Earl of Northumberland, was head of a great house which was much older. The Percys had been attainted after the Yorkist victory in 1461 and saw the family earldom given to a Neville, brother of Warwick, but were restored to favour when Warwick rebelled in 1470. Henry Percy formed a good working relationship with Richard when the latter had been King Edward's Viceroy in the North, but by 1484 he found his retainers slipping away into royal service. He was sounded out by Henry Tudor's representatives, and cannot have found it easy to choose where his loyalties should lie.

Thomas, Lord Stanley, was in an even more ambivalent position. His great-grandfather had been a soldier of fortune under Richard II, and since then the family had risen, through deft political moves and good governance of their estates, to form a solid regional power base in Lancashire and Cheshire. Stanley's father was ennobled in 1456 and died soon afterwards, but his son showed all the family flair for backing the winning side. If, from one viewpoint, this was sheer dynastic self-interest, from another it was a refusal to allow the oscillations of national politics to affect the lives of ordinary folk in the family's domains.

Lord Stanley's eldest son George had married the daughter and heiress of Lord Strange, thereby inheriting that title, and his brother Sir William Stanley had done almost as well for himself by marrying the widowed Countess of Worcester. The Stanleys had supported Richard during the autumn rising of 1483 and prospered by it, with grants of lands and offices. But by the summer of 1485, even if the King was unaware of just how deeply Lord Stanley's wife, Margaret Beaufort, was involved in Henry Tudor's preparations, he knew that the family had divided loyalties. When Stanley was sent off to raise troops his son, Lord Strange, was retained at court as a hostage.

Preparations for War

Richard had kept court in Westminster over the winter of 1484–5, and in the spring moved, by way of Windsor and Kenilworth, to Nottingham. Although the King was fond of hunting in nearby Sherwood Forest, he was drawn to Nottingham for excellent strategic reasons. He had improved its already strong castle, which was within easy distance of his own power base north of the Trent, and from it he hoped to dominate the Midlands. The Duke of Norfolk controlled East Anglia, Brackenbury's men garrisoned the Tower of London, and Lovell, at Southampton, watched the south coast. South Wales, an obvious source of Tudor support, was the responsibility of the King's brother-in-law, the Earl of Huntingdon, who had done his best to rally the local gentry.

A manuscript illustration of the Yorkist victory at Tewksbury (1471). In the foreground are the rival archers, wearing helmets and quilted jacks: some have placed spare arrows on the ground to help them shoot more rapidly. Behind them are the armoured men-at-arms. The lance, couched under the arm, was effective in the first impact of a charge: thereafter horsemen used sword, mace or battle-axe.

In June, sensing that invasion was imminent, Richard declared that the former Earls of Oxford and Richmond – deprived of their titles as attainted traitors – had allied themselves with the French. He went to issue commissions of array, ordering his officers to muster men and collect money for their pay. Knights, esquires and gentlemen were to hold themselves in readiness to support the King 'upon peril of losing their lives, lands and goods'.

Details of Henry Tudor's final preparations are obscure, but it is likely that he began to assemble arms, supplies and ships at Rouen in the spring. His army was built round a solid core of perhaps five hundred exiles, many of them, like his brother the Earl of Pembroke, the Earl of Oxford and Sir Edward Woodville, men of military experience. The bulk of Henry's army consisted of foreign troops, some provided by Charles VIII of France and others serving for pay – or, in the case of some Frenchmen, simply to get out of prison. One mercenary captain, Philibert de Chandee, was on good terms with Henry and remained in England after Bosworth; and strong tradition suggests that Bernard Stuart and Alexander Bruce led a contingent of Scotsmen in French service.

This modest force would be insufficient to defeat Richard, and Henry knew that he would have to attract support as soon as he landed. He had been in close contact with his English backers, had reason to expect that his arrival would inspire risings in many parts of the country, and knew, from messages from his mother, that the Stanleys were likely to throw their weight behind him. Yet the venture was still very risky. Richard was an accomplished soldier, and at Nottingham he was well placed, like a spider on his web, to react promptly to a landing. Henry could not afford an early reverse, which would dissuade potential supporters from declaring for him and push the undecided into Richard's arms.

The invasion fleet sailed on 1 August, and on Sunday 7 August Henry landed, just before nightfall, at Milford Haven in South Wales. His choice of Wales should come as no surprise. Although the country had lost its independence, national sentiment remained powerful. Proud and stubborn minor gentry had fought with distinction in the English armies of the Hundred Years War. Welsh soldiers had played their part in the Wars of the Roses, and a Welsh contingent, after a heroic struggle, suffered at Warwick's hands at Edgecote.

Henry and his uncle knew South Wales well, and although the Herberts, the dominant family, supported Richard, there had been wide-spread promises of support. We cannot be sure whether Henry actually spoke Welsh, but his years in exile at a Breton court which took pride in its Celtic culture can only have strengthened Henry's consciousness of his

Welsh roots. His appearance fanned a flame already kindled by bards who sang of a national revival:

> We are looking forward to the coming of Henry:
> Our nation puts its trust in him.

Shortly after landing, Henry knighted a select group of his companions, and marched through Haverfordwest and Llanbadarn to Machynlleth. Parties of gentlemen and yeomen rallied to him as he went, but there was disturbing news that Rhys ap Thomas and William Herbert, with their own retinues and levies from South Wales, were moving parallel with the rebels. This shadow-boxing may have been designed to persuade Richard that the landing had already been contained, to buy more time for a decision by ascertaining that Henry was in earnest, or simply to demonstrate the worth of those two contingents when they at last joined Henry at or near Welshpool. More Welshmen trooped in to a muster on Long Mountain, outside the town, and on 15 August Henry demanded the surrender of Shrewsbury. The town capitulated after a brief show of resistance, but only the next few days would show whether the rebellion, so strong in Wales, could be exported into England.

Richard received news of the landing on 11 August at his hunting lodge at Beskwood, near Nottingham. The *Croyland Chronicle* declares that 'the king rejoiced, or at least seemed to rejoice, writing to his adherents in every quarter that now the long wished-for day had arrived.' Fresh summonses were sent out to commissioners of array, noblemen and gentlemen, and the King's committed followers called out their own adherents. The Duke of Norfolk wrote to his 'well-beloved friend John Paston', head of a family of Norfolk gentry:

Wherefore I pray that you meet with me at Bury [St Edmunds], for, by the grace of God, I purpose to lie at Bury as upon Tuesday night [16 August] and that you bring with you such company of tall men as you may goodly make at my cost and charge, besides that which you have promised the king; and, I pray you, ordain them with jackets of my livery, and I shall content you at your meeting with me.

Paston's response is an index of the difficulties facing Richard. There is no evidence that he brought any men badged with the white lion of the Norfolks to the muster, and the fact that he became Sheriff of Norfolk two months later was fair reward for judging the mood of the country so well. Even gentlemen already on their way to the King at Leicester were not to be trusted. Brackenbury brought a contingent of southern gentlemen up from London, but both Sir Thomas Bourchier and Sir Walter Hungerford slipped away at Stony Stratford to join the rebels.

Richard was confident enough to celebrate the Feast of the Assumption of the Blessed Virgin Mary in some style on 15 August, but soon afterwards he heard first of mass defections in Wales, and then of the fall of Shrewsbury. A party of his closest adherents, including Lovell, Catesby and Radcliffe, had already joined him, and it was clear that Norfolk was levying men as ordered. The Earl of Northumberland was proving less prompt, and a royal summons for troops from York, issued on 16 August, may reflect the fact that Northumberland was not raising the North as Richard had hoped.

The Stanleys were even more ambivalent. As soon as he heard of the landing, Richard had summoned Stanley to Nottingham, but the peer replied that he had sweating sickness and could not come. Stanley's son, Lord Strange, tried to escape, but was caught and interrogated. He admitted that his uncle Sir William Stanley and a family henchman Sir John Savage had conspired with Henry, but swore that his father was loyal. He wrote, no doubt with Richard's encouragement, to tell his father of his plight and to urge him to join the King with all his forces.

Henry could have struck straight from Shrewsbury to London, but instead marched eastwards, drawing closer to the Stanleys and keeping open a line of retreat into Wales. At Newport he was joined by Sir Gilbert Talbot, a landowner of some importance and uncle to the Earl of Shrewsbury, with 500 men. This was Henry's first substantial English contingent, and it must have been most welcome.

At Stafford Sir William Stanley rode in for a brief meeting. He had marched down from Holt on the Welsh border, while his brother, who had set off from Lathom in Lancashire, was moving on a converging course further to the east. We do not know what was said, but it is likely that Sir William pointed out that his brother could not declare for Henry till the last possible minute without condemning Lord Strange to death. Lord Stanley's force probably reached Lichfield on 17 August and then moved eastwards, falling back in front of Henry and giving the impression that it was making for Richard's muster at Leicester.

Henry's advance persuaded the King to leave Nottingham on 20 August, although his army was still incomplete. Other contingents joined him at Leicester, to produce what the *Croyland Chronicle* exaggeratedly calls 'a number of warriors…greater than had ever been seen before in England collected together on behalf of one person.' The Duke of Norfolk and the Earls of Northumberland, Surrey, Lincoln and Shrewsbury were present, as well as several other peers.

We cannot be sure if this portrait of Richard III by an unknown artist, probably painted after his death, is an accurate likeness. Its close resemblance to a contemporary portrait suggests that it is. Richard was a good soldier and an accomplished administrator. His 'book of hours', a private book of devotions for daily use, has survived, and suggests that he was devout in a solid and unflamboyant way. He was certainly not the hunchbacked monster created by Shakespeare, but the circumstances of his accession and the fate of the princes in the Tower help make him one of the most controversial of English kings.

Henry Tudor's claim to the throne was not strong, but he was able to profit from French assistance, strong support in Wales, and existing divisions within the political nation to defeat Richard III at Bosworth and become Henry VII. The support of the powerful Stanley family was crucial though, interestingly, one of the Stanleys was subsequently executed for treason to Henry. He was not the warrior prince of Shakespearean mythology, but a painstaking administrator: this portrait hints at the sharp and unemotional brain behind the austere face. Henry was feared rather than loved, and there was popular rejoicing when he died.

On Sunday 21 August – 'the Lord's Day before the feast of Bartholomew the Apostle' – Richard led his host across the old Bow Bridge out of Leicester towards Atherstone. He marched through Peckleton and Kirkby Mallory to Sutton Cheney whence, hearing from his scouts that Henry was moving towards White Moors, he pushed on up to the commanding ground of Ambion Hill, west of Sutton Cheney.

Henry had made a formal entry into Lichfield on 20 August with as much show as he could muster. He seems to have spent that night between Lichfield and Tamworth, accidentally separated from his army, which was mightily relieved to see him when he rode into its camp next morning. On 21 August he was near Atherstone, possibly at Merevale Abbey: three months later he repaid the villages of Atherstone, Fenny Drayton, Mancetter and Witherley for corn taken by his men.

He met Lord Stanley some time on 21 August. Again, we cannot be sure what passed between the two men. A Scot, Robert Lindsay of Pitscottie, writing almost a century later but drawing on oral tradition, maintains that Stanley was bribed. It is safe to say that Stanley was assured that Henry would not be niggardly in rewarding him, and it is likely that Henry offered battle the following day confident that the Stanleys would support him. That night more men slipped away from Richard's army: Sir John Savage the younger, Sir Simon Digby and Sir Brian Sandford all brought their detachments to join Henry.

Shakespeare, writing with Henry's grand-daughter on the throne, had good reason to paint Richard's last hours as dark as possible. But other near-contemporary accounts also testify that the King had a poor night's sleep, and the *Croyland Chronicle* adds that his camp was so badly organized that he was unable to take communion. A strong local tradition suggests that he breakfasted on fresh water from a spring now called King Richard's Well. Desertions over the past weeks and his doubts about the Stanleys, and perhaps Northumberland too, cannot have lifted his spirits. However, his army, at least 10,000 strong and perhaps as large as 15,000, outnumbered the 5000 under Henry's direct command, and even if the Stanleys' 5000 men fought against him he probably still had the edge.

The Battlefield

It is rarely easy to be absolutely sure of the location of medieval battles – Hastings is a happy exception. In the case of Bosworth, although contemporary accounts speak of a battle in Redmoor Plain, and of Richard being killed at Sandeford, neither placename now survives. John Gillingham observes that the most one can say for certain is that the action took place between the villages of Market Bosworth to the north, Sutton Cheney to the east, Stoke Golding to the south and Upton to the west. Attempts to produce detailed maps are, he warns, 'quite worthless'.

The Bosworth Battlefield Visitor Centre disagrees, and sets out the traditionally accepted site of the field between Ambion Hill and the village of Shenton. D. T. Williams' booklet *The Battle of Bosworth Field* confirms this siting and Michael Bennett's comprehensive *The Battle of Bosworth* follows suit, although its author notes, in a postscript, his suspicion that the traditional site is wrong.

In 1985 Colin Richmond suggested that the battle was fought closer to Dadlington and Stoke Golding than was generally thought, noting that the church wardens of Dadlington had received royal permission to collect money 'for the building of a chapel of St James, standing upon a parcel of the ground where Bosworth field, otherwise called Dadlington field…was done'. Many skeletons were found in 1868 and about 1950 when graves were being dug in Dadlington churchyard. These may of course have been the remains of those killed following the battle, but, as we shall see, the death of Richard ended the fighting relatively swiftly, leaving little reason for pursuit and slaughter. It is clear that a marsh featured in the battle, and Peter J. Foss has argued, in *The Field of Redemore*, that this is most likely to have been west of Dadlington and north of Stoke Golding, where 'there is a band of alluvial flatland subject to periodic flooding'. Crown Hill, where Henry was traditionally crowned after the battle, is on the edge of Stoke Golding. Lastly, although the term Redmoor or Redemore has vanished from modern maps, the first-ever Ordnance survey map, printed in 1834, calls the area between Ambion Hill and Dadlington 'Radmore Plain'.

It is safe to say that Richard's army spent the night on Ambion Hill, and then descended into a plain to give battle, finding a marsh partly screening the enemy front. I favour placing the battlefield just north-west of Dadlington, but acknowledge that this is far from certain. We can be no more positive about the dispositions of the rival armies. Sunrise that morning was at 5.15, and Richard would have wished to move his army off Ambion Hill (too confined a field for such a great force) as soon as he could. Polydore Vergil, who based his version of the battle on eyewitness accounts, describes how Richard 'drew his whole army out of their encampments, and arrayed his battle-line, extended at such a wonderful length…'

It is likely that Richard followed the custom of the age and formed three divisions, or 'battles'. The evidence suggests that Norfolk commanded the leading and Northumberland the rearward battle, very possibly with Brackenbury in the centre. The fact that Northumberland took little part in the action has persuaded some commentators that the battles were intended to form up one behind the other. Given the numbers at Richard's disposal it is more likely that he would have wished to deploy his divisions side by side to make best use of his superiority. Northumberland's battle, arguably destined for his left flank, may have halted short of its intended location for a number of reasons. Perhaps it had not had time to deploy before fighting broke out, or perhaps Northumberland was treasonably cautious. Richard himself, with 'a select force of soldiers', doubtless from his own household, was on the slopes behind Norfolk.

As his own army prepared for battle, Henry sent a messenger asking Lord Stanley to join him, perhaps in accordance with plans agreed the previous day. Polydore Vergil tells us that Stanley replied that his step-son should deploy first, and he would then 'be at hand with his army in proper array', a response which can scarcely have cheered Henry. There is as much doubt surrounding the location of the two Stanley contingents as there is over other details of the battle. Lord Stanley seems to have spent the night near Higham on the Hill, just north of Nuneaton, and to have been on the march north-westwards when he received Henry's request: he probably halted near Dadlington. This line of march would be fully in accordance with Stanley's double game: he would appear to be joining Richard, but would be well placed to support Henry if he chose to do so. Some sources place his brother north of the battlefield, but it is unlikely that the Stanleys would have wished to fight separately – if, indeed, they were to fight at all. Sir William Stanley, described in one ballad as 'hindmost at the outsetting' is most likely to have been just south of his brother, perhaps near Stoke Golding.

The Fighting Begins

Henry wisely gave command of his main battle to the experienced Earl of Oxford. Polydore Vergil declares that there were two smaller flanking battles, under Sir John Savage the younger to the left and Sir Gilbert Talbot to the right. Henry himself, with a handful of horsemen and some infantry, was a good distance behind Oxford's battle.

Vergil tells us that there was a marsh between the armies 'which Henry deliberately left on his right, to serve his men as a defensive wall'. Jean Molinet, a Bugundian court historian, writes that Richard's artillery engaged the front of Henry's army, causing it to edge round to its left and come up towards Richard's right. The King's men gave 'a great shout' as battle was joined, and the archers on both sides let fly. Oxford's change of direction had given him the advantage of the prevailing wind, which blew from the south-west, and meant that his men did not have the sun in their eyes: his bowmen may consequently have been a good deal more effective than Norfolk's. But there was little time for an archery contest before the two vanguards were at hand-strokes.

The Duke of Norfolk's men, with the slope behind them, must have hit the Earl of Oxford's line hard, but the Earl had expected this and ordered his men to close up and not shift more than 10 feet (3 m) from their standards which were planted in the earth. After the failure of their initial attack, Norfolk's men 'broke off from fighting for a little while', and there are suggestions that some of them, their hearts never really in the battle, began to slip away.

As Norfolk's line wavered, Oxford's pushed forward, supported by Savage and Talbot, and there was a period of vicious hand-to hand fighting. We cannot tell how long it lasted – Vergil says the whole battle took only two hours – nor discern much of its detail. However, it was during this phase of the battle that most of the individual combats that were to pass into legend seem to have taken place, and these often reflected pre-existing animosity between combatants. For example, Oxford had beaten Norfolk's division at Barnet, only to be captured because the other flank had collapsed, and while Oxford was a prisoner Norfolk had secured most of his land. Molinet reports that Norfolk was captured at Bosworth and sent to Oxford, who had him killed, but it is more likely that the Duke fell as his men were pushed back, the less committed breaking first, leaving only Richard's most confirmed supporters and their immediate entourages fighting against worsening odds.

Northumberland's division was not engaged. The *Croyland Chronicle* records that 'no engagement could be discerned, and no battle blows given or received'. This may be because Northumberland had deliberately decided not to fight, or may reflect the fact that, hampered by the lengthy deployment of Richard's army from Ambion Hill, he was still too far back to be able to engage. The latter is more likely for, although Northumberland had probably been less than wholehearted in his support for Richard, he spent some time in prison after Henry's victory – scarcely a fair reward for calculated inaction.

From his vantage-point Richard would have seen Norfolk's division beginning to crumple. Some of his companions urged him to flee, and Salazar, a Spaniard in his service, said: 'Sire, take steps to put your person in safety, without expecting to have victory in today's battle, owing to the manifest treason in your following.' But Richard would have none of it. If he could kill Henry he might yet win: he quickly assembled a group of knights and gentlemen and led them 'from the other side,

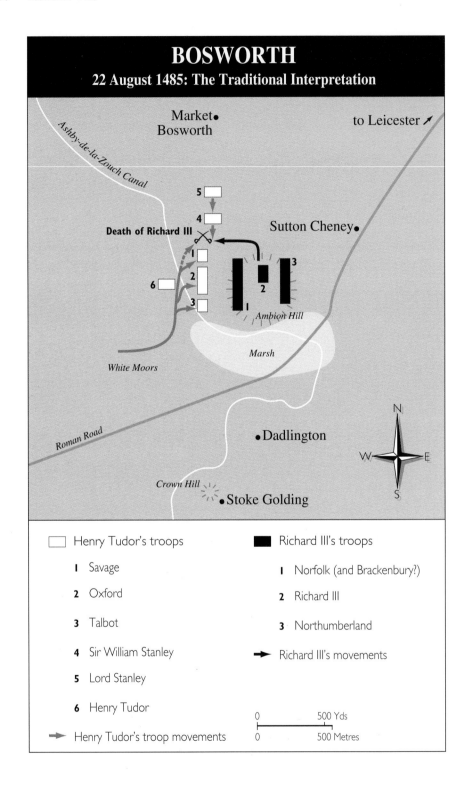

BOSWORTH
22 August 1485: The Traditional Interpretation

Market●
Bosworth

to Leicester ↗

Ashby-de-la-Zouch Canal

5

4

Death of Richard III

Sutton Cheney●

1

2

6

3

3

2

1

Ambion Hill

Marsh

White Moors

Roman Road

●Dadlington

N
W — E
S

Crown Hill

●Stoke Golding

Henry Tudor's troops	Richard III's troops
1 Savage	1 Norfolk (and Brackenbury?)
2 Oxford	2 Richard III
3 Talbot	3 Northumberland
4 Sir William Stanley	➡ Richard III's movements
5 Lord Stanley	
6 Henry Tudor	
➡ Henry Tudor's troop movements	

0   500 Yds
0   500 Metres

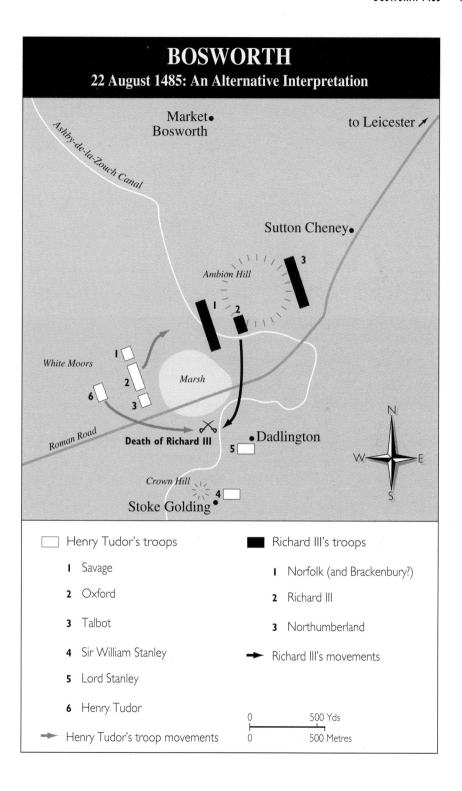

BOSWORTH
22 August 1485: An Alternative Interpretation

Market●
Bosworth

to Leicester ↗

Ashby-de-la-Zouch Canal

Sutton Cheney●

Ambion Hill

3

1

2

White Moors

1

2

6

Marsh

3

Roman Road

Death of Richard III

⚔

Dadlington

5

N

W   E

S

Crown Hill

4

Stoke Golding●

Henry Tudor's troops	Richard III's troops
1 Savage	1 Norfolk (and Brackenbury?)
2 Oxford	2 Richard III
3 Talbot	3 Northumberland
4 Sir William Stanley	➡ Richard III's movements
5 Lord Stanley	
6 Henry Tudor	
➡ Henry Tudor's troop movements	

0   500 Yds

0   500 Metres

beyond the battle-line' against the knot of men surrounding his rival. The fact that Richard's horse became stuck in a bog makes it likely that this charge took place around the battle's southern flank, and that the King stumbled upon the marsh which had protected Oxford's right flank.

The Death of Richard

Even those who had no love for Richard, or were writing when Henry or his descendants were on the throne, cannot deny Richard the honour of his last moments. He killed Henry's standard-bearer and hacked his way towards the pretender with sword or axe. His henchmen fought and died beside him, most dragged from their horses by foot-soldiers: Sir Percival Thirlwall, holding the royal standard, had his legs hewn from beneath him. Richard and his knights may even have managed to reach Henry had Sir William Stanley not chosen this moment to intervene. His force had probably edged in towards Henry's right rear once the fighting began, and when Richard charged it was well placed to deliver what was in effect the battle's deciding blow. Richard and his supporters had no chance against these fresh troops. The Warwickshire priest John Rous, who wrote about the battle not long afterwards, described Richard as 'cruel beyond measure'. But he went on to say: 'though small in body and feeble of limb, he bore himself like a gallant knight and acted with distinction as his own champion until his death, shouting oftentimes that he was betrayed, and crying "Treason! Treason! Treason!".'

Richard's death put an end to the fighting. Some of his men made off, while others, Northumberland amongst them, surrendered on the field. Casualties had been relatively small: Molinet suggests 300 on either side, and Vergil writes that about a thousand of Richard's men had fallen to scarcely a hundred of Henry's. Norfolk, Brackenbury and Radcliffe were amongst the dead, while Brandon was the only notable fatality in Henry's army.

After the battle Henry withdrew to what Vergil calls 'the nearest hill', by tradition Crown Hill near Stoke Golding. It was said that Richard's crown, which had slipped from his helmet during his last struggle, was found beneath a thorn-bush. Henry was crowned by Sir William Stanley or his brother, and the assembled throng bellowed 'God save King Henry! God save King Henry!'

Previous pages: **The view from Ambion Hill, looking north across the traditional battlefield, towards the high ground from which the Stanleys may have attacked. The field is well laid out, with explanatory signboards and banners marking the positions of various contingents. *Inset:* Sutton Cheney church, where Richard is believed to have heard mass before the battle.**

A View of the Field

We can still find traces of Richard, although his last resting-place is unknown. His naked body was slung across a horse, taken back to Leicester and exposed for two days in the church of St Mary of the Annunciation in the Newarke, to make it clear that Richard had indeed been killed, before being buried unceremoniously in the monastery of the Grey Friars near St Martin's Church. It has been said that the King's bones were thrown into the River Soar at the time of the dissolution of the monasteries, but it is more likely that they lie in Leicester in the vicinity of Grey Friars Street. A fine bronze statue of the King stands in Castle Gardens, looking towards Bow Bridge.

Legend affirms that when Richard rode out across Bow Bridge the day before the battle his spur clipped a stone pillar. A wise woman declared that where his spur struck his head should be broken, and when the King's body was carried across the bridge after the battle his head hit the same stone. The old bridge was demolished in 1861 and the plaques commemorating this incident were added to its less than elegant replacement. A plaque in nearby Castle Street marks the five hundredth anniversary of the battle.

Middleham Castle, in North Yorkshire, was known as 'the Windsor of the North'. Once owned by the Nevilles, it was acquired by Richard in 1471: its chapel and gatehouse survive. The nearby market cross with a double flight of steps bears Richard's boar badge. Richard's only legitimate son, Edward, was born at Middleham, and is buried, beneath a crowned effigy, at Sheriff Hutton, about 12 miles (19 km) north of York. Richard was a frequent visitor to Raby Castle, which had also belonged to the Nevilles: it is still inhabited and can be visited on summer afternoons. Barnard Castle is now a spectacular ruin above the River Tees, but the oriel window in the great chamber has Richard's white boar carved above it.

The Bosworth Visitor Centre

The Bosworth Visitor Centre is at Ambion Hill, Sutton Cheney, 2 miles (3.2 km) south of Market Bosworth and 16 miles (26 km) south-west of Leicester. There is an exhibition hall, film theatre, cafeteria and bookshop. The latter is especially well-stocked, and usually has copies of Peter J. Foss's *The Field of Redemore,* the best analysis of the debate on the battlefield's location, which has the merits of not only being cheap but also of fitting comfortably into a jacket pocket.

There is a Battle Trail which is helpfully laid out with information boards and banners marking the positions of the various contingents. The

Visitor Centre favours the traditional interpretation of the battlefield, with which I happen to disagree, but it is eminently worth a visit: its well-made models give a good impression of the men who fought at Bosworth. It also offers special events with a medieval theme on summer Sundays, and there is an annual re-enactment of the battle. The Battlefield Line runs steam and diesel trains from Shenton Station, an easy walk from the Visitor Centre, to Shackerstone, where there is a railway museum, via Market Bosworth.

The Alternative Battlefield

The alternative battlefield lies south of Ambion Hill, with the Ashby-de-la-Zouch Canal and a disused railway line curling across it. It is easily viewed by leaving the Battle Trail and walking south along the old railway line, crossing the canal and then walking about 200 yards (180 m) east along the tow-path. A natural bowl lies south of the canal, and looking across it the churches of Dadlington (to the left) and Stoke Golding (to the right) appear on the high ground on its far side. The fields are lush, with a stream, edged by willows, running through them. The Roman road from Stoke Golding to Fenny Drayton (still called Fenn Lanes) is built up to cross this depression.

My interpretation would place the marsh in this area. Oxford's division would have swung north to avoid it, and the fight between Oxford and Norfolk would have taken place just to the south-west edge of Ambion Wood, perhaps where the old railway now crosses the canal.

Contemporary accounts say that Richard was killed at Sandeford. The suffix 'ford' on a place-name need not refer only to river or stream crossing. It could also indicate a causeway, and it may well be that the Roman road crossed the wetlands in this area on a causeway: even now it is taken over several streams on substantial culverts. There was a Sand Pit Close just south of Fenn Lanes, where the Roman road swings north-eastwards near Greenhill Farm, in 1849. My best guess, and it can be no more than that, places the last mêlée somewhere near the irregular quadrant between the Roman road, the minor road to Dadlington, the canal, and the footpath connecting Fenn Lanes to the towpath. This interpretation would leave the victorious Henry in a good position to retire to Crown Hill, to the south, and would account for the presence of bodies in Dadlington Church.

The happy combination of footpaths and minor roads enables the visitor first to view the area from the towpath south of Ambion Wood, and then drive along Fenn Lanes to Dadlington. The churchyard offers a good view of Ambion Hill, and the pub opposite provides wholesome and copious bar food. A footpath connects the north-west edge of Dadlington with Fenns Lanes, enabling the zealous vistor to walk off lunch and continue the process of battlefield speculation.

Richard's Well, on Ambion Hill, marks the spring where Richard is believed to have drunk before the battle: the Richard III society holds a service there on 22 August each year. By tradition Richard heard mass in the church of St James, Sutton Cheney, on the morning of the battle, and a memorial there urges us to:

Remember Before God

RICHARD III

King of England
and those who fell
at Bosworth Field
Having Kept Faith
22 August 1485
Loyaulté me lie

Naseby
1645

Background

Whatever his failings, Charles I was no coward. On the morning of his execution in January 1649, a month so cold that the River Thames froze, he wore two shirts, lest any shivering be misunderstood. But on 14 June 1645, he was preparing to charge at the head of his cavalry reserve when:

the earl of Carnwath, who rode next to him…on a sudden laid his hand on the bridle of the King's horse, and swearing two or three full mouthed Scots' oaths (for of that nation he was) said, 'Will you go upon your death in an instant?' and, before His Majesty understood what he would have, turned his horse around… Upon this they all turned their horses round and rode upon the spur, as if they were every man to shift for himself.

It is likely that the battle was already lost. Yet perhaps Charles could, even then, have tilted the balance of the day by throwing himself into the scales: had he failed, he might have met a more fitting end on Naseby field than on a scaffold in Whitehall.

The Tudors
It was less than a century and a half since Richard III had died at Bosworth, but in that time England had been transformed. John Guy suggests that the nation 'was economically healthier, more expansive and more optimistic under the Tudors than at any time since the Roman occupation of Britain.' Its population grew from 2.26 million in 1525 to 4.1 million in 1601; agriculture flourished and prices rose. Yet it was not a comfortable era to

This plate from a pre-Civil War drillbook shows a musketeer, match glowing, blowing loose powder from his priming pan. Charges hang from his bandoleer. By 1645 dress was less elaborate and musketeers had discarded the forked musket-rest. The matchlock musket *(left)* was the most common firearm of the period. Although cumbersome and inaccurate it was robust and simple to maintain.

live through, as dispossessed countrymen flocked to the towns or strove to survive as vagabonds.

Henry VII (Henry Tudor) inaugurated the political stability which made this economic success possible. Although he began with important advantages, his reign was not secure at its outset. Richard III had removed most contenders for the throne, and the Earl of Warwick, a possible claimant, was in Henry's custody. Henry's judicious marriage to Edward IV's daughter Elizabeth of York helped mollify many Yorkists. However, in 1487 Viscount Lovell, the Earl of Lincoln and disaffected Yorkists invaded from Ireland, using a boy called Lambert Simnel to masquerade as the Earl of Warwick. They were defeated at Stoke, where Lincoln was killed. Lambert Simnel was more fortunate: he was taken into royal service as a kitchen-boy.

It was typical of Henry's wily nature that he dated his reign from the day before Bosworth, making traitors of those who fought against him. Yet he was relatively merciful, and Sir William Catesby was one of the few executed after the battle. There was heavier retribution after Stoke, but discontent continued to bubble up. Northumberland was murdered on a tax-collecting expedition in 1489, allegedly because of 'his disappointing of King Richard at Bosworth', and Sir William Stanley, whose defection had done much to win the battle, was executed for treason six years later. Another impostor, Perkin Warbeck, who claimed to be Richard of York, one of the princes who died in the Tower of London, was seized and later executed, and the real Earl of Warwick was beheaded to deter future imitators.

Historians once wrote of a 'Tudor revolution in government' instituted by Henry VII, but most would now recognize that Henry adapted existing mechanisms and enforced old obligations rather than developing new ones. He made ruthless use of royal patronage, awarding titles, lands, offices and pensions, in order to control the political nation. Command of castles and garrisons was concentrated in reliable hands, and noblemen who kept liveried retainers were heavily fined. Henry watched royal finances like a hawk, and some of his methods of raising money from his subjects scarcely fell short of extortion.

It is small wonder that Henry's death in 1509 was greeted with universal rejoicing. His son Henry VIII, who succeeded him, made what might have seemed a good start by marrying his late brother's widow, Catherine of Aragon; and by executing his father's two most unpopular ministers. For the first years of his reign, when Cardinal Wolsey was his chief minister, the King spent much of his time hunting, dancing or playing the lute, though his appetite for glory led him into costly wars against France.

His attempt to divorce Catherine, who had failed to produce a living male heir, in order to marry Anne Boleyn, precipitated the real crisis of Henry's reign. Henry's failure to persuade the Pope to agree to a divorce encouraged him to claim supremacy over the English Church, and in the early 1530s the Church's connection with Rome was legally severed and Henry was established as its head. Shortly afterwards the monasteries were dissolved, and though the Crown obtained their lands, most were sold to cover Henry's profligate expenditure.

The break with Rome sealed Wolsey's fate, and Thomas Cromwell, who master-minded the dissolution, was soon jettisoned. The King's headstrong character and poor judgement was reflected in a succession of royal marriages, and Henry wooed the British Isles no less roughly. A northern rising, the Pilgrimage of Grace, was brutally suppressed. Wales was effectively annexed, and in 1542 Henry assumed the title of King of Ireland, though he still tried to govern through the chiefs who controlled the country beyond Dublin. The Scots were beaten at Flodden in 1513 and Solway Moss in 1542, but their nationalism could not be expunged and their 'auld alliance' with France repeatedly threatened to open up war on two fronts.

The reign of Henry's devoutly Protestant son Edward VI was dominated by two protectors. The first, Edward Seymour, Earl of Hertford and then Duke of Somerset, pursued expensive wars with France and Scotland and provoked rebellion at home. In 1549 he was overthrown by the Earl of Warwick, who elevated himself to Duke of Northumberland. Northumberland made peace with France and Scotland, and might be more favourably remembered but for an attempt to win the throne for his daughter-in-law Lady Jane Grey, daughter of the Marquess of Dorset and next in succession after Henry VIII's daughters Mary and Elizabeth. Although the dying Edward disinherited his sisters, Jane ruled for only nine days before Mary entered London: Northumberland and his chief adherents were executed.

Henry VIII's quarrel with Rome had been principally political, but there were other pressures on the Church. Resentment of its privilege and wealth was an undercurrent throughout the age, and there were demands for religion to be more accessible and to reflect the mood of reform and humanism that was sweeping the Continent. Henry's ecclesiastical revolution had not been accompanied by doctrinal change, but under Edward Protestant theologians flocked into England and reformers dominated the Church.

Mary, a devoted Catholic, brought the kingdom back into obedience to Rome and burnt several leaders of Edwardian Protestantism. Many opponents escaped abroad, from whence they poured a stream of propaganda against the Queen and her advisers. Mary married Philip, son of the Holy Roman Emperor Charles V, and when Philip became King of Spain in 1556 England was dragged into war with France. In 1558 the French took Calais, the last relic of English victories in the Hundred Years War: its loss was bitterly resented.

Mary died childless in November 1558, and was succeeded by her sister Elizabeth, fruit of Henry VIII's liaison with Anne Boleyn. She was to rule for 44 years, in a reign replete with military and political triumphs. The Anglican church was firmly established, and in 1588 England survived its sternest test when the Spanish Armada, intended to seize control of the English Channel and convoy the Duke of Parma's army from Holland, was defeated. Plots and risings were suppressed, and local government, run by the gentry, was conducted with exemplary efficiency.

Yet all this success rested on weak foundations. Despite the Queen's parsimony, royal income, aided by parliamentary subsidies, could not keep pace with growing costs. The religious settlement was popular neither with extreme Protestants nor with Roman Catholics. A long war in Ireland ended in English victory, but did not create the conditions needed for lasting peace. Too many workers chased too few jobs, and the population grew faster than food resources.

The Stuarts

It would have been astonishing had these pressures not come to a head under that unlucky dynasty, the Stuarts. James I, son of Mary, Queen of Scots, was already unpopular in Scotland, where he had reigned since 1567, because of his favouritism. He was an intelligent man who hoped for a genuine union between England and Scotland and a wide measure of religious toleration. He made little progress in religious or constitutional matters, partly because of an unwise affair with George Villiers, Duke of Buckingham, but handed over a stable kingdom to his son Charles I in 1625.

The chaste and chilly Charles was a stark contrast to his scruffy father. He cleaned up a sleazy court, sharpened royal administration and ensured that the Crown could 'live of its own' in peacetime, albeit by exploiting some obsolete feudal practices. After clashing with Parliament he ruled without it, and the mid-1630s saw him apparently triumphant. However, religious conflict helped tarnish this image. William Laud, Archbishop of Canterbury, did not merely offend Puritans by attempting to make them conform with the 1559 Prayer Book, but alienated many others by striving to increase the Church's wealth and jurisdiction.

Attempts to extend Laud's religious reforms into Scotland provoked resistance which flared into outright war, and it was the two Bishops' Wars (1639–40) that highlighted the weakness of Charles's position. He could not fight without parliamentary subsidies, and summoning Parliament unleashed demands for the redress of financial and religious grievances and the punishment of the King's 'evil counsellors'. A rising in Ireland, where rebels massacred several thousand Protestants, added to the mood of crisis.

Long-term economic, religious and social pressures contributed to the breakdown. Yet Charles might still have averted it, had he shown better judgement or behaved with greater determination. He acquiesced in the execution of the Earl of Strafford, who was accused of planning to use an Irish army against Parliament, the imprisonment of Laud (who was later executed), and gave in to most of Parliament's demands. Yet when the Grand Remonstrance, a condemnation of Charles's rule, was passed by a narrow majority in the Commons, Charles tried to arrest five leading members of the Opposition. It was a humiliating fiasco, and on 10 January 1642 he left London to the mercy of a hostile mob and his enemies in Parliament. He was never to return as a free man.

The Civil War Begins

The process of taking sides in the Civil War was infinitely more complex than the simple terms Royalist or Parliamentarian imply. If men at the political or religious extremes found it easy to decide where their loyalties lay, it was harder for most of the political nation. Sir Edmund Verney, for example, was a Puritan and hoped that the King would yield to Parliament's demands, but declared: 'I have eaten his bread and served him near thirty years, and will not do so base a thing as to forsake him; and choose rather to lose my life (which I am sure to do) to preserve and defend these things which are against my conscience to preserve and defend.' He was killed at Edgehill, the first battle of the war: his eldest son fought for Parliament and two others for the King.

Economic interests, religious sensibilities, political, personal, family and local loyalties all played their parts, and many strove to remain neutral until they were drawn into the conflict. Lines of cleavage could be wafer-thin. Sir William Waller and Sir Ralph Hopton were close friends, had served together in the Thirty Years War (1618–1648), and were members of the Parliamentary opposition. Yet Hopton felt that ultimate sovereignty resided in the monarch, and Waller did not. They commanded rival armies in the South-West, personal friendship rising above what Waller called 'this war without an enemy'.

Charles I and his younger son James, Duke of York, the future King James II. Like most portraits of Charles, this painting by Sir Peter Lely catches his regal chilliness. Behind this austere exterior lay a man who found it hard to adopt a settled course of action and was often powerfully influenced by unreliable advisors.

On 20 August 1642 Charles raised his royal standard at Nottingham, an act which symbolized the outbreak of war. Both sides had been raising troops for months, but hoped that outright war could be averted. On 23 October there was an inconclusive battle at Edgehill between the King's main army and Parliament's principal force under the Earl of Essex. The King pushed on to take Brentford, only to find his route to the capital blocked at Turnham Green. He established his capital at Oxford instead, and both sides spent the winter in fruitless negotiation and preparing for a renewal of the fighting.

The war's inherent localism was evident in 1643, when the Royalists secured the South-West, taking Bristol, the country's second port, on 26 July. They were unsuccessful at Gloucester, and fought a drawn battle at

Newbury against the Parliamentarian army that had marched out from London to relieve Gloucester. In the North the Royalist grandee the Duke of Newcastle strengthened his grip on much of Yorkshire, despite spirited opposition from Lord Fairfax and his son Sir Thomas. In East Anglia the Parliamentarian Eastern Association gained the upper hand, with Oliver Cromwell, a Huntingdonshire squire and MP, establishing a growing military reputation. The year's most important event was political: in September the Solemn League and Covenant, an alliance between Parliament and the Scots, was signed, and the Scots began to raise troops. They could not afford to be single-minded in their commitment to their allies, however, because the Marquis of Montrose, Charles's captain-general in Scotland, won a string of remarkable victories over the Covenantors.

The year 1644 was also indecisive. Although Charles fought a successful campaign in the West Country, totally defeating Essex's army, on 2 July his nephew Rupert was beaten by the allies at Marston Moor, the war's largest battle, and York fell shortly afterwards. On 27 November a promising Parliamentarian plan misfired at the second Battle of Newbury. The acrimonious debate which followed it highlighted the lack of resolve in the Parliamentarian command.

'Gentlemen,' pleaded the Earl of Manchester, 'I beseech you let's consider what we do. The King need not care how oft he fights... If we fight 100 times and beat him 99 he will be King still, but if he beats us but once, or the last time, we shall be hanged, we shall lose our estates, and our posterities be undone.'

'My Lord,' replied Cromwell, 'if this be so, why did we take up arms at first? This is against fighting ever hereafter. If this be so, let us make peace, be it never so base.'

Changes in Military Organization and Weaponry
Parliament's alliance with the Scots, its possession of most major ports, and its control of the fleet and the wealth and manpower of London, and a central tract of territory meant that it was likely to win a war of attrition. It could not do so, however, without an army capable of closing the deal. The inquiry into failure at Newbury soon deepened into an examination of the conduct of the war in general, and on 23 November the Committee of Both Kingdoms, with both English and Scots members, directed the Commons 'to consider a frame or model for the whole militia'. The Self-Denying Ordinance, which excluded members of both Houses of Parliament from military command, passed the Commons on 9 December. The Lords initially threw it out, but the Committee of Both Kingdoms had already sketched out a force under central command with a strength of some 22,000 men. This

was to become the New Model Army, instrument of Parliament's victory.

There had been no standing army under the early Stuarts. In Elizabeth's reign the general obligation of Englishmen to serve in time of need was reflected in the organization of county militias, known as trained bands. These were sometimes efficient, especially in counties liable to invasion, with their training administered by professional soldiers, but there is little doubt that if Parma had landed in the Armada in 1588 his tough veterans would have made short work of them. Troops were specially raised for overseas expeditions: in 1585, for instance, the Earl of Leicester led 6000 men to help the Dutch against the Spanish.

Britain exported military talent. Well-born young men served abroad as gentlemen volunteers, and scions of impecunious gentry went off to make their fortunes in the wars. Irishmen fought for France or other Catholic powers, and there were Scots and Englishmen on both sides during the Thirty Years War. When the Civil War broke out hundreds of these men returned to provide a leaven of military experience on both sides. With them came foreigners, like the King's nephews Rupert and Maurice, sons of the Elector Palatine and Charles's sister Elizabeth of Bohemia. Some professionals imported the culture which had helped make the Thirty Years War so bitter and destructive. 'I care not for your cause,' said one. 'I come to fight for your half-crown and your handsome women.'

Historians debate whether the term 'military revolution' accurately describes the changes in organization and weaponry which took place at this time. If they were spread over too long a period (and embodied too much of what had gone before) to constitute a real revolution, they were nonetheless profound. Armies became bigger, coming more firmly under the control of states in whose formation they played a crucial part. The proliferation of gunpowder weapons was accompanied by the need for drill. Military organization took on characteristics which are with us still: the titles of many modern military ranks and bodies date from this period.

Infantry formed the bulk of armies. About two-thirds of foot-soldiers carried the matchlock musket, loaded by tipping black powder down its barrel, following this with a ball, and tamping the charge down with wadding – tow, paper or even grass. It was fired when the match, a length of smouldering cord held in the jaws of the cock, was dropped into the priming pan, thus igniting the weapon's charge. Misfires or accidents were common, and rainy or windy weather might render the musket useless.

The musket fired a bullet weighing 12 to the pound, lethal at up to 400 yards (365 m) but really effective at much less, perhaps 150 yards (137 m). A musketeer had once fired his weapon from a forked rest, though this was obsolete by 1645, and carried spare charges in tubular containers hung from his bandoleer. He wore a sword, though for close combat he generally took to 'clubbing them down', swinging his musket by the barrel.

The musketeer relied for close protection upon the pikeman. The pike was a long spear with a regulation length of 18 feet (5.5 m), although there were complaints that men cut their pikes down to make them less cumbersome. In Elizabeth's time pikemen had worn a gorget at the throat, a cuirass (breast- and back-plate), a steel helmet and tassets covering the thighs, but gorgets and tassets were abandoned at the start of the Civil War and it is possible that the New Model Army's pikemen were not issued with any armour. The crux of infantry battle came when the foot came to 'push of pike'. Musketeers would try to get off a volley just before impact, 'doubling their ranks' so that two or three ranks fired at once.

At the start of the war, in 1642, some cavalry had worn armour, but by 1645 most troopers on both sides wore a cuirass and a lobstertail helmet: the latter was certainly not confined to Parliamentarian cavalry. Some preferred a broad-brimmed felt hat with a metal 'spider' beneath it to protect the skull. A stout leather buff-coat was worn under or instead of the cuirass. Cavalrymen carried a long, straight sword and a pair of wheel-lock pistols, fired when a toothed wheel revolved against a piece of iron pyrites held in the jaws of the cock. Some had carbines, short muskets.

Cavalry tactics had been warmly debated. Disciples of the Dutch school maintained that each rank of horsemen should trot up to pistol range of their enemy, fire, and wheel about to reload. At the other extreme, followers of the Swedish school argued that cavalry achieved the best results by shock action: pistols ought not to be used until horsemen had charged home. By the time of Naseby the Swedish school was in the ascendant, although commanders might provide cavalry with firepower by attaching groups of 'commanded musketeers' to them.

The dragoon was a hybrid. Although he was mounted, his horse was primarily a means of transport rather than a fighting platform, and was much cheaper than the cavalryman's steed. He had no armour, wore a cloth rather than a buff-coat, and carried both sword and musket. In the advance dragoons moved with the vanguard to hold key features or defiles until the infantry came up; and in retreat they often formed part of the rearguard. Dragoons, and the infantry who guarded the train of artillery, were usually equipped with the more modern snaphance musket, forerunner of the flintlock which was later to become the standard infantry weapon.

Artillery was still comparatively poorly developed. Cannon graduated from the tiny robinet, with its ¾ lb (0.3 kg) ball, through falconet, falcon, minon, saker, demi-culverin, culverin, demi-cannon and cannon, to the

Far left: This Victorian painting of the execution of Charles I outside the Banqueting House in Whitehall (Horse Guards now stands almost directly opposite) catches the mood of that freezing day well. Musketeers and pikemen surround the temporary scaffold. Although pikemen traditionally wore armour, there is no evidence that the New Model's pikemen had it at Naseby. The horsemen are members of a cavalry regiment. *Left:* Many cavalrymen on both sides wore a stout leather buff-coat, thick enough to turn a sword-cut, with breast- and back-plate over it. The lobstertail helmet drew its name from the articulated plates covering the neck. By the time of Naseby cavalrymen were trained to charge home with their swords, using point and edge in hand-to-hand combat.

cannon royal which fired a 63 lb (27 kg) ball. The 5-pounder (2.3 kg) sakers and 9-pounder (4 kg) demi-culverins were the most commonly used field guns. They were usually positioned in groups, and were unlikely to move during the course of an action. Smaller, more mobile pieces, would deploy in the intervals between bodies of infantry.

Stubby, high-trajectory mortars, with their exploding bombs, were useful in siege warfare, but field-guns fired solid roundshot which trundled through the enemy's ranks, killing and wounding as they went. At close range, gunners used caseshot, a canister of small balls which spread in a wide arc on leaving the muzzle. Each gun was manned by the gunner, his mate, and a number of labourers or matrosses.

The New Model Army

The regiment, named after its colonel, was the standard unit of horse and foot. The New Model Army's infantry regiments had an establishment strength of 1200 men divided into ten companies. The colonel's company, commanded by his captain-lieutenant, was 200 men strong, the lieutenant-colonel's 160 and the major's 140: other companies were commanded by captains and numbered 100 men apiece. Each company had its own colour, carried by the ensign, the most junior of its three commissioned officers. Cavalry troops, the equivalent of companies, had a standard each, and dragoon companies a guidon. Regiments of horse or foot were often brigaded together under a general or senior colonel.

A captain-general or lord-general commanded an army, with a lieutenant-general as his second-in-command, and each of the major arms – horse, foot and guns – might have a general and lieutenant-general, though not all posts were usually filled. The foot also had a sergeant-major-general (soon abbreviated to major-general) and the horse a commissary-general.

Convention decreed that armies formed up with their foot in the centre, with its most senior regiment on the right, the next most senior to the left, and so on. Cavalry stood to the flanks, with the senior cavalry general on the right flank and his junior on the left. Amongst the staff were the scoutmaster-general (responsible for the collection and processing of intelligence) and the carriage-master-general, who supervised the baggage train.

Civil War armies were poorly administered, with the arrival of pay and rations far from certain. Soldiers were entitled to a daily ration or cash instead. Sir James Turner tells how:

they allow so much bread, flesh, wine or beer to every trooper and foot soldier, which is ordinarily alike to both, then they allow to the officers, according to their dignities and charges, double, triple and quadruple portions... The ordinary allowance for a soldier in the field is daily, two pound of bread, one pound of flesh, or in lieu of it, one pound of cheese, one pottle of wine, or in lieu of it, two pottles of beer.

The soldier who received this was fortunate. All too often he was reduced to living at 'free quarter', billeted on civilians who fed and sheltered him (paid either in cash or with debentures which could in theory be cashed in but were often worthless). Horses too had to be fed: the New Model's baggage-train contained over a thousand horses, not to mention the mounts for senior officers and the cavalry, all munching their way through fodder.

When the New Model was raised its officers and men were promised 'constant pay', and this was to be furnished by a monthly assessment on property levied in 17 counties. Officers were to receive 'respited pay' – payment only partly in cash, with the remainder secured by a debenture until the end of the war. Initial delays in collection meant that pay was in arrears: nevertheless, the New Model was better-paid than its Royalist opponents.

Sir Thomas Fairfax who became the New Model's commander-in-chief, was a 33-year-old Yorkshireman whose dark hair and swarthy features earned him the nickname 'Black Tom'. He had served in Holland and as a colonel of foot in the first Bishop's War before commanding the horse under his father Lord Fairfax in Yorkshire in 1642–3. At Marston Moor he had led the right wing, which was roughly handled by the Royalist cavalry. Fairfax was a dashing and enterprising commander with abundant common sense. When the lord-general's regiment claimed that its status exempted it from rearguard duties, Fairfax is reported to have simply dismounted and led it to the rear of the army.

Sir Thomas Fairfax, Lord-General of the New Model Army. Fairfax was a tough fighting Yorkshireman whose personal contribution to victory at Naseby was considerable. He had little taste for politics, and did not sign Charles's death-warrant.

Oliver Cromwell was the New Model's lieutenant-general, commanding its cavalry, at Naseby. He succeeded Fairfax as lord-general and later became Lord Protector and head of state. This portrait of him by Robert Walker shows him in armour, probably rather more than he would have worn at Naseby. He holds the baton which marks him out as a senior officer. A page is tying his sash. Officers on both sides wore silk sashes, sometimes so wide that they could make improvised stretchers. Royalist sashes were red, Parliamentarian sashes orange-tawny. Cromwell was not a vain man and, when painted by Lely, urged the artist to show him 'warts and all'.

Oliver Cromwell, Fairfax's lieutenant-general, had also been lieutenant-general to the Earl of Manchester in the Eastern Association. He was 12 years older than Fairfax, and had no pre-war service but had risen from captain of horse by sheer merit. Part of his skill lay in personnel selection. 'I had rather have a plain russet-coated captain that knows what he fights for and loves what he knows,' he affirmed, 'than that which you call a gentleman and is nothing else.' Although he was an MP he was to be exempted from the Self-Denying Ordinance (which excluded Members of both Houses of Parliament from military command) to become lieutenant-general shortly before Naseby. His commissary-general, appointed on the eve of the battle, was his close associate Henry Ireton, who became his son-in-law the following year. Philip Skippon, a veteran of the Dutch service who had commanded the London Trained Bands and then served as major-general to the Earl of Essex, was responsible for the New Model's infantry.

The New Model was to comprise 12 regiments of foot with a strength of 1200 men apiece; 11 regiments of horse, each 600 strong; and 1000 dragoons in ten companies. The artillery train, under Lieutenant-General Thomas Hammond, included at least three demi-culverins, a mortar, nine sakers and three smaller guns. Three regiments each of horse and foot came from Essex's army, two of foot from Waller's and nine of horse and four of foot from the Eastern Association's. Other regiments were disbanded to bring the New Model up to strength, and some men were drafted in from civilian life. Fairfax and Skippon spent much of April 1645 in the far from painless business of 'New Modelling', and it is thanks to their practical common sense that the process went as well as it did.

The New Model has been the subject of such varied judgements that it is difficult to assess it objectively. It has been hailed, on the one hand, as a force with a strong political and religious identity, and on the other as just another seventeenth-century army, irregularly paid and indifferently fed: the truth embodies elements of both extremes. In 1645 it was not, as its critics opined, 'an army of sectaries', officered by low-born men of extreme Independent rather than moderate Presbyterian views. Denzil Holles, a leading member of the pre-war Opposition, concluded that the army was more of a danger than the King, and complained:

All of them, from the general (except what he may have in expectation of his father's death) to the meanest sentinel, are not able to make a thousand pounds a year [from the rent of their] lands; most of the colonels are tradesmen, brewers, tailors, goldsmiths, shoemakers and the like. These to rebel against their masters!

There was only a measure of truth in Holles's complaint. Parliament had to approve Fairfax's list of officers, and the Lords objected to two colonels – the 'dangerous' Independents Edward Montague and John Pickering, as well as 40 captains. The list eventually scraped by with a majority of just one. Some officers were not gentlemen: Lieutenant-Colonel Thomas Pride of Harley's Regiment had been a drayman before the war and Lieutenant-Colonel John Hewson of Pickering's a cobbler.

Remodelling gave Fairfax and his generals complete control over the appointment of officers, subject to parliamentary approval, and the quality of its officers was one of the New Model's greatest strengths. John Rushworth, writing after Naseby, declared that:

from the beginning I was confident, a blessing from heaven did attend this army, there were in it so many pious men, men of integrity, hating vice, fighting not out of ambitiousness or ends, but aiming at God's glory and the preservations of liberty and religion, and the destruction of the enemy.

Nonetheless, there were complaints that competent officers had been 'put out' because of their religious or political views, and Joshua Sprigge, an army chaplain, agreed that some 'were better Christians than soldiers and wiser in faith than in fighting'.

The rank and file was more uneven in quality. At one extreme the horse, particularly the old Eastern Association regiments, was very good. At the other, the infantry was patchy. About half the foot-soldiers had been conscripted, and they deserted in large numbers. Thus, while the New Model, in its newly issued red coats, struck Sir Samuel Luke as 'the bravest that I ever saw for bodies of men, both in numbers, arms or other accoutrements', its commander was warned by an unnamed great person that 'he was sorry that I was going with the army, for he did believe we should be beaten'.

The Royalists
Many Royalists cracked jokes about the 'New Noddle', though these could scarcely conceal the fact that their own army had been harrowed by three years of war and now lacked a large enough territorial base to make good its losses. Nevertheless, the King's cause seemed far from hopeless at the outset. Detachments of sturdy foot still trudged in from Wales, nursery of the Royalist infantry; a cessation of hostilities in Ireland enabled the King to use 'Irish' troops in England, though at terrible risk, for Parliament had decreed that they were to be killed if captured; and in Scotland the Marquis of Montrose was tying down a growing proportion of the Scots army.

The key strategic question of early 1645 was the use to which the King's main army should be put, and there was no unanimity amongst the men who debated it. Charles was captain-general but, though he had performed well in the West Country in 1644, he was ill-suited to command in the field. He was weak and indecisive, often influenced by the last person to advise him, yet could turn stubborn over what he regarded as issues of principle. He was a poor judge of men, and in 1645, when there were good arguments for concentrating to meet the New Model, he gave an independent command in the South-West to that engaging drunkard and womanizer, George, Lord Goring.

Charles's lieutenant-general and nephew, Prince Rupert, had begun his military service at the age of 14. He had a considerable reputation before the war, and his many achievements during it had earned him the respect of his own men and the hatred of his enemies. Unfortunately not all the latter were in Parliament's ranks. Rupert had allies, notably his brother Maurice, commanding in Wales and the Marches, and Colonel Will Legge, Governor of Oxford. Amongst his opponents was George, Lord Digby, one of the King's secretaries of state, who exercised great influence over Charles. The King had decided to establish his son Charles, Prince of Wales, at Bristol with his own council, and many of his more level-headed advisers had been sent off with the prince, strengthening the malign influence of Digby.

In March 1645 Charles wrote to his wife Queen Henrietta Maria that there was 'a great division... amongst his own friends upon the conditions of peace out of the universal weariness of the war'. Rupert and his supporters favoured streamlining the Royalist chain of command in much the same way as Parliament had with the New Model, and fighting for a compromise peace. Digby, in contrast, encouraged Charles to believe that the war could be won. He was not alone, for in January, Montrose, with another stunning victory behind him, had told the King:

Forgive me, sacred Sovereign, to tell your Majesty that, in my opinion, it is unworthy of a King to treat with rebel subjects... Through God's blessing I am in the fairest hopes of reducing this kingdom to your majesty's obedience, and... I doubt not before the end of this summer I shall be able to come to your Majesty's assistance with a brave army.

Campaign and Battle

Rupert's plan of campaign for 1645 was robust. Garrisons around Oxford would be pared down to strengthen the field army, while artillery and engineer stores would be concentrated in the city. The army would then concentrate on Worcester and move north to relieve besieged Chester, drawing recruits from Wales as it went. It could raise more men in Lancashire and in Yorkshire, and then perhaps even join Montrose in Scotland. Speed was of the essence, for there was everything to be gained by moving before the New Model was ready.

Royalist preparations so alarmed the Parliamentarians that Cromwell, who arrived at Windsor ready to relinquish his commission under the terms of the Self-Denying Ordinance, was immediately given a brigade of cavalry and sent off to disrupt them. On 24 April he beat the Earl of Northampton's cavalry brigade at Islip Bridge, and went on to summon the garrison of Bletchington House to surrender. The governor, Colonel Francis Windebank, was unnerved by the presence of his young wife and some of her friends, and immediately gave up to save his guests from the horrors of an assault which Cromwell, with no infantry at his disposal, was in a poor position to deliver.

Two days later, Cromwell's horse, swinging north and west of Oxford, dealt with some Royalist cavalry and then overwhelmed 350 foot-soldiers at

Bampton-in-the-Bush. He summoned Faringdon Castle to surrender, but its governor replied 'You are not now at Bletchingdon.' Although Cromwell brought up infantry from the Parliamentarian garrison of Abingdon, when he attempted to storm Faringdon he was beaten off. News that Goring was on his way from the South-West persuaded Cromwell to fall back, but in the space of a few days he had unsettled the Royalists and, no less importantly, swept up many heavy draught horses which were to have been used for moving the train of artillery but had not yet been taken into Oxford.

The Siege of Oxford

If the King's Council was unsure of how to prosecute the war, Parliament's Committee of Both Kingdoms scarcely had any better idea. The Scots, in the North, demanded help against Langdale's marauding cavalry, and there were urgent requests that besieged Taunton should be relieved. On 28 April the Committee ordered Fairfax to march to the relief of Taunton, and he set off two days later. He was at Blandford in Dorset on 8 May, with Cromwell well off to his right flank in case the Oxford army moved south. He now received new orders. The King's army was moving north, and he was to detach a brigade to relieve Taunton and take the remainder of the New Model towards Oxford. Fairfax obediently sent Colonel Weldon with four regiments of foot and one of horse to Taunton and set off northwards.

Rupert and Maurice had reached Oxford on 4 May, and Goring rode in the following day. The King left Oxford on 7 May with his lifeguard, the Oxford infantry and the artillery, and the next day Sir Marmaduke Langdale brought his Northern Horse down to a general rendezvous on Bradford Down. A council of war was held in Stow-on-the-Wold that evening.

Rupert reiterated the case for marching on Chester: if it fell, then it would be impossible to bring any more troops over from Ireland. The weakened and disillusioned Scots could be dealt with, and only then should the Royalists risk fighting the New Model. Langdale supported him: his own men were happier closer to home. Digby and Goring favoured tackling the New Model head on. Rupert seems to have suggested a compromise: Goring would return to the West to hold up the New Model while the rest of the army marched north. The Earl of Clarendon claims that Rupert hoped to be rid of Goring because 'he was like to have most credit with the king in all debates' and got on well with Digby. Goring was happy with the scheme, which would give him an independent command, and even if Rupert was less devious than Clarendon suggests the arrangement suited him too, for Goring's fondness for the bottle had made him increasingly unreliable. It was a disastrous decision, for whatever Goring's failings he was a superb cavalry leader, and his horse would have made a real difference at Naseby.

The Royalists marched north, joined by reinforcements as they went. The most substantial contingent, 3300 infantry, appeared at Evesham on 9 May. With it came Lord Astley, major-general of the foot, 'as fit for the office he exercised,' records Clarendon, 'as Christendom yielded and was so generally esteemed.' He was a short, white-haired man – Elizabeth of Bohemia had called him 'my little monkey' – 66 years old but in sprightly good health. Jacob Astley's enormous experience in the Dutch service, personal courage and forthright honesty earned him wide respect. He deserves remembering for the brief prayer he uttered before leading the Royalist foot forward at Edgehill: 'O Lord! Thou knowest how busy I must be this day. If I forget thee, do not thou forget me – march on boys!'

Cromwell, still without a commission in the New Model, shadowed the Royalists, at first hoping that Fairfax would join him, but soon hearing that the New Model had been ordered to besiege Oxford. He was told to send Colonel Vermuyden with a brigade of horse to support the Scots contingent in Derbyshire, and then fell back to join Fairfax.

On 20 May the King was at Market Drayton, where he heard that the Parliamentarians had raised the siege of Chester. Thus far the campaign was going his way. Parliament had hoped that the Scots and local forces would prevent the King from moving north, but the Scots, concerned for their lines of communication and well aware that Montrose was on the rampage in their homeland, withdrew from Derbyshire into Westmorland. The Midlands and the North were dangerously exposed, and Charles's arrival transformed the local balance of power.

After hearing the good news from Chester, Charles decided to march eastwards, hoping to draw cavalry out of the Royalist enclave of Newark to strengthen his own horse and then to move on to raise the sieges of Pontefract and Scarborough. The Scots were very relieved at his change of direction: 'I was much afraid,' wrote one, 'that the north of England should have joined with him, and fallen first on our army, and then on Scotland.'

Fairfax, meanwhile, was stuck fast before Oxford, able to cut off the city but too short of heavy guns to begin a formal siege. He asked why 'we should spend our time unprofitably before a town while the King hath time to strengthen himself and by terror to enforce obedience of all places where he come.' Although the city was well defended and provisioned, Sir John Culpepper, who had been left there, warned Digby that 'the temper of those within the town, the disaffection of the townsmen...and the vast importance of the place and persons within the town' made it imperative for Oxford to be relieved.

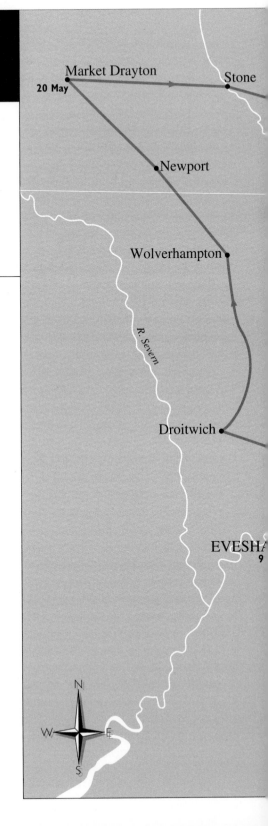

THE NASEBY CAMPAIGN

1645: Main Armies Only

Royalist troop movements

New Model troop movements

0   10 Miles
0   10   20 Kms

Market Drayton

20 May

Stone

Newport

Wolverhampton

R. Severn

Droitwich

EVESHA
9

N
W — E
S

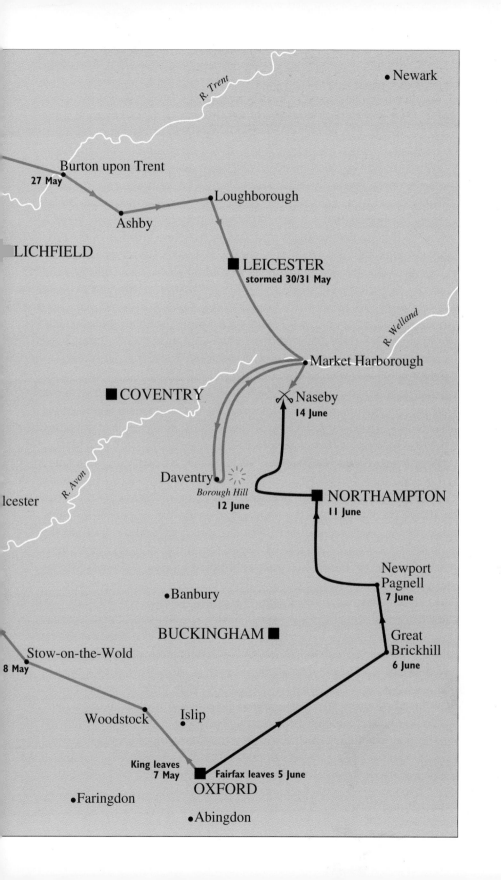

Newark

R. Trent

Burton upon Trent
27 May

Loughborough

Ashby

LICHFIELD

■ LEICESTER
stormed 30/31 May

R. Welland

Market Harborough

■ COVENTRY

⚔ Naseby
14 June

R. Avon

Daventry

Borough Hill
Borough Hill
12 June

lcester

■ NORTHAMPTON
11 June

Banbury

Newport
Pagnell
7 June

BUCKINGHAM ■

Great
Brickhill
6 June

Stow-on-the-Wold

8 May

Woodstock   Islip

King leaves
7 May   Fairfax leaves 5 June

•Faringdon   OXFORD

•Abingdon

A council of war, held at Burton upon Trent on 27 May determined that the best way to raise the siege of Oxford would be 'to fall upon some place possessed by the Parliament'. This would draw Fairfax away from Oxford and would bring about battle on the most favourable terms. Sir Charles Gerard was told to bring his horse across from Newark, and Rupert ordered Goring to make for Market Harborough with his horse and any spare foot, pausing at Oxford to collect the remainder of the artillery. Knowing that Goring might not obey an order from Rupert, Digby reinforced the summons with one of his own. 'For God's sake use diligence and come as strong as you can,' he urged. 'In my conscience it will be the last blow in the business.' He did not know how right he was.

The Siege of Leicester

Leicester, with a population of about 4000, was prosperous but weak, and would have preferred to continue 'uneasy neutrality' than stand a siege. Its castle had been re-fortified, and the adjacent Newarke suburb was surrounded by medieval walls. The town itself had lost its walls, though their gates remained, and earth and timber defences had been thrown up in their place. Some prominent buildings outside the defences which might offer cover to a besieger had been demolished, but many had survived, doubtless because of the influence of their owners.

There were about 600 foot and 420 horse in the garrison, with some 900 well-disposed townsmen ready to assist them. Although the County Committee had reported that Leicester was short of cannon, no more had been sent by the time the Royalists arrived, and the defenders had only nine. The garrison was fortunate that two experienced officers from the New Model, Colonel Sir Robert Pye and Major James Innes, were fortuitously caught up in the siege and were able to advise the governor, the inexperienced Colonel Grey.

Leicester was cut off by Langdale's horse and then, on 29 May, surrounded by the Royalist foot. Rupert threw up a six-gun battery on Raw Dykes, south of the town, facing the walls of the Newarke. The next day he sent a trumpeter to demand the town's surrender, and when the governor asked for more time 'the battery began to play...and made such a breach, that it was thought counsellable, the same night to make a general assault with the whole army, in several places, but principally at the breach...'

The defenders, working frantically, built a retrenchment behind the breach, and when the assault came they fought like tigers, repulsing three Royalist attacks. The attackers did better elsewhere, using primitive hand-grenades to drive back the defenders, and scaled the defences in three separate places. Pye led a cavalry counter-attack, and garrison and townsmen fought with extraordinary determination. A Royalist officer wrote of how:

they fired upon our men out of their windows, from the tops of the houses, and threw tiles upon their heads...finding one house better manned than ordinary, and many shots fired at us out of the windows, I caused my men to attack it, and resolved to make them an example for the rest; which they did; and breaking open the doors, they killed all they found there without distinction.

The attackers, their blood up, drew no easy distinction between soldiers and non-combatants. The Parliamentarian press reported that all Scots in the garrison were killed out of hand and many women murdered or ravished. Even if the butchery was on a lesser scale than hostile reports suggested, there is no doubt that the organized pillage which followed the storm was extreme by the standards of the Civil War. It was claimed that 140 cartloads of goods were sent off to Newark, and when the Mayor turned out to greet the King on 1 June his silver mace was snatched as he awaited the monarch's arrival.

The fall of Leicester and its horrific aftermath sent shock-waves through Parliamentarian garrisons in the Midlands and greatly encouraged the Royalists. Even before the fall of Leicester Cromwell had been sent up to the Isle of Ely to put its defences in order in case the Royalists struck deep into East Anglia, and on 2 June Fairfax was at last ordered to raise the siege of Oxford and march towards the Eastern Association.

A Royalist council of war at Leicester reiterated the usual arguments. Rupert was for marching north, and perhaps coming to terms with the Scots who were increasingly disillusioned with Parliament's shift away from Presbyterians towards the Independents. The courtiers argued in favour of returning to Oxford – they did not yet know that the siege had been lifted – and fighting the New Model if they met it. Charles decided to go back to Oxford, and dawdled south-west to Daventry, a change of direction which produced a temporary mutiny amongst the Northern Horse. There he heard that Fairfax had left Oxford, and told the Queen: 'I may without being too much sanguine affirm that since this rebellion my affairs were never in so hopeful a way.'

Rupert was less cheerful. Goring had still not appeared. Leicester had cost the army perhaps 700 killed and wounded, a garrison had been left to hold it, and some men had disappeared with their loot. Although he could not have known it, Parliament had at last given Fairfax a free hand, and on 8 June his council of war had decided to make the King's army their fixed object. Fairfax was marching north, bent on battle.

The Armies Converge

The Royalists remained around Daventry throughout the second week in June, awaiting the return of a cavalry escort (which had taken a provision convoy into Oxford and would return with ammunition to replenish that expended at Leicester) and plundering villages for miles around. Rupert had secured the huge Iron Age hillfort on Borough Hill, which dominated western Northamptonshire, but his army was widely spread.

Fairfax reached Newport Pagnell on 7 June, and then moved more cautiously. Sir Samuel Luke, the town's governor, received regular reports from surrounding garrisons and was well aware of the Royalist progress, and Fairfax's scoutmaster-general, Major Leonard Watson, sent his own mounted scouts well ahead of the New Model. Fairfax still had important changes to make to his command structure. He was able to persuade Parliament to grant Cromwell a lieutenant-general's commission regardless of the Self-Denying Ordinance. Vermuyden's brigade, which had been sent on a fruitless mission to join the Scots, rejoined the army in Newport Pagnell, and its commander announced that he wished to go abroad: this left the way clear for Ireton's appointment as commissary-general, Cromwell's second-in-command.

The New Model reached Northampton on 11 June, and that day Fairfax ordered Skippon to frame a 'form of battle' in brigades of horse and foot which would be its standard disposition for battle. On 12 June he was at Kislingbury, about 7 miles (11 km) as the crow flies from Borough Hill. That evening the King was hunting in the deer park at Fawsley, 3 miles (5 km) south of Daventry, when he heard that Parliamentarian horse had surprised Colonel Carey's cavalry regiment at Flore, only 5 miles (8 km) to the east. Rupert drew the army together in a general rendezvous on Borough Hill at midnight and kept it stood to arms all night, but Fairfax had no intention of attacking such an advantageous position.

The Oxford convoy rejoined the Royalists that night, and not long after first light they were on the move, marching through Daventry in a column perhaps 6 miles (10 km) long. They were heading for Market Harborough and Melton Mowbray, whence they would make for Newark to obtain reinforcements before heading north. This is an index of just how badly the Royalists had misjudged the tactical situation: with the New Model so close there was no real prospect of escaping without a battle. They probably swung north-eastwards up the Avon valley, through the Kilworths and Husbands Bosworth, to reach Market Harborough after a march of some 23 miles (37 km). The King spent the night in the Old Hall at Lubenham, and Rupert was in Market Harborough itself. The army was in the town and surrounding villages, with a cavalry outpost in Naseby, to the south-south-west.

The New Model spent the night in and around Guilsborough, and a cavalry patrol drove the Royalists out of Naseby: one source says that troopers of Rupert's Lifeguard were surprised playing quoits, while another has them caught at dinner in Shuckburgh House, opposite the church. News of this clash brought the King to a council of war at Rupert's headquarters, traditionally the King's Head Inn. We should not be surprised that there was a difference of opinion. Although there are contradictory accounts, it seems certain that Rupert and his supporters favoured marching north (though with the New Model so close it is hard to see how guns and baggage could have been transported safely), while Digby and the courtiers wanted to offer battle. The King backed Digby, and if Rupert had advocated caution he subsequently gave little sign of it, and the next few hours saw him galvanized with all his old enthusiasm.

The Royalists were numerically weaker than the New Model. Glenn Foard, whose *Naseby: The Decisive Campaign* is unlikely to be bettered as a scholarly assessment, reckons that there were between 9500 and 12,500 Royalists and 15,200 to 17,000 Parliamentarians, depending on the method of calculation. As to quality, the Royalists had more experienced officers, though the composite character of their army meant that it contained more smaller units than the New Model. If few of the New Model's officers had served on the Continent, most had been in arms during the war. Both armies contained some recently drafted, part-trained men. There were more of these in the New Model than the King's army, and Fairfax used some local forces to compensate for the brigade sent to Taunton. Within each army there were sharp differences in quality, and the best, like Rupert's Bluecoats or Cromwell's own regiment of horse, were amongst the finest of the age.

The battle was to be fought north of Naseby, largely on unenclosed open fields. There was pasture near the villages, but for the most part the fields were composed of unhedged cultivated strips of brown loam with patches of gorse at their fringes. A walled rabbit warren, with a warrener's cottage, stood a little over a mile (1.6 km) due north of Naseby, and the battlefield's left flank was defined by robust hedges on the edge of the enclosed pasture fields of Sulby. The Naseby–Sibbertoft road (then as now) divides the battlefield. The ground rises north of Naseby to cross the long ridge of Mill Hill–Fenny Hill. North of this lies the long valley of Broad Moor, with Dust Hill, connected to the Sibbertoft plateau by a narrow neck of land, behind it.

The Royalists were on the move well before first light, and drew up on 'rising ground of very great advantage', the ridge south of East Farndon crossed by the Naseby road. There was no sign of the enemy, and Francis

Ruce, the scoutmaster-general, was sent forward but failed to find any trace of them. It is probable that another report then arrived saying that the New Model was retreating. Rupert at once set off southwards with a party of horse supported by musketeers, whether to check on the reports or, as his enemies were to maintain, because his natural impetuosity impelled him to risk a battle whatever the terms, we cannot be sure. As he passed through Clipston he saw the New Model forming up to the south-west, blocking the road in the area of New House Farm.

Both armies then edged westwards, probably with the New Model beginning the process first and making for Mill Hill. Rupert summoned his own army, possibly because he thought that, as the Parliamentarians were pulling back off the ridge, Fairfax was trying to get away. The Royalists came forward, as Colonel John Okey of the New Model's dragoons put it, 'in a very stately way in a whole body towards us...' By mid-morning the rival armies were arrayed on the low ridges on either side of Broad Moor, their western flanks resting on the Sulby hedges and their eastern flanks bordering the thicker furze where the ground begins its long ripple down towards the Naseby–Clipston road.

The Battle is Joined

There are two good contemporary plans of the battle, one published by Streeter in *Anglia Rediviva*, an account by the Parliamentarian chaplain Joshua Sprigge, and the other a manuscript sketch by the Royalist engineer Sir Bernard de Gomme. Glenn Foard's analysis now enables us to place the armies with some confidence. The Parliamentarians were in two main lines, Cromwell's horse on the right and Ireton's on the left, with Skippon's foot in the centre. A 'forlorn hope' (in this context a forward screen) of musketeers stood to Skippon's left front, and Lieutenant-Colonel Pride commanded a rearguard behind his centre. Cromwell's strong right wing formed three lines rather than two because the ground was too broken up with furze and rabbit holes to enable it to extend further to the east. The baggage train, escorted by its snaphance-armed guard (matchlocks and powder barrels were an unwise combination) was probably on the north-west edge of Naseby. The New Model's field-word, to aid identification in battle, was 'God is our Strength', and some Parliamentarians wore a piece of white linen or white paper in their hats.

The Royalist deployment was more complex. Rupert drew his army up in three lines, with musketeers between the cavalry, and a regiment's worth of cavalry interleaved between the infantry brigades. The former was a continental practice designed to give firepower to cavalry, and the latter was intended to shore up the outnumbered infantry. Rupert

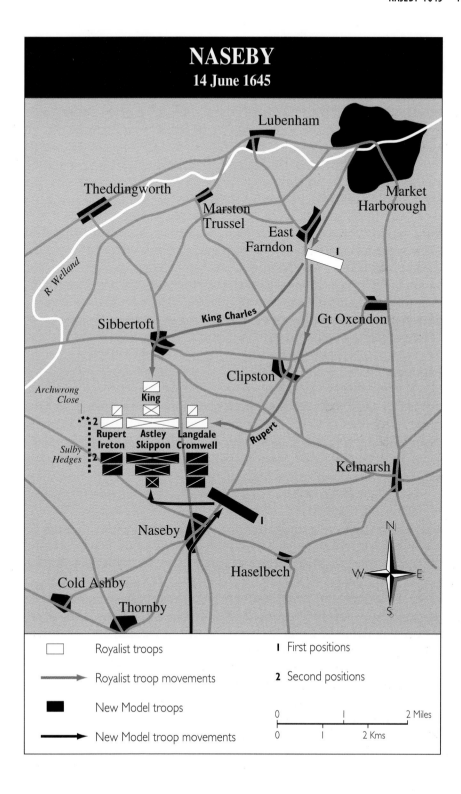

NASEBY
14 June 1645

Lubenham

Theddingworth

Market
Harborough

Marston
Trussel

East
Farndon

R. Welland

King Charles

Sibbertoft

Gt Oxendon

Clipston

Archwrong
Close

King

Rupert
Ireton   Astley
Skippon   Langdale
Cromwell

Rupert

Sulby
Hedges

Kelmarsh

Naseby

Haselbech

Cold Ashby

Thornby

N
W   E
S

	Royalist troops		First positions
	Royalist troop movements	2	Second positions
	New Model troops		
	New Model troop movements		

0   1   2 Miles

0   1   2 Kms

commanded five regiments of horse on the right, and Langdale his under-strength Northern Horse on the left. Jacob Astley's foot formed three tertias or brigades commanded by Sir Bernard Astley, Sir Henry Bard and Sir George Lisle. The King, well back on the slopes of Dust Hill, was surrounded by a mixture of horse and foot including his own Lifeguard and Prince Rupert's Bluecoats. The baggage train was well back, and recent finds of coinage suggest that it might have been east of Sibbertoft, near the Sibbertoft–Clipston road. 'Queen Mary' was the Royalist field word, and many Royalists had put beanstalks in their hats, taken from the bean fields they had crossed during their advance.

The New Model formed up just south of the crest-line so that it was not visible to the Royalists, although the 'forlorn hope' on the forward slope and senior officers on the crest-line must have made the general outline of deployment clear enough. Cromwell, struck by the importance of the Sulby hedges, found Colonel John Okey of the dragoons issuing ammunition to his men behind the Parliamentarian lines, and ordered him to secure the hedged close on the army's left. Recent evidence of musket-balls and pewter tops from the charge-boxes on bandoleers suggests that the close in question was Archwrong Close, well forward of the Parliamentarian left, not simply a hedge-line at right angles to the main line of deployment as was once believed. Okey moved fast, and on arrival one man in ten held the horses while the other nine prepared to defend the hedges with their muskets. Rupert reacted immediately with infantry and cavalry, but Okey reported that: 'it pleased God that we beat off both the horse and foot on the left, and the right wing, and cleared the field, and kept our ground.'

It may be that the dragoon battle goaded the Royalists into attacking, or that Rupert hoped to catch the Parliamentarians before they were fully formed up. In any event, between 10 and 11 a.m. both armies advanced, drums beating and colours flying. Fairfax halted his men on the crest, but the Royalists came on, receiving a spattering of shot from the 'forlorn hope' of musketeers, which fell back up the hill. Both armies had cannon drawn up between their front-rank infantry regiments. The Royalists fired at most a round or two apiece, and although the Parliamentarian guns fired more, their effect was no more than irritating.

It was axiomatic that horse under attack should not receive the charge standing still, but advance to meet it, and when Rupert led his wing forward Ireton's men moved down the slope. This advance, the boggy ground around a stream in the valley bottom, or perhaps a parish boundary hedge, caused Rupert to pause before he thundered up the slope 'at full career', taking the fire of Okey's men in his right flank as he did so.

Although this attack was launched by the best of the Royalist horse the result was no foregone conclusion, for the Parliamentarians did not break at first impact but fought back hard. In fact Ireton's right-hand units had the better of the encounter, enabling Ireton to lead them in against the Royalist foot. However, his horse was killed, and he was run through the thigh with a pike, gashed in the face by a halberd, and taken prisoner. Rupert charged again, this time breaking both Ireton's lines, driving many – but by no means all – of his troopers in disorderly flight to the south and pounding after them.

Astley's foot came on no less gallantly than Rupert's horse. The Parliamentarians advanced to the crest-line to meet them – Clarendon says that 'the Foot on either side scarcely saw each other till they were within carbine-shot' – and fired a volley, which seems to have done little damage. The Parliamentarians held the first attack, but the second, supported by the cavalry attached to the infantry for just this purpose, proved more serious, and Sir Edward Walker saw how the Royalist foot 'falling in with sword and butt end of musket did notable execution; so much as I saw their colours fall and their foot in great disorder.' Pickering's and Montague's regiments broke and ran, opening a gap in the centre. Though Skippon's, on the left, was terribly hard hit, assailed in front by the King's foot and in its left flank by some of Rupert's horse, it fought on.

The Royalists flooded through the gap ripped in the Parliamentarian centre, over-running six guns. They now had only the second line to beat, and as Skippon led it forward he was hit under the ribs by a musket ball which pierced his armour. However, as Fairfax wrote: 'he continued in the field with great resolution: and when I desired him to go off the field he answered, he would not go as long as a man could stand…' His personal example helped avert disaster, for the second line held. Archaeological evidence suggests that most of the firing took place at this stage in the battle, with the foot on both sides firing steadily. The wind was blowing from the north-west, a disadvantage for the Parliamentarians as the powder-smoke blew back in their faces.

It was only on the eastern flank that the Parliamentarians gained an early decisive advantage. Although Langdale's horse was much-criticized for its failure, it is clear that the northerners fought hard against the first wave of Cromwell's attack: Whalley's regiment suffered more casualties

Overleaf: **Streeter's 1647 engraving of the battle in *Anglia Rediviva*, written by the Parliamentarian chaplain Joshua Sprigge, is an important source. Although not wholly accurate, it helps us relate the armies to the ground and helps us understand their layout. The obelisk north-east of Naseby stands on the site of the windmill.**

than any other Parliamentarian cavalry regiment, and its commander 'had his coat cut in many pieces'. But Langdale faced impossible odds: he was outnumbered at least two to one by the New Model's best cavalry, charging with the advantage of the slope. Cromwell sent part of his force after Langdale, to prevent him from rallying, and had the bulk of it available to throw against the Royalist infantry.

Once battle was joined all along the line, Fairfax rode from place to place giving orders, and was personally involved in the cavalry attack on the unbroken third line of foot, which included Rupert's Bluecoats who 'stood to it very stoutly' and received the charge 'like a wall of brass'. Fairfax had already had his helmet knocked off. He met his Lifeguard, commanded by Captain Charles D'Oyley, wheeling away from a body of foot, probably the Bluecoats, which they could not break. Fairfax took some troopers and charged from the rear while D'Oyley attacked from the front. The infantry broke at last, and Fairfax cut down an ensign, whose colour was picked up by a trooper who boasted about his valour. D'Oyley reprimanded the man, but Fairfax replied: 'I have honour enough, let him take that to himself.'

Many historians – myself included – have written of the rapid collapse of the Royalist foot once the horse from Cromwell's victorious right wing surged in against it. However, musket-ball scatters, discovered by metal-detectors, suggest that parties of Royalists, horse and foot alike, fought on across Broad Moor and Dust Hill although the day was clearly lost. Some may have been Irish who 'chose rather to die in the field than be hanged' but the overall picture can only pay tribute to the King's foot, who, as a Parliamentarian admitted, 'did as gallantly as ever men on earth could do'.

It was now that the King was dissuaded by Lord Carnwath from charging with his remaining horse, and as he wheeled from the battlefield there was a temporary panic. It seems likely that the shaken horse soon rallied and charged, but the odds were hopeless and they fell back once more.

Rupert now returned to the field. He had chased the broken portion of Ireton's wing for some miles, and, in the process, encountered the Parliamentarian baggage train. The guard commander mistook Rupert for Fairfax, doffed his hat and asked how the day was going, and only realized his mistake when Rupert asked him if he would surrender. Although John Rushworth says that the guard 'gave fire and instantly beat them off', several members of the train were killed and wounded, suggesting that Rupert may have made a more determined attack. Rupert did manage to rally most of his men before he returned to the battlefield, but when he arrived he found that all was already lost. He could do nothing for the infantry, and he joined the King's party only to find that they were faced by a reconstituted Parliamentarian army. Sir Walter Slingsby admits that: 'they being horse and foot in good order, and we but a few horse only, and those mightily discouraged, that so we were immediately made to run...' The Royalists fled with Fairfax's horse in hot pursuit: 'happy was he that was best mounted'. A substantial musket-ball scatter on high ground north of the Sibbertoft–Clipston road suggests that some of the infantry made a last stand, but it was a hopeless venture.

The Aftermath of the Battle
Near Clipston the pursuing Parliamentarians caught several hundred women from the baggage train: some were killed and the others marked as whores by having their faces slashed or noses slit. Although they were described as 'Irish women, of cruel countenance', armed with long knives, it is likely that they were Welsh and that the knives were for no more sinister purpose than to prepare food for the infantrymen they followed. Of more political significance was the capture, in the King's coach, of the royal correspondence, which was later published as *The King's Cabinet Opened* and contained damaging admissions about Charles's dealings with the French and Irish.

The pursuit went on to the gates of Leicester, and only about 4000 Royalists escaped. Fairfax marched on to Market Harborough, regrouped his army and told Parliament of its staggering victory. He was soon complaining that the sheer quantity of booty taken at Naseby had induced many of his men to desert, and his infantry were only at half their establishment strength. The New Model had lost perhaps 300 men killed in action and another 44 who died of wounds. Royalist losses were much heavier: perhaps 1000 killed; as many seriously wounded; and 5000 captured. What made Naseby decisive was the destruction of the King's 'old infantry'. Charles was never to have an army approaching such quality again.

Although Charles got clear of the battlefield, halted briefly at Leicester, and then set off for Hereford where he began to raise fresh infantry, his cause was lost. Fairfax marched into the West Country, beat Goring at Langport on 10 July and then attacked Bristol, held by Prince Rupert. With his defences pierced, Rupert surrendered on favourable terms, but found himself exiled by his infuriated uncle. The King's last armies were snuffed out, and on 20 March 1646 Lord Astley, on his way to Oxford with 3000 foot, was caught by superior forces at Stow-on-the-Wold. The brave old gentleman surrendered at last. As he sat on a drum he told his captors: 'You have done your work, boys, and may now go play, unless you will fall out amongst yourselves.'

They were prophetic words. A second Civil War, with the captive Charles supported by the Scots, ended with Cromwell's victory at Preston in August 1648. Cromwell was fast becoming the most powerful figure on the Parliamentarian side, and his conviction that Charles was inherently untrustworthy encouraged him to press for the King's execution in January 1649. A third Civil War saw Charles II's Scots supporters defeated at Dunbar in 1650 and Worcester a year later. Cromwell strove without success to find a lasting constitutional settlement, and eventually became Lord Protector in 1657. When he died the following year there was nobody of his status who could hold the reins of power, and the monarchy was restored in May 1660.

A View of the Field

Time and the antics of town planners have not dealt kindly with Leicester, but the Castle Park area, south-west of the city centre, has retained several areas of interest. The original gateway into the Newarke was built during the fourteenth century, used for the storage of arms during the Civil War and subsequently known as the Magazine. It stands in a sprawl of main roads on the south-eastern edge of Castle Park, and now houses the museum of the Royal Leicestershire Regiment.

The Newarke
About 200 yards (180 m) to the west is the Newarke Houses Museum, maintained by Leicester City Museums. It is devoted to the social history of Leicester during the last 500 years. The room on the right of the entrance was panelled in the seventeenth century, possibly to repair damage suffered during the siege. It contains contemporary furniture and artefacts, amongst them a cuirass (breast- and back-plate) and lobstertail helmet of the Naseby period. Upstairs is the militia gallery, which contains the town's armour and some Civil War pottery hand-grenades –'grenadoes' to the men who used them. Leave the museum, turn right and right again to gain access to the gardens. The wall behind them is part of the original defences of the Newarke, and its soft stone is still pierced by the loopholes cut in 1645 to enable Parliamentarian musketeers to fire on the Royalists.

Naseby Field
The field of Naseby was remarkably unspoilt until the recent construction of the A14 across its southern edge. Despite this piece of insensitivity the

battlefield remains easy to interpret, although one must always remember that there were almost no hedges in 1645. Many fields still show signs of the distinctive ridge and furrow field system which characterized pre-enclosure agriculture. There are good examples, for instance, where the little road to Marston Trussel heads north from the Sibbertoft–Clipston road.

An obelisk about 1 mile (1.6 km) north-east of Naseby, on the Market Harborough road, bears a plaque whose inscription warns of the importance of kings not exceeding their just prerogatives. The A14, which clips along noisily just to its north, is on the approximate site of the New Model's first position. The Royalist first position was probably along the road between East Farndon and Great Oxenden – line up the two church towers and you have it – with Market Harborough lying in the valley behind it: it remains 'rising ground of great advantage'.

The little road which heads due north from Naseby goes squarely across the battlefield. Just off its western verge, 1½ miles (2.4 km) from the village, is a memorial which pays tribute to Cromwell but actually stands just forward of the New Model's infantry line. A panel helps the visitor interpret the ground. Broad Moor, a natural amphitheatre, though a tiny stage for such an important play, falls away to the north, and Dust Hill rises on its far side. The woods, Naseby Covert due east and Long Hold Spinney to the north-east, post-date the battle. Both, however, are helpful guides to its dimensions: Cromwell's horse formed up where Naseby Covert now stands, and Langdale's Northern Horse on the ground now covered by Long Hold Spinney. There is no public access to Archwrong Close, seized by Okey's dragoons at the start of the battle, but a bridleway running south-west from the southern edge of Sibbertoft passes just north of it and gives a good feel for the western edge of the battlefield.

Naseby Village

Naseby Battle and Farm Museum, in Purlieu Farm just south of the village, is open on Sunday and Bank Holiday afternoons between Easter and the end of September. It contains some relics and a model of the battle; and a sword, probably dating from 1645, hangs in Naseby church. Naseby Hall, where some of Rupert's troopers were surprised the night before the battle, was demolished to make way for a newer building, but its dining table – 'Cromwell's table' – is also in the church. It looks modest enough, but run a hand over its gnarled surface, close your eyes, and you can almost catch the whiff of sweat and tobacco, and hear those sunburnt troopers, in their buff-coats and top-boots, toasting 'Charles, King of England, and Rupert of the Rhine'.

CHAPTER 4

The Boyne
1690

Background

The Boyne was not a big battle. It was not even the bloodiest battle of the Williamite War in Ireland – that honour goes to 'Aughrim of the slaughter', fought a year later. Yet it struck a particular chord. It was the only battle where the contenders for the British throne, James II and William III, met in person, and they did so on the banks of a river which courses through Irish history. Its images are compelling: William's Dutch Guards marching to the river to the accompaniment of the popular tune 'Lilliburlero'; asthmatic little William crossing the water on horseback under fire; and the Duke of Berwick, James's illegitimate son, leading charge after charge.

But the Boyne has cut a deeper groove in history than its military importance might suggest. To the Protestants of the North it became symbolic of the defeat of Catholicism. Although the battle itself was fought on 1 July, calendar changes adopted in the eighteenth century pushed anniversary celebrations on to 12 July. The Boyne anniversary is the highlight of the 'marching season', when flute bands in their distinctive liveries parade through the streets of Northern Ireland. The Loyal Orange Institution, whose members originally swore to 'support and defend the king and his heirs as long as he or they support the Protestant ascendancy' makes much of the Boyne and its victor, and William, splendidly mounted on a white charger, is an enduring piece of Orange ideography. The battle lives on in songs, one of which concludes:

Orangemen remember King William
And your fathers who with him did join
And fought for our glorious deliverance
On the green grassy slopes of the Boyne.

Above: James II had fought bravely on land and sea in his youth, but the Boyne campaign found him past his best, probably because his expulsion from England in 1688 had done serious damage to his self-confidence. *Left:* He is said to have worn this armour at the Boyne: the sliding grille protecting his face is pierced with the royal arms. He holds a commander's baton, and would have carried a pair of holster pistols, one visible here, as well as a sword.

The English Conquest of Ireland

The fate of Ireland was bound up in all the battles described thus far. After the Norman conquest of England, Norman lords sailed to Ireland and established themselves there: the great keep of Carrickfergus Castle, overlooking Belfast Lough, is one of their enduring monuments. But Norman rule was never comprehensive. Gaelic chieftains remained powerful, and over the next three centuries increased their influence through intermarriage with Norman families and military victory. By 1435 the Irish Council reported to Henry VI that his writ ran only in a small area around Dublin: the Pale, a fortified barrier, was built to defend it.

English kings styled themselves lords of Ireland, and it was only Henry VIII who assumed the title of king. He declared that English laws automatically applied in Ireland, and that the Irish Parliament could legislate only with his consent. In practice he exercised little real power beyond the Pale, and relied heavily on the support of the Gaelic chiefs.

In Elizabeth's reign periodic rebellions by the Gaelic chiefs, together with the risk that Ireland, scarcely touched by the Reformation, might provide a springboard for a Spanish attack on England, persuaded the Queen to embark on full-scale conquest. It was a bitter war, with its share of English reverses. In 1598 Sir Henry Bagenal was defeated by Hugh O'Neill, Earl of Tyrone, at Yellow Ford on the River Blackwater, a rout 'so disastrous to the English and successful in action to the Irish as they shaked the English government in this kingdom till it tottered, and wanted little of fatal ruin.'

O'Neill was a charismatic commander, and the Irish Council believed that, under his leadership, the Irish sought 'to recover their ancient land and territories out of the Englishmen's hands, and [strive] for the restoring of the Romish religion, and to cast off English laws and government...' Although O'Neill developed his force from guerrilla bands into something approaching a regular army, he was ground down by the weight of numbers deployed by Elizabeth's Lord Deputy, Lord Mountjoy. In September 1601 3500 Spaniards landed at Kinsale, just south of Cork, and on Christmas Eve the allied Spanish and Irish advanced to attack Mountjoy's camp. It was badly beaten in what emerged as the war's decisive battle, and by 1603 the English conquest of Ireland was complete.

Under James I 'plantations' of Protestant Scots and English migrants were established in the North. 'Make speed, get thee to Ulster, serve God and be sober,' urged one Norfolk gentleman who took possession of a grant of land in Fermanagh. James gave great tracts of land to the City of London, whose livery companies built a walled city at the old settlement of Derry, renamed, like the county around it, Londonderry.

The English Civil War and the Restoration

In October 1641 the Irish of Ulster rose against English rule, and stories of the atrocities committed by the rebels made a powerful contribution to the air of crisis on the eve of the English Civil War. During that struggle Charles I concluded a truce or 'cessation' with the rebels in order to employ Irish troops in England. Parliament riposted by ordering any Irish taken in arms to be executed without further ado.

Parliament's victory in England left Ireland in the hands of unrepentant Royalists, and in 1649, Cromwell, who had succeeded Fairfax as Lord-General, departed to bring them to heel. In the process he added a new layer to the dreadful strata of atrocity and counter-atrocity which were coming to characterize Irish history. The garrisons of Drogheda and Wexford were amongst those that resisted him, and both were massacred when the towns were taken.

Although it can be argued that Cromwell was not departing from the strict rules of war at the time – defenders put their lives at risk if they continued to fight once their walls were breached and assault was imminent – the assaults on Drogheda and Wexford were brutal, even by the standards of the age. At Drogheda some of the defenders took refuge in a church, which was fired. Cromwell wrote that one of them yelled from the midst of the flames 'God damn me, God confound me; I burn, I burn', while another, who jumped from the tower, was spared 'for the extraordinariness of the thing'. The governor, a testy veteran called Sir Arthur Aston, was beaten to death with his wooden leg; and captured priests, as Cromwell admitted, 'were knocked on the head promiscuously'.

Cromwell ruthlessly suppressed the Roman Catholic Church in Ireland, destroying its buildings and transporting its priests to Barbados. The lands of most 'Irish papists' east of the Shannon were confiscated, and their former owners sent 'to Hell or Connaught' on its far side. With the restoration of Charles II in 1660 the Irish Catholics, many of whom had bravely supported the King and his father, Charles I, hoped to have their lands returned and their Church revived.

Neither proved easy. It was impossible to restore land to the Catholics without alienating the new owners, whose support underpinned the Restoration settlement. The eventual compromise, which gave back about a third of the confiscated land, pleased nobody, and left much of the Catholic nobility and gentry potentially disaffected. The plight of the Catholic Church was no more encouraging. The established church, the Church of Ireland, catered for perhaps 100,000 of Ireland's 300,000 Protestants – most of the rest were Scots Presbyterians, mainly living in the North. The land's 800,000 Catholics were severely handicapped by being unable to take the oath of supremacy required of holders of public office, civil and military, for it acknowledged the king's supreme authority in all matters spiritual and temporal. Catholic clergy were poor and sometimes persecuted, notably during the 'popish plot hysteria' towards the end of Charles II's reign.

James II Comes to the Throne

The accession of Charles's Catholic brother, James II, in 1685, offered hope to the Catholics. Despite James's initial desire not to alienate Irish Protestants, it soon became clear that changes were under way, and in January 1687 Richard Talbot, Earl of Tyrconnell, a Catholic landowner who, as a young officer, had managed to escape the carnage of Drogheda, arrived as Lord Deputy (in effect, Viceroy). His appointment elated Catholics and depressed Protestants, and the delight of the former is mocked in the doggerel set to Purcell's tune 'Lilliburlero' by Thomas, Lord Wharton:

> Ho, Brother Teague, dost hear the decree?
> Dat we shall have a new deputy.
> Ho, by my shoul, it is de Talbot,
> And he will cut de Englishmen's throat.

If Tyrconnell's aims were in fact less sanguinary than Wharton suggested, he certainly lost no time in restoring Catholics to political and military dominance. The Irish army was purged of its Protestant officers, enabling both native Irish and 'old English' to return to a profession which was regarded as natural for a gentleman. The removal of Protestants from the civil administation was less rapid and less thorough, and nothing was done about the vexed question of land settlement.

In England, James II sought to repeal anti-Catholic legislation, and, recognizing that the weight of the political nation was firmly against him, tried to gain approval of both Catholics and Protestant dissenters, granting freedom of worship to the latter and reorganizing local government so as to give them greatly increased power. In 1685 a rising by James's nephew, the Duke of Monmouth, attracted considerable support in the West Country, but was put down at Sedgemoor.

More generally, opposition was muted both by the memory of recent civil war and by the belief that James's unpopular policies would be short-lived. The King was 50 years old. His second wife, Mary of Modena, had no surviving child and had not given birth for several years. It was assumed that when he died his Protestant daughter Mary, married to the Dutch ruler William of Orange (himself son of James II's sister Mary), would succeed him.

William Lands in England

The birth of a son and heir, James Edward, in June 1688, changed the prospect at a stroke. The opposition leaders invited William to come to England, and William was prepared to take the risk of doing so because victory would enable him to mobilize Britain's financial, naval and military resources against his long-standing enemy, Louis XIV of France. William landed at Torbay on 5 November. James advanced to Salisbury to meet him, but was held up by a series of nosebleeds and displayed alarming behaviour which encouraged many senior officers, like John Churchill (the future Duke of Marlborough and the real architect of victory at Sedgemoor), to desert him.

James might yet have won. As a young man he had fought bravely on land and sea, but now his nerve deserted him and he fled to London. He was soon captured, allowed to escape, inconveniently recaptured and permitted to escape once more: the crown was then offered jointly to William and Mary. Most modern historians take a cautious view of the 'Glorious Revolution' of 1688, which was in many respects what Paul Langford terms 'a palace coup than a genuine shift of social or political power'. But the settlement, based as it was on the legitimization of an evidently illegitimate act, did embody the crucial notion of contract between rulers and ruled. William and Mary reigned not because of Divine Right, but because of the will of the people as expressed by Parliament.

If the revolution was largely bloodless in England, it was less so in Scotland, where James's supporters – the Jacobites – had to be defeated by force of arms. In Ireland its consequences were even more bloody, although the slide into conflict was slow. News of James's fall aroused fears in Catholics and Protestants alike, but Tyrconnell did his best to preserve calm, and it briefly seemed that he might negotiate with William.

William sent out Richard Hamilton, a scion of the Irish noble house of Ormonde, major-general in James's army and a close personal friend of Tyrconnell's, in an effort to persuade the Earl to surrender. Hamilton, however, seems to have urged him to hold out, and Tyrconnell raised fresh troops, asking James (exiled in France) to send both money and arms.

By April 1689 Tyrconnell controlled all Ireland with the exception of parts of Ulster. Derry had declined to accept a Jacobite garrison; in Enniskillen the local Protestants formed their own garrison under Gustavus Hamilton; and the Earl of Mountalexander headed a 'Supreme Council' based in Hillsborough in County Down. Richard Hamilton was sent north to subdue Ulster, dispersed Mountalexander's troops with little difficulty, and snapped up the smaller garrisons, leaving only Londonderry and Enniskillen in Protestant hands.

James II Lands in Ireland

James landed in Ireland on 12 March 1689, the first English king to visit for more than 300 years. Although Louis XIV's advisers were divided as to the wisdom of the expedition, Louis eventually decided that it was very much in his interest to support the Irish Jacobites. They would be a thorn in William's flesh, and would prevent him from concentrating British resources against France. Ireland might be a springboard from which James could invade Scotland, where he still enjoyed substantial support, or even England itself. News of James's arrival alarmed William's English supporters. 'If Ireland be lost,' warned one MP, 'England will follow.'

James arrived at Kinsale in a fleet of 22 ships. With him came numerous Irish, Scots and English supporters, his two illegitimate sons (the Duke of Berwick and the Grand Prior of France), a substantial contingent of French troops under General Conrad von Rosen, and the Comte d'Avaux (an experienced diplomat who was to give James political guidance and to report back to Louis). James went straight to Cork, where he rewarded Tyrconnell by making him a duke. He was greeted on his journey from Cork to Dublin 'as if he had been an angel from heaven', and entered Dublin Castle beneath a banner which read:

Now or never
Now and forever.

As soon as he arrived in Dublin, James summoned a parliament which was to meet on 7 May. All but six members of the House of Commons were Catholics, and most of them looked forward to repealing the anti-Catholic laws, reforming the land settlement, strengthening the economy and generally making Ireland less dependent on England.

James and his English advisers were less enthusiastic, because such changes would make it harder for James, once fully restored to his throne, to control Ireland. Measures which gratified Irish Catholics would be almost guaranteed to offend many of James's potential supporters in England. James saw Ireland, just as Louis hoped, as a stepping-stone to his restoration in England. His Irish supporters hoped for much more than he would willingly grant.

The land settlement was duly overturned, offering the prospect of the recovery of land confiscated by Cromwell and not restored under Charles II, although military events moved too quickly for a large-scale redistribution to take place. An act of attainder condemned James's opponents as traitors, subject to the death penalty and the confiscation of their property. Parliament agreed to grant James a subsidy to prosecute the war, although it proved difficult to collect. A shortage of precious metal compelled

James to mint coins from brass and copper, and Tyrconnell later complained to Mary of Modena that even base metal was so scarce that 'we are forced to coin our brass guns for want of it'.

Not only did James and his Irish supporters have different ambitions, but political squabblings distracted them from conducting what was by now a war. In late April a French fleet disembarked Irish regiments raised in France in Bantry Bay, and had rather the better of a battle with an English squadron. It was typical of James that he did not know quite what to make of the encounter. While a French victory was in his interests, he could not bear to think of his old fleet being defeated, and when told that the English had been beaten he snapped, 'It is the first time, then.'

Changes in Military Organization
Each of Charles II's three kingdoms had its own army, and it was the Irish army, Protestant under Charles but transformed into a Catholic force by Tyrconnell, that formed the basis of James's army. Its establishment varied little throughout the war, and in 1689 comprised a Lifeguard, seven regiments of cavalry, eight of dragoons and 45 of foot.

There was initially much variation in the establishments of individual units, with some infantry regiments having up to 45 companies, but soon most foot regiments comprised 13 companies, each with a theoretical strength of 62 private soldiers, five non-commissioned officers (or NCOs) and three officers – captain, lieutenant and ensign. The regiment's three field officers, its colonel, lieutenant-colonel and major, were also company commanders. Its wartime strength was 43 officers, 65 NCOs and 650 privates, but detachments, casualties and desertion would reduce this. The cavalry regiment, whose six troops corresponded to infantry companies, was supposed to number 527 officers and men, but was only likely to produce 3–400 on the battlefield. Dragoon regiments had 10 or 12 companies, and in the Jacobite army they had retained their old role of acting essentially as mounted infantry, using their horses for transport to the battlefield, where they generally fought on foot.

In the armies of the age, colonels were more than mere regimental commanders. Their regiments usually took their colonel's name, and the regiment's colours – once a colour for each company, but now generally a colour for each field officer – might bear devices from the colonel's coat of arms or be the hue of his livery. Colonels were responsible for raising and equipping their regiments and had much influence, sometimes amounting to effective control, over the appointment of their officers. Often they held other senior military or political appointments which kept them away from their regiments, so that the real work was done by the lieutenant-colonel. If all went well there was money to be made from a colonelcy, for even if pay was in arrears, an astute colonel might pocket the difference between the money granted for clothing and equipment and the real cost of items purchased.

Because most Catholics had been excluded from British military service for a generation, James's experienced colonels were officers who had served in other European armies. Perhaps the best-known is Patrick Sarsfield. The first Sarsfield to arrive in Ireland had done so in the retinue of Henry II in 1172, but since then the family had intermarried with the native Gaels: Sarsfield's father married Anne O'Moore, daughter of Rory O'Moore, one of the leaders of the 1641 rebellion. Sarsfield was typical of the 'old English', deprived of their lands in the Pale by Cromwell and packed off to Connaught, resentful over the land settlement and religious discrimination, and with a cultural identity blurred by five centuries in Ireland .

In the 1660s and 1670s a series of legal actions failed to give the Sarsfields posession of their old estate, and Patrick decided to become a soldier. As a Catholic he could not hold a commission in the British Isles, so he became an officer in an English regiment raised to fight for Louis XIV as part of a secret agreement concluded between Charles II and Louis in 1670. Still unable to hold a commission in England, he fought bravely at Sedgemoor as a gentleman volunteer, was rewarded with a captaincy and was specifically exempted from taking the oath of allegiance and supremacy. He was a lieutenant-colonel in 1688, and showed characteristic flair in a patrol action near Wincanton.

As he approached, an enemy officer shouted: 'Stand! For who are ye?'

'I am for King James,' replied Sarsfield, 'Who are you for?'

'I am for the Prince of Orange.'

'God damn you!' came the reply, 'I'll *prince* you!'

Sarsfield had the better of the skirmish, which hardly guaranteed him a future in William's army, and he joined James in France.

Not all the Jacobite colonels were men of Sarsfield's experience, but were given regiments because of their political clout or personal wealth. Lord Bellew had a 6000 (2400 hectare) acre estate but no prior military service, while his neighbour Lord Louth had 4000 acres (1600 hectares) and had joined the army as a captain only in 1686. Usually inexperienced colonels were given veteran lieutenant-colonels – Lord Galway, for instance, had Laurence Dempsey, who had served in Portugal and France. Over 200 Frenchmen served as officers in the Jacobite army, one (the Marquis de Boisseleau) commanding a foot regiment.

As Diarmuid and Harman Murtagh have observed, 'a regiment resembled a business, managed by the colonel, with the other officers as junior partners. They tended to be drawn from the colonel's relatives, neighbours, "conections", and, very probably, those who were prepared to invest in the enterprise.' There were 10 other Plunketts besides the colonel in Lord Louth's regiment, and Colonel Art MacMahon's regiment was officered by MacMahons and O'Reillys, with a leavening of Bradys and Duffys.

Changes in Weaponry

In the 45 years separating Naseby from the Boyne the art of war had moved on apace. The matchlock musket was being superseded by the flintlock, whose charge was ignited by the sparks from a flint which struck a steel frizzen when the trigger was pressed. Flintlocks were more reliable than matchlocks, but more expensive to manufacture and maintain, and the Jacobite army was always short of them. The proportion of pikemen to musketeers was declining. Sir Edward Dering's regiment, in William's service, had two-thirds musketeers to one-third pikemen in 1689, but by 1691 the English regiments which left Ireland for Flanders had only 14 pikemen per company (less than a quarter of their strength).

The development of the bayonet contributed to the pikeman's demise. The first bayonets were fitted with tapered hilts which simply plugged into the musket's muzzle, and it was not until the early eighteenth century that the socket bayonet, which fitted over the muzzle, became generally available. The musket could not be fired when its plug bayonet was fixed, a fact which contributed to the defeat of a Williamite force by the Scots Jacobite John Graham of Claverhouse, Viscount Dundee, at Killiecrankie in July 1689. Government muskets were – not for the last time – no match for the broadswords of charging Highlanders, but Dundee himself was shot dead in the moment of victory and the rising soon collapsed without him.

The Jacobite army was constantly under-equipped. Not only were most of its muskets matchlocks, but there were never enough even of them, and

Most of William's musketeers carried the new flintlock musket, known as a 'dog-lock' because of the catch (dog) that holds it safely at half-cock. The hilt of the plug bayonet was simply inserted into the musket's muzzle when required.

in 1689 there were reports that whole regiments were equipped with sharpened sticks, clubs or even scythes. In March 1690 Tyrconnell complained that he was short of 20,000 muskets and had so little gunpowder that two-thirds of his men had never fired a shot. Eight major arms convoys arrived from France, but Louvois, the Minister of War, had never been in favour of the enterprise, and even Louis regarded it as simply a means of diverting William from the Continent. There were never enough French arms, and those that appeared were usually old or in poor repair. Private purchase was sometimes more successful: flintlocks and cannon were bought in Portugal, and Mary of Modena pawned her jewellery to buy 2000 muskets.

The Jacobite foot-soldier looked very similar to his opponent. He wore a full-skirted coat, long waistcoat, shirt, cravat, loose-fitting breeches, woollen stockings, brogues, and a broad-brimmed hat. One company in each regiment contained grenadiers, who needed to sling their muskets over their shoulders in order to throw their hand grenades (cast-iron globes filled with gunpowder and ignited by a burning fuse), and so wore low caps instead of hats. Most Jacobite regiments, in common with their English opponents, wore red coats, although white, grey and perhaps blue were also used. There was much variety in the colour of the coat's lining and the wide, turned-back cuffs. The Jacobite cavalry impressed friend and foe alike. At the start of the war it was well-mounted and had the best of the officers. Cavalrymen wore long coats, breeches and high jackboots, and carried a sword, a pair of flintlock pistols and a flintlock carbine. Dragoons carried sword and musket, and wore short boots and a cap similar to that worn by grenadiers in the infantry.

James was poorly provided with artillery. Shortage of guns was one reasons for his failure to take Londonderry, and at the Boyne he had perhaps 16 field-guns. He was scarcely better off for engineers or doctors, and Ireland's notoriously poor roads caused constant difficulties for his transport train which comprised 170 wagons and 400 carts in 1691.

The Jacobite army was of uneven quality. It lacked experienced officers, was wretchedly paid, and shortage of modern weapons told against its infantry. Yet it often fought remarkably well. John Stevens, an Englishman who served as an officer in the Grand Prior's Regiment, commended the army's 'courage and resolution', adding, 'Let not any mistake and think I either speak out of affection or deliver what I know not; for the first I am no Irishman to be anyway biased, and for the other part I received not what I write by hearsay, but was an eyewitness.' 'Never was an attack made with more bravery and courage, and never was it known that the Irish fought with more resolution' was a Williamite's verdict on Jacobite performance at Aughrim.

The Sieges of Derry and Enniskillen

By the time James arrived Tyrconnell had done his work well and all the country, except Enniskillen and Derry, was in Jacobite hands. In April he approached Derry, hoping that his presence would persuade the citizens to open their gates, but was disappointed: on18 April he was fired upon and some of his entourage were killed. After a council of war it was decided that James would return to Dublin while the French Lieutenant-General Maumont besieged Derry, with Richard Hamilton as his second-in-command.

The siege of Derry was the first major act of the Williamite war. The city's governor, Lieutenant-Colonel Robert Lundy, fled in suspicious circumstances – his effigy is burned annually – and Henry Baker and the Reverend George Walker were appointed joint governors. The able-bodied male citizens, some 7500 men, were formed into eight regiments, each assigned to a sector of the walls. Cannon were positioned along the walls, covering the gates, and on the tower of St Columb's Cathedral.

The besiegers, numbering perhaps 20,000 men, had too few cannon to breach Derry's walls, but fired mortar bombs into the city – George Walker thought that at least 600 people were killed by them – and tried to starve out the defenders. On 21 April the defenders mounted a sortie against Pennyburn, a mile (1.6 km) north of the city, killing Maumont in the process. Early the following month a small fort built round a windmill on the southern edge of the city was captured by the Jacobites and then recaptured by the garrison.

Rosen arrived with reinforcements in June, and the besiegers tightened their grip, blocking the River Foyle with a wooden boom to prevent relief by water. Bad weather and shortage of food added to the discomfort of besiegers and besieged alike. Walker admitted that one extremely fat man feared that he would fall victim to cannibalism, and from the other side of the lines a French officer wrote that 'the troops are tired and many of them are ill...' On the evening of Sunday 28 July the boom was broken and two merchant ships full of provisions reached Derry. With no prospect of starving the city into submission, the Jacobites abandoned the siege.

Enniskillen, the other centre of Protestant resistance, was also besieged. Although it lacked Derry's stout walls, its position, on an island where Upper and Lower Lough Erne join, gave it great natural strength. Its defenders were never as closely besieged as the garrison of Derry, and were able to make damaging raids against Jacobite lines of communication. In July Viscount Mountcashel and Major-General Anthony Hamilton (Richard's brother) launched a deliberate attack on Enniskillen, trying first to take Crom Castle on Upper Loch Erne. They were badly beaten there, and the victors capitalized on their success by attacking Mountcashel at Newtownbutler.

The Enniskilleners were tough adversaries – 'I have seen them, like mastiff dogs, run against the bullets,' said one amazed Englishman – and the force of their assault was too much for Mountcashel's men. Mountcashel himself was dangerously wounded and then captured: perhaps 2000 of his men were killed and another 500 taken. The defence of Derry and Enniskillen, and the battle of Newtownbutler, raised Protestant morale, and hard on their heels came more good news: William was sending an expedition to Ireland.

Schomberg Arrives in Ireland

William had originally hoped to persuade Tyrconnell to capitulate; he then offered the Jacobites religious toleration and security of property, but confiscation of their land if they did not submit. This had no effect, and it became clear that he would have to recapture Ireland by force of arms. William was not confident enough of the English regular army's loyalty to use it in such an attempt. Instead, he brought over Dutch troops, supplemented by English regiments specially raised for the expedition, and officered by Irish Protestants in exile in England. Other regiments were recruited from French Huguenots, who had been forced to emigrate when Louis XIV had revoked the Edict of Nantes (which had given them religious freedom) in 1685. In command was the 74-year-old veteran Frederick Hermann, Duke of Schomberg. He had served in the Portuguese, Brandenburg and French armies, becoming a marshal of France in 1675 but, a Protestant, leaving France in 1685. He had been William's military commander in 1688: active, experienced and methodical, he was a natural choice for command in Ireland.

Schomberg landed in Bangor Bay in mid-August, and at once laid siege to Carrickfergus Castle, which surrendered on terms after a stout defence. Word of Schomberg's arrival, coming hard on the heels of bad news from Derry and Enniskillen, provoked something approaching a panic in Dublin. James considered returning to France, but soon decided to go forward to Drogheda, ordering Tyrconnell to follow with the army, while Berwick delayed Schomberg's advance around Newry by breaking up the roads and laying waste the countryside.

In early September Schomberg ground to a halt at Dundalk, and the adversaries remained facing one another, in growing discomfort from sickness and bad weather, till early October when James withdrew to Ardee, and thence to Dublin, and Schomberg fell back to winter quarters of his own in Lisburn. The campaign had proved utterly inconclusive, and William was not pleased. He concluded that 'nothing worth while would be done' unless he went to Ireland himself, though he was reluctant to do so because it would keep him from the Continent during the 1690 campaigning season.

Campaign and Battle

Both sides built up their forces for the coming campaign. In 1689 William had begun negotiating the hire of troops from the King of Denmark, and in March 1690 1000 Danish cavalry and 6000 infantry, commanded by the Duke of Wurttemberg-Neustadt, arrived in Ireland. More English, German and Dutch troops arrived over the next two months, and steps were taken to improve the regularity of the army's pay and supply of rations.

William was assisted by the fact that his navy was able to control the Irish Sea so that convoys could cross without interference. Sir Cloudesley Shovell, the enterprising commander of the squadron of warships protecting communications with Ireland, was delighted that the French made no serious attempt to interfere. He made several raids on Jacobite bases, and even managed to cut out a 20-gun frigate from Dublin Harbour.

The Jacobites, meanwhile, exchanged a brigade of Irish infantry under Lord Mountcashel (who had succeeded in escaping from Enniskillen) for a brigade of French under the Comte de Lauzun. Mountcashel's men formed the nucleus of the many 'Wild Geese' who were to serve France, especially after the final collapse of the Jacobite cause in Ireland in 1691.

Louis XIV got the best of the deal. Lauzun was ambitious, inexperienced and on bad terms with Louvois, the Minister of War, whose support was essential. D'Avaux was recalled to France at the same time, and was not sorry to go, as he expected to fall out with Lauzun, and he may well have been right, for it was soon reported that the Count had boxed the ears of the Governor of Dublin. Three of Lauzun's five regiments were French, one was Walloon (from what is now Belgium) and the remaining one, Zurlauben's, was German. Some were Protestants, who deserted to William after the Boyne, and they were far less well-equipped than the reinforcements William was sending to Ireland. Nor was this all. Lauzun had been told to remain on the defensive and play for time, for Louis now saw little hope of James re-establishing himself in England.

William Arrives in Ireland

William sailed from Hoylake in Lancashire on 11 June and, escorted by Shovell's squadron, reached Carrickfergus three days later. With him came another 14,000 men, a train of artillery from Holland, a full war-chest and a veritable galaxy of notables. William was 39 years old, the son of William II, Prince of Orange and Stadholder of the United Provinces of the Netherlands, and his wife Mary, eldest daughter of Charles I of England. William's father had died shortly before his birth, and the House of Orange had lost its power to an oligarchy of wealthy citizens which failed to make preparations to meet the rising power of Louis XIV. When the French attacked in 1672 'the United Provinces collapsed like a bad soufflé', and three provinces were actually over-run. William inspired the defence, and the following year he began the counter-offensive by taking the town of Naarden.

William's recovery of the lost provinces made him a national hero. 'The hereditary establishment of his offices made him, in all but name, a constitutional monarch,' wrote his biographer Stephen Baxter, and 'the Prince had become a professional soldier and a very hard man.' In 1672 he married Mary, daughter of James Duke of York, the future James II. Although the marriage developed into a love match, the princess was shocked by the first sight of her future husband. He was half a head shorter than she was, hunchbacked, pockmarked and asthmatic: his only remarkable feature was a pair of brilliant eyes.

It may have been William's unprepossessing appearance as much as their own unfamiliarity with monarchy that gave the people of Belfast pause for thought when William entered the city. One eyewitness said that

Above: **The Norman castle at Carrickfergus had been taken by Schomberg in August 1689: William arrived with substantial reinforcements on 14 June 1690.** *Above right:* **Sir Godfrey Kneller's formal portrait of William sets out the sharp lines of his features, but does not reveal that he was short, stooped and pockmarked. William was a brave man and a seasoned soldier: on campaign he lived with his troops in a portable 'cabin' designed by Sir Christopher Wren.**

they 'did nothing but stare, never having seen a king before in that part of the world; but after a while some of them beginning to huzza the rest all took it (as hounds do a scent).' William declared that he had not come to let the grass grow under his feet, and he made plans to move his 36,000 men south as quickly as he could. He himself made for Dundalk by way of Newry and the Moyry pass, sending part of his army via Armagh and Newtownhamilton.

The Jacobite Advance
James had set off for Dundalk with the main body of his army, some 26,000 strong, on 16 June. His men were optimistic: 'Some were so open

as to tell their Protestant friends very lately that they would be glad to go to mass within this twelve months.' They believed that the French fleet would sever William's communications with England, or that their would be a Jacobite rising there. Lauzun was more hard-headed. James was short of supplies and his men were poorly armed: if he went forward to Dundalk he risked being cut off from Dublin. Although a Jacobite screening force fought a brief delaying action in the Moyry pass, James wisely decided not to hold it in strength because he risked being outflanked by the advance from Armagh.

In truth James had few options. The ground between Dundalk and Dublin is generally low and easily crossed. All its rivers flow eastwards to the sea and must therefore be crossed by an invader moving southwards, but neither the Fane, Glyde and Dee in County Louth, nor the Nanny in County Meath are serious obstacles. If James moved westwards he would simply uncover Dublin, for William could advance directly on it, keeping himself supplied by sea.

James knew that he was outnumbered, and, misled by information from a prisoner taken in the Moyry pass, may well have believed William to be stronger than he actually was. But as he was to maintain:

What induced the king to hazard a battle on this inequality was that if he did not there he must lose all without a stroke, and be obliged to quit Dublin and all Munster, and so be reduced to the province of Connaught, where having no magazines he could not subsist very long, it being the worst corn country in Ireland. Besides his men seemed desirous to fight, and being new raised would have been disheartened still to retire before an enemy and see all their country taken from them without one blow for it, and by consequence be apt to disperse and give all for lost.

James's only chance was to face William behind the best obstacle he could find: the Boyne water.

Yet even the Boyne was far from perfect. James acknowledged that the position he chose was 'an indifferent good one (and indeed the country afforded no better)'. It had two chief disadvantages. The first was that the Boyne swings north near Rossnaree to loop round Oldbridge before resuming its journey eastwards to the sea through Drogheda. Classical military theory warns against defending the curve of a river which faces the enemy, for an opponent who attacks where the river bends is effectively behind the defenders of the loop, who risk being cut off if the attack succeeds. In James's case this warning was particularly appropriate, for the small town of Duleek, where the road to Dublin from Oldbridge crosses the River Nanny, actually lay closer to attackers across the Boyne at Rossnaree than to the defenders at Oldbridge.

Worse still, the Boyne was fordable in many places, although the practicability of these fords remains a matter of debate. Lauzun observed that when the Jacobites crossed the river at low tide on 29 June their drummers continued beating, without having to lift their drums to protect them from the water. He then rode along the course of the river to Slane, finding it fordable everywhere. However, given Lauzun's instructions only to risk a battle on favourable terms, and the part he was to play in persuading James to flee, he is scarcely an impartial witness. Two of his French subordinates found the river a much more formidable obstacle, and the commissary Coubertin thought that only the ford at Rossnaree offered a realistic prospect of crossing upstream of Oldbridge.

The Williamites were certainly impressed by the Jacobite position. William's confidant the Earl of Portland believed that the King found the fords 'not only difficult, but almost impracticable', and Captain Robert Parker of Lord Meath's Regiment thought that 'it would be a difficult matter to force them from their ground, unless some measures were taken before the battle which might oblige them to break up the order they were drawn up in'.

The Deployment of the Armies
The most recent terrain analysis of the battlefield of the Boyne, conducted by Donal O'Carroll in 1990, concludes that the position did indeed have considerable natural advantages, but that these were not properly appreciated by James. The Oldbridge area and the lofty Donore Hill to its south were its vital ground, and the only realistic prospect of outflanking this came from the Slane/Rossnaree area. Even if an attacker did cross the river at Rossnaree, it would be no easy matter for him to reach Duleek because of the very boggy ground. The battlefield, O'Carroll sensibly maintains, 'had a potential for defence that would have belied later events'.

William's army reached the Boyne early on 30 June and encamped near Tullyallen, facing James's main body on Donore Hill. 'His troops had marched out properly,' wrote a Danish officer, 'and were divided by brigades very advantageously on the other side of the river. The crossing a little way off [Oldbridge] was strongly held by the enemy.' William's Dutch guards, in their distinctive blue coats, were engaged by Jacobite cannon covering the crossing. When William's guns arrived in the afternoon they were brought onto action on 'a furry bank over against the pass', probably the rising ground just north of Oldbridge, and took on the

MUNSTE

Jacobite guns, apparently persuading James to move his headquarters back to the ruined church atop Donore hill.

William himself went down to the river shortly afterwards, looked at Oldbridge ford and then rode upstream. He dismounted to relax, and no sooner was he back in the saddle than a cannon ball, possibly fired from one of a pair of field-pieces brought forward with a party of cavalry and concealed behind a hedge, 'grazed upon the bank of the river, and in the rising slanted upon the King's right shoulder, tore out a piece of his coat, and tore the skin and flesh, and afterwards broke the head of a gentleman's pistol.' William made light of it, quipping that it could have come nearer, but spent the evening riding about his camp to show his men that he was not badly hurt.

William held a council of war that night. It was clear to all present that their choices were limited to an attack at Oldbridge, an outflanking move by way of Slane/Rossnaree, or a combination of the two. There was a bridge at Slane, but the Jacobites had in fact broken it down; though the bridges at Drogheda were intact, the town was strongly held. Schomberg favoured making a feint at Oldbridge and sending the bulk of the army upstream to find a crossing. Count Solms, commander of the Dutch contingent, disagreed, and recommended throwing the whole army across the river at Oldbridge.

William hit upon a judicious compromise. A strong detachment of cavalry, infantry and dragoons, some 10,000 men in all, probably under the overall command of Lieutenant-General James Douglas, would march upstream towards Slane/Rossnaree. Douglas expected to make for Slane bridge, but was to be redirected to Rossnaree. Schomberg's son, Count Meinhard Schomberg, moved first with part of the force, making for the ford at Rossnaree. The remainder of the army was to cross at Oldbridge. This plan would give William the flexibility of exploiting success at either crossing, and he might have hoped that news of young Schomberg's approach would persuade James to weaken his strong position around Donore: this is precisely what happened.

Schomberg's party moved off at about 5 a.m. on the morning of 1 July, and reached the river at Rossnaree perhaps an hour later. They found the ford defended by Colonel Neil O'Neill's dragoon regiment. As commissary Coubertin pointed out, the ford was so important that it merited a strong garrison, and O'Neill, under orders to 'defend that pass as long as he could, without exposing his men to be cut to pieces', had no realistic prospect of stopping Schomberg.

Schomberg sent 100 elite mounted grenadiers down to the ford to draw the defenders' fire, and followed up with his Dutch dragoons, driving O'Neill's men back. O'Neill himself, who proudly celebrated his ancestry by dressing like an Irish chief rather than a colonel of dragoons, was mortally wounded. With Schomberg's cavalry across, his infantry followed, and an officer was sent back to tell William the good news. William then ordered Douglas to support Schomberg with the remainder of the flanking force.

The threat to his left induced James to shift troops across to strengthen it. He sent off two regiments of cavalry, one of them Sarsfield's, together with Lauzun and his French infantry, followed by some of the Irish infantry until about half the Jacobite army was on its way towards Rossnaree. James expected that the whole Williamite army would follow young Schomberg, but when he rode forwards he found Tyrconnell with the right wing of cavalry and two brigades of infantry facing William's men at Oldbridge.

James then rode westwards and joined Lauzun's force near Corballis. It was drawn up perhaps 500 yards (460 m) from the Williamites, with boggy ground and two deep, high-banked ditches between the armies. The Williamite Lord Meath complained that 'a damned deep bog lay between us; we could not pass it', and Colonel Richard Brewer 'thought the Devil himself could not have got through'. James had now checked the flanking attack, but at the price of weakening his centre, and while he was talking to Lauzun a messenger arrived with the worst possible news: the Williamites had crossed the Boyne at Oldbridge.

The Battle Begins
The first crossing began just after 10 a.m., when William's Dutch guards, nearly 2000 strong, advanced to the strains of 'Lilliburlero'. The Reverend George Story tells how 'the Dutch beat a march till they got to the river's side, and then, the drums ceasing, they went in some eight or ten abreast'. When they were about halfway across the defences of Oldbridge blazed into life, and 'a whole peal of shot came from the hedges, breastworks and houses'. The fire was not notably effective, but when the Dutch reached the shore the Royal Regiment of Foot took them on hand to hand, Major Arthur Ashton rushing forward to pike a Dutch officer as he scrambled from the water, only to be shot a moment later. 'The fighting was so hot,' recorded Story, 'that many old soldiers said they never saw brisker work.'

The Dutch guards pushed the Jacobites out of Oldbridge and then formed up on its far side. While they were doing so, other Williamite troops prepared to cross downstream; as they marched to their crossing-points Tyrconnell launched his cavalry against the Dutch while he prepared to meet the fresh attacks. The charge was led by James's natural son the Duke of Berwick, whose horsemen 'rushed sword in hand' upon the guards. William, watching through a telescope from the other side of the river, was, according to his Secretary at War, George Clarke, 'in a good deal of apprehension for them, there not being any hedge or ditch before them nor any of our horse to support them, and I was so near His Majesty as to hear him say softly to himself "my poor guards, my poor guards, my poor guards".' The Dutch formed square and stood their ground with musket and bayonet, bringing down horse and rider. William was mightily relieved, and 'breathed out as people used to after holding their breath upon a fright or suspense, and said that he had seen his Guards do that which he had never seen foot do in his life.'

The two Huguenot regiments of Cambon and Caillemotte, together with William's northern Irish foot (notably Gustavus Hamilton's Enniskilleners), Nassau's Dutch regiment and two English regiments crossed a little downstream from the guards. Lieutenant-General Richard Hamilton led some Jacobite foot against them, only to see his inexperienced men break and run as the Williamites crossed. He galloped across to some nearby cavalry and led them in a series of charges which not only checked the Williamite advance but forced some of the infantry back into the river, and came close to breaking Caillemotte's regiment. Colonel de la Caillemotte, mortally wounded, was carried back across the river, shouting: *'À la gloire, mes enfants, à la gloire'*.

His men were at their last gasp when the Duke of Schomberg rode up, drew his sword, pointed at the Jacobites and reminded the Huguenots of the miseries inflicted on them by Catholics. *'Allons, messieurs,'* he cried, *'voila vos persecuteurs'* – 'Come, gentlemen, there are your persecutors.' The appeal worked and Caillemotte's men rallied.

The Duke of Wurttemberg-Neustadt led his Danish troops across the river at Yellow Island, almost a mile (1.6 km) downstream from Oldbridge, carried on the shoulders of his grenadiers. 'Where your Majesty's Guards crossed,' he later reported to the Danish King Christian V, 'the water was so deep it came up to their armpits. We marched across by division. The bottom was very boggy.' No sooner did the Danish guards reach the southern bank than they were bravely attacked by Jacobite horse – 'the Irish cavalry behaved very well,' wrote Wurttemberg-Neustadt, 'but the foot behaved very badly.' The guards beat off the charge and formed a bridgehead where they were joined by the Danish cavalry, de la Mellonière's Huguenot regiment and Cutts' English regiment in Dutch pay.

William's men were now across the river in such strength that Tyrconnell's plight was hopeless. Nevertheless, he sent all his cavalry

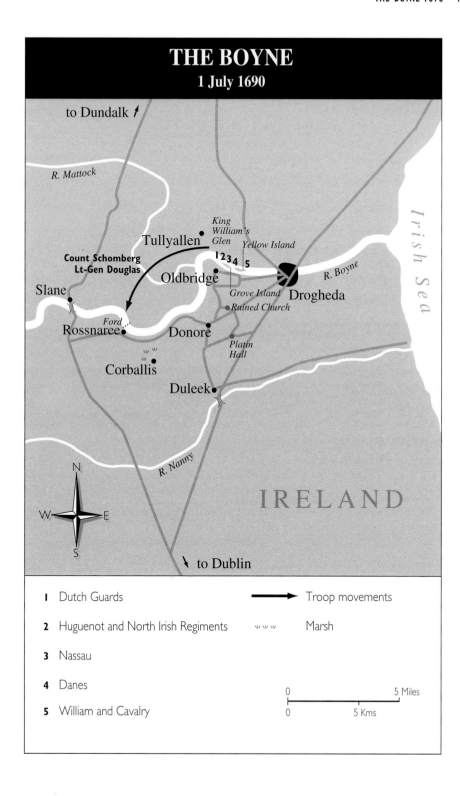

THE BOYNE
1 July 1690

to Dundalk

R. Mattock

King William's Glen

Tullyallen

Yellow Island

Count Schomberg
Lt-Gen Douglas

1 2 3 4 5

Oldbridge

R. Boyne

Slane

Grove Island   Drogheda

Ruined Church

Ford

Rossnaree

Donore

Platin Hall

Corballis

Duleek

R. Nanny

N
W   E
S

IRELAND

Irish Sea

to Dublin

1	Dutch Guards	→	Troop movements
2	Huguenot and North Irish Regiments	ⅳ ⅳ ⅳ	Marsh
3	Nassau		
4	Danes		
5	William and Cavalry		

0   5 Miles
0   5 Kms

William's cannon, north of the Boyne, support the crossing at Oldbridge. Many Jacobite regiments and the French brigade had been shifted from the high ground opposite to deal with the crossing at Rossnaree, well to the right of this picture.

forward in a desperate attempt to thrown the Williamites back into the river in a charge which excited the admiration even of its intended victims. 'The enemy's horse fought wonderfully bravely as ever men could do,' acknowledged James Douglas, while Sir Thomas Bellingham wrote that: 'The enemy's horse of Tyrconnell's regiment behaved themselves well but our Dutch like angels.'

Berwick's horse was killed under him, but the Duke was helped to safety by a trooper. Old Schomberg was less fortunate. He was with the Huguenots and Enniskilleners when a bullet hit him in the neck. The Danish ambassador thought that it was fired 'by our men, who were crossing the river and discharging their pieces as they advanced', though the Jacobites were to claim that the fatal shot was fired deliberately by Sir Cathal O'Toole. Schomberg fell from his horse and 'died immediately without uttering a word'. Another distinguished casualty was George Walker, once Governor of Londonderry and now Bishop-Elect of Derry, serving as chaplain with the Enniskilleners. William had no time for warrior-priests and, when told that Walker had been killed, asked sarcastically: 'What took him there?'

Although William had not been pleased with Schomberg's performance the previous year, he realised that news of the Duke's death might have a detrimental effect on his men's morale, and determined to cross the river himself. He had already ordered Godart de Ginkel to find a ford below Yellow Island and cross there with his cavalry regiment and two regiments of dragoons.

William reached the river while the crossing was still in progress and, seeing Lord Walter Dongan's Jacobite dragoons riding down to intercept Ginkel, organized covering fire from two field-guns and some Danish infantry. Dongan was killed and his men were driven off. William then crossed the river. He could not wear a cuirass because of the wound he had received the previous day, carried his sword in his left hand because his right arm was so sore, and was a prominent sight in the sash and star of the Order of the Garter. The Danish ambassador admitted that at this stage in the battle he and a colleague fell back behind the King, 'not deeming it our duty to expose ourselves to musket shots and sabre cuts'.

The crossing was so boggy that William had to dismount, and the stress of tramping through the mud brought on an asthma attack. Yet he was soon back in the saddle, leading his cavalry in an effort to cut off the Jacobite infantry around Oldbridge. Once again the Jacobite cavalry bore the brunt of the battle, checking the pursuit and falling back onto the slopes of Donore. Even Tyrconnell now realized that the game was up, and decided to withdraw to Duleek, ordering Richard Hamilton to keep the Williamites back as best he could.

William, anxious to press the Jacobites, approached the Enniskillen cavalry regiment, commanded by an Englishman, Colonel William Wolseley. The troopers did not recognize him in the dust and smoke until Wolseley saw the star and sash and shouted: 'It's the King!' William stood up in his stirrups and cried: 'Gentlemen, you shall be my guards today. I have heard much of you. Let me see something of you!' Then he led them up Donore hill towards Hamilton's rearguard.

There was a desperate fight around Donore Church. 'The place was unfortunately full of holes and dung pits and the passages narrow,' recalled Sir Robert Southwell:

but above all the dust and smoke quite blinded them. His Majesty was here in the crowd of all, drawing his sword and animating all that fled to follow him… Nay one of the Inniskilleners came with a pistol cocked to His Majesty till he called out 'what, are you angry with your friends?' The truth is the clothes of friends and foe are so alike that His Majesty had the goodness to excuse all that passed.

Richard Hamilton was wounded and captured, and William rode over to see him, asking him if he thought the Jacobites would charge again.

'Yes, upon my honour, I believe they will,' replied Hamilton, 'for they have a good body of horse still.'

'*Your* honour?' riposted William, mindful of the fact that he had sent Hamilton to Ireland in 1689 to persuade Tyrconnell to surrender.

James heard of the defeat of his right wing at about 2 p.m., and whispered to Lauzun that their only hope was to charge the younger Schomberg's detachment before their soldiers found out what had happened and became disheartened. Lauzun and his cavalry commander, the Marquis Lery de Girardin, agreed that the ground made this quite impossible. However, his second-in-command, the Marquis de la Hoguette, was soon to write that the bog and ditches could have been crossed. It is, however, likely that he wrote with a view to discrediting Lauzun, for even the fiery Patrick Sarsfield believed that 'it was impossible for the horse to charge the enemy.'

The Jacobite Retreat

At this moment the Williamite dragoons mounted, and Schomberg's force turned right and began to march southwards as if to gain the Dublin road. This manoeuvre threatened to outflank the whole Jacobite army, and Lauzun at once ordered de la Hoguette to march off by the left flank and make for Dublin. James claimed that Lauzun pressed him to take his own regiment of horse, which was then at the head of the column, and some dragoons, head straight for Dublin, and then 'to go with all expedition to France to prevent his falling into the enemy's hands...' Lauzun pressed the cavalry to go faster, and when de la Hoguette remonstrated that this would imperil the infantry, Lauzun retorted that all that now mattered was saving the King.

The retreat speedily got out of hand. Lieutenant Stevens describes how the Grand Prior's Regiment of Foot had begun to withdraw, in good order, down a sunken road leading towards Duleek, when a fleeing cavalry regiment burst upon them:

so unexpected and with such speed, some firing their pistols, that we had no time to receive or shun them, but all supposing them to be the enemy (as indeed, they were no better to us) took to their heels, no officer ever being able to stop the men after they were broken...some throwing away their arms, others even their coats and shoes to run lighter.

There was a dreadful scramble when the two retreating wings collided at Duleek, where a single bridge crossed the narrow River Nanny. De la Hoguette later told Louvois that: 'The Irish troops were not only beaten;

A later print showing the flight of James II from the Boyne. Most senior officers wore broad-brimmed hats rather than helmets (see page 121). James was hustled from the field by Lauzun, commanding the French contingent, who was anxious to prevent him from being killed or captured.

they were driven before the enemy like sheep.' Colonel Conrad von Zurlaben reported that his French comrades-in-arms behaved little better, and it was his own bluecoats, mainly German and Swiss, who helped the Jacobite cavalry cover the retreat.

William did not press his beaten enemies. The Jacobite Colonel O'Kelly claims that it was because James's men fell back in such good order. This may have been true of Zurlaben's regiment, the cavalry, and some gunners, probably French, who checked the pursuit for an hour and a half near Duleek, but it scarcely applies to the rest of the army. Bishop Burnet suggests, more plausibly, that William believed that James's army would disintegrate and there was little to be gained from a vigorous pursuit with the attendant loss of life. Jacobites found on the field were certainly shown little mercy: 'they shot them like hares amongst the corn and in the hedges as they found them in their march,' admitted George Story. The Danish envoy noted that Count Schomberg had received no orders to cut off the Jacobite retreat, and that William himself may have wished 'to put into practice Caesar's maxim and leave his enemies a golden bridge' over which to retire.

The first fugitives from the Boyne reached Dublin at about 5 p.m. that afternoon, and the trickle soon became a flood. James himself arrived at 10 p.m., accompanied by 200 of Sarsfield's horse. It was said that the Duchess of Tyrconnell offered him food, but he replied that after such a breakfast he had little stomach for supper. He consulted such Privy Councillors as could be found and asked them whether he should return to France (he later made much of the fact that amongst his letters from Mary of Modena was one advising exactly that). Tyrconnell soon arrived and recommended withdrawal to France, and Lauzun sent a note with the same suggestion.

Early the next day James told some of his leading supporters that the Irish had played him false. 'When it came to a trial,' he bleated, 'they basely fled the field and left the spoil to the enemy...henceforth I never determined to head an Irish army, and do now resolve to shift for myself, and so, gentlemen, must you.' He rode south at once, and a St Malo privateer took him from Duncannon to Kinsale, where he had landed a year before. He paused long enough to write orders for Tyrconnell, telling him that he was now Viceroy, and then, on 4 July, left Ireland for ever.

William's army had spent the night of 1 July on the battlefield. The most senior officers slept in their coaches, but most officers and men bivouacked, as best they could, in the field. Some made bonfires of discarded pikes and muskets to keep themselves warm, and others poked about in the Jacobite camp, finding gold watches and silver dinner-services. Surprisingly few soldiers had been killed: most estimates suggest that about 1000 Jacobites and 500 Williamites perished.

The Decline of the Jacobites

The Boyne did not end the war, which dragged on for another year. William was repulsed from Limerick in August, after a spectacular raid by Sarsfield crippled his siege train, and returned to England almost immediately, leaving the conduct of the war in the hands of Godart de Ginkel, whom he created Earl of Athlone. Tyrconnell and Lauzun left for France, and in May 1691 the former returned with a new French commander, the experienced Marquis de St Ruth.

It was like 'pouring brandy down the throat of a dying man', and the Jacobite cause enjoyed a last revival. On 12 July St Ruth was engaged in a desperate battle at Aughrim when a cannon ball killed him. His army, fighting remarkably well until then, panicked, and may have lost as many as 7000 men killed, including 400 officers. After Aughrim the decline was rapid. The Jacobites fell back on Limerick, where Tyrconnell died of a stroke, and his successors squabbled hopelessly. Ginkel laid siege to the city, and on 3 October the adversaries signed a draft treaty.

The Treaty of Limerick allowed the French to return home and guaranteed safe conduct to Jacobites who wished to do the same or to serve abroad. Jacobite estates would not be confiscated, and Catholics would receive 'not less toleration' than they had enjoyed under Charles II. The treaty was not ratified. A million and a half acres (600,000 hectares) were confiscated, and penal laws bore down on Catholics and dissenting Protestants alike.

It is small wonder that when the Irish brigade spearheaded the successful French attack at Fontenoy in 1745 that its soldiers shouted: 'remember Limerick and English treachery!' Sarsfield was long dead, mortally wounded at Neerwinden in Holland in 1693. His last words were 'If only it was for Ireland.' The Irish did not find it easy to forgive James for using them as a mere tool in his own political ambitions. He became *Seamus an Chaca*, 'James the shithead', and after the Boyne Irishmen fought to drive out the English, not in support of a King who had betrayed them.

Indeed, James must bear a great share of the blame for what happened that day, and many Irish officers could not but compare the soldierly William with the irresolute James. Let us leave the last word to the gallant Sarsfield. 'As low as we now are,' he declared, 'change but kings with us and we will fight it over again with you.'

A View of the Field

Drogheda

The pleasant little town of Drogheda is a good starting-point for a visit to the battlefield of the Boyne. It was held by the Jacobites during the battle, and its defenders surrendered on terms on 3 July 1690. Officers were allowed to keep their swords and the garrison was given safe conduct to Athlone.

The prominent Millmount Fort, on Duleek Street, south of the Boyne, is known locally as the cup and saucer. The hillock was fortified by the Normans in the twelfth century, and was Sir Arthur Aston's headquarters when Cromwell stormed the town in 1649, though the present pill-box tower dates from 1808 and was damaged in 1922. The tower offers an excellent view across Drogheda; and the Millmount Museum, in a converted barracks at the foot of the mound, has a small collection of material relating to the Battle of the Boyne.

Parts of Drogheda's medieval walls and gates survive. St Laurence Gate stands at the head of St Laurence Street at the eastern edge of the town, with a pub named after Patrick Sarsfield just outside it. Dr Oliver Plunkett, Roman Catholic Archbishop of Armagh, was implicated in the popish plot in Charles II's reign, and convicted of treason on the false witness of Titus Oates and others. He was hanged, drawn and quartered in 1681, and canonized in the 1980s. His head is now kept in an imposing shrine in St Peter's Church. Some may find this a macabre relic, but it is a striking symbol of the immediacy of Irish history.

Oldbridge

The N51 runs from Drogheda to Slane by way of Oldbridge. North of Oldbridge a narrow wooded valley, still known as King William's Glen, runs up towards Tullyallen: it provided the Williamites with an admirable covered approach to the ford. William's guns were probably deployed on the rising ground just east of the glen.

The Boyne is now crossed by an iron girder bridge and the village of Oldbridge, once on its southern side, has disappeared altogether: not even ruins remain. The river is deeper now than it was in 1690, but still looks eminently fordable just upsteam of the bridge, where a pleasant meadow is today the haunt of anglers rather than Dutch guardsmen and Jacobite foot.

A large overgrown plinth on the northern bank marks the site of a pillar dedicated to the Duke of Schomberg. For many years it was believed that this had been blown up by the IRA in 1922, but recent evidence suggests that post-prandial high spirits on the part of officers from the Free State Army's garrison in Drogheda were responsible.

The canal which parallels the Boyne at Oldbridge postdates the battle by almost two centuries. South of it a minor road runs parallel with the river, giving a good view of the Williamite crossings. The fierce cavalry charges came down from the high ground to the south, and the Dutch guards beat them off in the open ground just above Oldbridge Hall.

Donore and the Boyne

The ruins of the old church at Donore have all but disappeared, but the cemetery which surrounds them remains. It is reached down a long straight track which strikes northwards, through a farmyard, on a sharp bend where the road from Sheephouse, south of Oldbridge, nears Newtown Platin. It offers a superb view over the whole of the central part

William, crossing the Boyne on a white charger, is a popular image in some Protestant areas of Northern Ireland.

of the battlefield, and Drogheda itself is clearly visible to the north-east.

From the village of Donore, confusingly well to the west of the old church, a road follows the course of the Boyne: across the river is the grave at Newgrange, now recognized as dating from around 3200 BC and predating not only Stonehenge but also the pyramids. The Boyne Valley Visitors Centre (under construction when this book went to press) will include a full-scale replica of the tomb. The site of the ford at Rossnaree, bravely defended by Sir Neil O'Neill's dragoons, lies just east of Rossnaree House, and a well-used parking spot gives a good view of the river there. The road joins the main N1 at McGruder's Cross-Roads, and leads on to Slane, with its splendid bridge, damaged by the Jacobites in 1690. The gates of Slane Castle, famous for its rock concerts, can be seen from the bridge.

The difficulties facing the retreating Jacobites can easily be grasped by visiting Duleek, south of Donore and just off the road connecting Drogheda with the N2. The Nanny is much smaller than the Boyne, but a long causeway crosses meadows which remain liable to flooding. A stone memorial, its lettering worn with age, on the causeway's south-western end commemorates something older than the Battle of the Boyne: beaten Jacobites and victorious Williamites alike would have passed it on their way south.

CHAPTER 5

Dunkirk
1940

Background

The Commander-in-Chief did not mince his words. 'I must not conceal from you,' he warned the Secretary of State for War, 'that a great part of the BEF and its equipment will inevitably be lost even in the best circumstances.' Viscount Gort gave this chilly prognosis on 26 May 1940, as his British Expeditionary Force fell back across Belgium and northern France. Gort had earlier suggested that the BEF was making 'the retreat with which all British campaigns start'. As the campaign reached its climax he must have feared that the retreat would end in disaster.

Yet only 10 days later most of the BEF was safe. A total of 338,000 men – 120,000 of them French – had been evacuated from Dunkirk and the open beaches to its east. The Royal Navy had played its part, with destroyers like *Grafton*, *Javelin*, *Shikari* and *Wolfhound* as had Allied warships like the French *Bourrasque* and the Polish *Blyskawicz*. Passenger steamers, like *Lochgarry, Mona's Queen* and *Royal Daffodil* also made their valuable contribution. Then came a host of smaller craft: their types a naval architect's catalogue; their names a blend of the utilitarian and the whimsical.

There was the Isle of Wight Ferry *Fishbourne*; the eel boat *Johanna*; the motor cruiser *Silver Queen;* the London fire float *Massey Shaw;* the wherry *Medora;* the Belgian fishing boat *Lydie Suzanne,* the Margate lifeboat *Lord Southborough* and over five hundred more. Some survived, but many did not. The Thames estuary cockle-boat *Renown* spent a day under fire, ferrying troops out to larger craft. On her way home her engine broke down, and she asked for help from her sister ship *Letitia*, herself under tow. 'They made fast to our stern,' reported *Letitia*'s skipper:

That was at 1.15 am, and tired out, the engineer and seaman and signaller went to turn in, as our work seemed nearly done...at about 1.50 a terrible explosion

Above: The shriek of the *Stuka* dive-bomber was an abiding memory for Dunkirk survivors. Many came back to England, like those in the main photograph, on the decks of warships.
Left: The Victoria Cross, Britain's highest award for gallantry in battle, was won by Captain Ervine-Andrews, who helped defend the Dunkirk perimeter while evacuation went on.

Overleaf: Charles Cundall's dramatic painting shows most of the evacuation's key features. In the foreground small craft ferry troops to larger vessels. In the centre an improvized jetty helps men reach a coaster. In the background, burning oil tanks west of the port cast a pall of smoke over the scene.

took place, and a hail of wood splinters came down on our deck. In the pitch dark you could see nothing, and after the explosion we heard nothing. And we could do nothing, except pull in the tow-rope which was just as we passed it to the *Renown* about three-quarters of an hour before, but not a sign of *Renown*.

Though contemporaries exaggerated the contribution made by the little ships, they were an inseparable part of this tale of unlooked-for deliverance. The weather was unexpectedly calm; the German high command halted its tanks with victory within its grasp, and, terrifying though the *Luftwaffe* was, its attacks were less conclusive than its commanders hoped. It is small wonder that a relieved nation hailed the miracle of Dunkirk.

Britain Before the Second World War
The three and a half centuries since the Battle of the Boyne had seen Britain rise to become an imperial power. In the eighteenth century industry and agriculture burgeoned: the domestic market for manufactured goods grew, and exports tripled in the second half of the century. Britain emerged victorious from a long struggle with Revolutionary and Napoleonic France, and by the middle of the nineteenth century was at her apogee. The Royal Navy brooked no competition, and under its protection trade flourished and the largest empire the world had ever seen prospered.

There was a price to be paid for all this. Industrialization condemned much of the population to life in reeking, overcrowded cities, and it took decades for liberal politicians and medical reformers to improve matters. Periodic agricultural depressions brought misery to the countryside, and in Ireland failures of the potato crop – the staple diet for much of the population – resulted in famine. A series of reform bills widened suffrage, but it was not until after the First World War that women were able to vote.

The 1914–18 war itself did extraordinary damage to the old Britain. It was not simply that its human cost was horrifying: Britain lost 700,000 men killed, and tens of thousands of others were physically crippled or mentally scarred. The whole country was impoverished by the war, and industrial stagnation and mass unemployment cast a shadow over the inter-war period.

Yet the picture was not universally bleak. The working class, though blighted by the Depression, maintained its own cohesive character, and a growing middle class filed out into the orderly suburbs. Public entertainment, in music hall and cinema, on football field and cricket pitch, not only furnished 'opium for the people' but also helped give a sense of common values. The monarchy remained a powerful symbol of national unity. Even the crisis of 1936, when Edward VIII abdicated to marry Mrs Simpson, left it essentially untouched.

The coalition government under David Lloyd George, 'the man who won the war', was returned to power in 1918. It was swamped by a sea of troubles. The national debt rose alarmingly, leading to demands for better management of public expenditure. In Ireland, the nationalist Sinn Fein party won the majority of seats, and its MPs withdrew from Westminster to establish an unofficial parliament in Dublin. After a bitter campaign against the Irish Republican Army, Lloyd George negotiated with Sinn Fein leaders, and in 1922 the Irish Free State came into being, leaving just the six counties of Northern Ireland as part of the United Kingdom. Rising unemployment and harsh treatment of strikers reflected the government's failure at home; and growing disillusionment over the consequences of the Treaty of Versailles, which ended the First World War, testified to the unpopularity of its foreign policy.

Though the Conservatives won the 1922 election, the Labour Party, under Ramsay MacDonald, grew in strength. In 1924 MacDonald became the first Labour prime minister, but his minority government, at the mercy of its Liberal allies, proved short-lived. The Conservatives, under Stanley Baldwin, won the 1924 election, but in 1931 MacDonald was prime minister once again.

The collapse of the American stock market in October 1929 sent shock-waves across the whole of the western world; and in 1931 MacDonald's goverment could not reconcile conflicting demands to reduce spending and maintain social benefits. MacDonald stayed on as the head of a National Government consisting mainly of Conservatives and Liberals; an election later that year brought the National Government back with a huge majority.

MacDonald himself, his power base gone, was succeeded by Baldwin in 1935, and in 1937 Neville Chamberlain became prime minister at the head of a largely Conservative National Government. In domestic terms Chamberlain's solid managerial conservatism seemed to have much to offer; it was foreign policy that became his downfall.

The Lead-up to the Second World War
The Versailles settlement was a compromise. It was deeply humiliating to Germany which was stripped of territory and allowed an army of only 100,000 men. Yet the Europe it created was inherently unstable: states like Poland and Czechoslovakia could not realistically defend themselves

against major aggressors. The League of Nations initially seemed to offer the hope of creating collective security, but the United States declined to join and the League's voice soon counted for little.

The rise of extremist politics in Europe was bound up with the growing economic crisis. Benito Mussolini had taken power in Italy before the storm broke, but in Germany the rise of Adolf Hitler was made possible by mass unemployment and hyper-inflation. Some British politicians admired the achievements of Mussolini's Italy and Hitler's Germany, and argued that Germany formed a bulwark against Communist Russia. They also maintained that some of Hitler's early expansionist moves were only correctives to Versailles. When Spanish nationalists, under General Franco, rose against the republican government in 1936 the British Cabinet remained rigorously non-interventionist.

Chamberlain's attempts to maintain a working relationship with the dictators at first seemed to chime with popular opinion, but news from Spain and Germany helped change the mood. In September 1938, with war looming over the German threat to Czechoslovakia, Chamberlain went to Munich, came to an accommodation with Hitler, and returned to announce 'peace in our time'. Initial enthusiasm evaporated when Hitler invaded Prague, and Chamberlain was compelled to offer Poland security guarantees he had no means of honouring. When Hitler invaded Poland on 31 August 1939 a British ultimatum did not deter him, and when it expired, at 11 a.m. on 3 September, Britain found herself at war with Germany.

Shortages of British Troops and Arms
There had been over 3.5 million troops in the British establishment in 1918 (at the end of the First World War) but only 370,000 in 1920, and numbers fell further as the Treasury's axe bit. From 1919 successive governments followed the 'Ten Year Rule', declaring that defence planning must proceed on the assumption that there would be no major war for the next 10 years. The recent world war was officially described as 'abnormal', and both the forces and the domestic armaments industry were allowed to wither.

Hitler's repudiation of Versailles brought only a gradual response. As late as December 1937 the dispatch of an expeditionary force to support a European ally was accorded the lowest priority, well below the defence of the United Kingdom against air attack, the reinforcement of imperial garrisons and the sending of a force to an unspecified eastern theatre. However work had already been begun on new fighter aircraft, and British investment in radar – R(adio) D(etecting) A(nd) R(anging) – would pay dividends. In March 1939 the government announced the doubling of the part-time Territorial Army, and the following month it introduced limited conscription.

The future Field-Marshal Montgomery, shortly to command a division in the BEF, was scathing. 'In September 1939,' he wrote:

the British Army was totally unfit to fight a first class war on the continent of Europe. It must be said to our shame that we sent our Army into that most modern war with weapons and equipment which were quite inadequate, and we had only ourselves to blame for the disasters which early overtook us in the field when fighting began in 1940.

Numbers were scarcely impressive. The expeditionary force sent to France initially numbered four divisions, and was to rise to 13 by May 1940 when the French had 103 divisions and the Belgians 20. Equipment was patchy. Although the entire force was motorized, many vehicles had been commandeered from their civilian owners and breakdowns were frequent. The new Bren light machine-gun was on general issue, and the excellent 25-pdr field-gun was beginning to come on stream. There were relatively few armoured vehicles and initially only a single tank brigade which could take on German armour on anything approaching equal terms. And, partly because of inter-service rivalry in the inter-war years, the BEF's Air Component was weak even in May 1940, with four fighter, two bomber, two bomber reconnaissance and four army co-operation squadrons.

The paucity of tanks and aircraft did not simply reflect pre-war parsimony. The RAF placed greater emphasis on the air defence of the UK and the build-up of its strategic bombing force than on co-operation with the army. The army itself had flirted with the development of experimental mechanized units in the late 1920s but had failed to keep up the momentum. One leading advocate of mechanization, Major-General J. F. C. Fuller, described by Brian Bond as 'an eccentric genius with remarkable abilities', flared into prominence only to be retired prematurely in 1930. Another, Captain Basil Liddell Hart, successively military correspondent of the *Daily Telegraph* and *The Times,* sketched out ideas for an 'expanding torrent' of armour and was influential as adviser to Leslie Hore-Belisha, Secretary of State for war 1937-40. However, the army's leadership eventually decided in favour of gradual wholesale mechanization and motorization, rather than concentrating on specialist tank formations, and Liddell Hart was to write damningly of Britain's surrender of her lead in armoured warfare.

The French Army

The French also favoured caution. In their case, the size of their army and its limited resources (the Maginot Line, a fortified barrier covering parts of the Franco-German border, had made great demands on their defence budget) meant that in 1940 most French infantrymen still marched on foot like their fathers before them.

France had her share of forward thinkers: Colonel Charles de Gaulle had been struck off the 1936 promotion list because his book *Vers l'armée de métier* had recommended the establishment of a mechanized force composed of professional soldiers. France also produced some good tanks, and by May 1940 had six armoured or mechanized divisions and was forming a seventh. But her army remained firmly wedded to doctrine based on the tactics of the First World War: artillery conquered and infantry occupied. Most tanks were allocated to infantry support, and their design, armament and limited communications reflected this preference.

Germany Takes the Lead in Armoured Warfare

The *Reichswehr,* the 100,000-man army permitted Germany by the Treaty of Versailles, was largely officered by men who were militarily and politically conservative. However, they and their NCOs were trained to take responsibilities well above their formal ranks, making the *Reichswehr* a kernel for subsequent expansion; and collaboration with the Soviet Union enabled the Germans to familiarize themselves with tanks and aircraft forbidden them by Versailles.

The German army, too, contained advocates of mobility. Heinz Guderian was convinced that all arms formations, all of whose elements enjoyed the same cross-country mobility as tanks, would achieve 'decisive importance' in a coming war. The German army expanded rapidly after 1933, and in 1936 the first three panzer (armoured) divisions were formed. Many senior officers regarded them with suspicion, and feared that selective mechanization would consume resources better spread across the army as a whole.

Nevertheless Hitler's support helped advocates of mechanization, and the Germans gained experience of armour during the Spanish Civil War, when 'volunteers' fought for Franco. The invasion of Poland in 1939 helped develop panzer tactics still further. Guderian's slogan '*Klotzen, nicht Kleckern*' – 'Smash, don't tap' – applied, and divisions were concentrated into panzer corps so that tanks could be used en masse. The *Luftwaffe* prevented hostile aircraft from intervening, and lent powerful support to the ground battle, acting as 'flying artillery.' The Junkers 87

Stuka dive-bomber, with its gull-wing silhouette and banshee shriek, was particularly unnerving.

Campaign and Battle

Although Britain and France had declared war in response to Hitler's invasion of Poland, there was little they could do to help the Poles. The French launched a half-hearted offensive into the Saar, and then settled down to build up their forces for a long struggle. The BEF established itself in north-west France, with its headquarters in Arras.

The Allied Commanders
General Lord Gort, Commander-in-Chief of the BEF, was a descendant of Colonel Charles Vereker, MP for Limerick and commander of its militia, who in 1798 had distinguished himself against French troops who had landed to support the Irish rebels. Gort was born in 1886, commissioned into the Grenadier Guards in 1905 and won the Victoria Cross as an acting lieutenant-colonel in September 1918. Chief of the Imperial General Staff at the outbreak of war, Gort had, as his biographer puts it, 'done his conscientious best in work and surroundings that were uncongenial and with a Secretary of State [Hore-Belisha] he found even more so.'

The official history of the campaign declares that Gort 'was not an intellectual man nor had he the mind of an administrator: by temperament and training he was a fighting soldier...' He had a guardsman's respect for precision. One of his first conferences discussed which shoulder the steel helmet should be slung from when it was not worn on the head, and shortly before his evacuation – characteristically he took no more kit than a private soldier – he cut the medal ribbons from uniforms he left behind. When faced with the campaign's sternest decision 'he stood unmoved and undismayed', with a moral courage equal to his physical valour.

The BEF was part of General Billotte's No 1 Army Group, but in practice Gort received orders from General Georges, Commander-in-Chief North-East Front. The War Office directive emphasized that Gort was to 'carry out loyally' instruction issued by Georges, but 'if any order given by him appears to you to imperil the British Field Force...you should be at liberty to appeal to the British government before executing that order.' Georges' headquarters were at La Ferté-sous-Jouarre, about 40 miles (64 km) east of Paris. His own superior, the French Commander-in-Chief, General Maurice Gamelin, was based at the Château de Vincennes on the eastern edge of Paris.

The air chain of command was almost equally long. From January 1940 Air Marshal A.S. Barratt commanded both the BEF's Air Component and the Advanced Air Striking Force. He had previously been based at Coulommiers, east of Paris, with the Commander-in-Chief of the French Air Force, but now established a forward headquarters at Chauny, with General d'Astier de la Vigerie, whose Northern Zone of Aerial Operations was to support Billotte's army group. The Air Ministry ordered Barratt to use his aircraft 'in accordance with the day to day needs of the Allied situation on the Western Front as a whole', but to give Gort 'full assurance' regarding his own air support. It was, as the official history recognizes, a 'somewhat ambiguous directive'.

Planning the Campaign
Belgium had become neutral in 1936, and was not prepared to countenance planning with the British and French, but let it be known that, if attacked, she proposed to fight a delaying battle on the Albert Canal. This had been strengthened by forts, notably the mighty Eben Emael, and its defence would buy time in which the Allies might come to Belgium's aid.

Gamelin planned to meet an attack by holding fast along the Maginot Line and wheeling forward on his left to take up a position on the River Escaut (Scheldt) between Antwerp and Ghent. This plan would result in the Allies holding a long line but defending little of Belgium. Gamelin was considering modifying it when a copy of a German operations order fell into Belgian hands. It revealed that the Germans were indeed planning to move into central Belgium, and encouraged Gamelin to opt for the Dyle Plan, which took his left wing forward of Brussels, with the Breda variation, which would send a French army up to help the Dutch. The revised plan would throw 30 Allied divisions, including most of the armoured, motorized and light mechanized divisions, deep into Belgium.

By this stage the Germans had changed their minds. Their original plan, Case Yellow, had pushed the weight of the attack into Belgium, where Army Group B was to head for Brussels. Army Group A was to launch a subsidiary attack towards Namur, while Army Group C covered the Maginot Line.

Amongst the critics of this project were Hitler himself and Lieutenant-General Erich von Manstein, Chief of Staff of Army Group A. The latter argued that the attack should force 'a decisive issue by land', and the new plan, *Sichelschnitt* ('Sickle-cut'), went a long way towards meeting his suggestions. Army Group B was reduced in size, and would now form the 'matador's cloak' which would draw the Allies to the Low Countries. General von Rundstedt's Army Group A, with 45 divisions, would penetrate

General Lord Gort, Commander-in-chief of the BEF, studying a map with his Chief of Staff, Lieutenant-General Pownall, before the opening of the campaign. Gort had won a VC in the First World War, and in 1940 he showed considerable moral courage.

the hilly and wooded Ardennes. It would contain seven panzer divisions, in Guderian's XIX, Reinhardt's XLI and Hoth's XV Panzer Corps (the first two comprising Panzer Group Kleist) which would hit the Allied front between Sedan and Dinant on the River Meuse, the hinge between the static armies in the Maginot Line and the mobile force clattering forward into Belgium.

It was high risk. The attackers would be vulnerable to air attack as they wound through the Ardennes, and there was no guarantee that they would succeed in crossing the Meuse. But the potential pay-off was also high. If the Germans broke through and moved fast it would be hard for the Allies to regain the initiative.

Churchill Comes to Power

In April 1940 the Germans invaded Denmark and Norway. The Allied response was hopelessly uncoordinated, and its political backdraught blew Chamberlain from power. He was replaced by Winston Churchill, whose political career to date had been controversial. Churchill had been in both the Liberal and Conservative parties, and had held high office. As

DUNKIRK
1940: The Campaign

→ Planned German
movements

–·–·–·– Frontiers, 1940

0	10	20	30 Miles
0	10 20	30 40	50 Kms

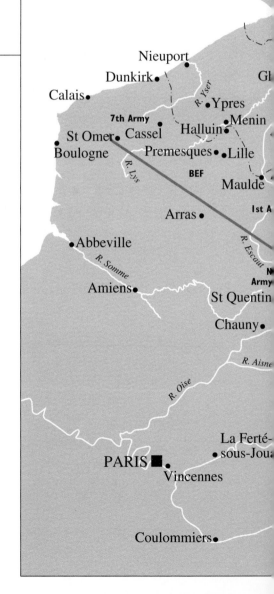

Nieuport

Dunkirk

Calais

R. Yser

Ypres

Menin

7th Army

St Omer • Cassel   Halluin

Boulogne

Premesques • Lille

R. Lys

BEF

Maulde

Arras

1st A

R. Escaut

Abbeville

R. Somme

N

Army

Amiens

St Quentin

Chauny

R. Aisne

R. Oise

La Ferté-
sous-Joua

PARIS ■

Vincennes

Coulommiers

AMSTERDAM

NETHERLANDS

Rotterdam

Breda

Antwerp

Army Group
B

Albert Canal

R. Dyle

R. Senne

Louvain

Eben
Emael

BRUSSELS

BELGIUM

GERMANY

R. Rhine

Liège

embloux

Namur

R. Ourthe

Charleroi

ns

Dinant

Army Group
A

A   r   d   e   n   n   e   s

my

Trier

Sedan

2nd Army

LUXEMBOURG

Army Group
C

Longwy

Maginot Line

3rd Army

Marne

R. Meuse

Châlons-sur-Marne

No 2
Army Group

FRANCE

N

W   E

S

First Lord of the Admiralty on the eve of the First World War he did much to prepare Britain for a conflict he regarded as inevitable. Blamed for the failure of the Gallipoli expedition in 1915, he resigned and fought on the Western Front before returning to serve in Lloyd George's coalition government. Chancellor of the Exchequer under Baldwin, he then spent 10 years in the political wilderness, attacking appeasement and inaction in the face of the threat from Germany. He was brought back into the government on the outbreak of war, and his pugnacious manner made him a popular choice as Chamberlain's successor.

Churchill was not always an easy man to deal with. He often intervened directly in the conduct of operations, and did not always grasp tactical realities. 'A scandalous (i.e. Winstonian) thing to do, and in fact quite impossible to carry out,' complained Gort's Chief of Staff, Lieutenant-General Henry Pownall of one proposed manoeuvre. For all this, Churchill was the man of the hour, an inspirational war leader at a time when Britain's fortunes were approaching their nadir.

The German Advance

The Germans attacked on 10 May. Their aircraft wreaked havoc in France and the Low Countries (Belgium and the Netherlands), attacking airfields and strafing troops on roads and railways. Half the Belgian aircraft were destroyed before they could get airborne, and some French airfields suffered severely. Special forces, some in Allied uniforms, attacked key points. Eben Emael was blinded by a glider assault group that landed on top of it, and surrendered the next day. General von Rundstedt's men plunged into the Ardennes, brushing aside Belgian *Chasseurs Ardennais* and a French cavalry screen, and reached the Meuse on 12 May.

The Allies, meanwhile, advanced into Belgium as planned. However, when the French 7th Army reached Breda it found that the Dutch had already been pushed back to Rotterdam. Things went from bad to worse on 13 May. Guderian crossed the Meuse at Sedan, and Major-General Erwin Rommel's 7th Panzer Division, which had gained a foothold on the far bank on the previous day, established a solid bridgehead near Dinant. A French mechanized corps, brought up behind the Sedan front on 14 May, was ordered to contain the breakthrough rather than counter-attack; and while it struggled with Guderian's flank guard the panzers swung westwards, making for the Channel coast.

When his army advanced, Gort had moved forward to keep in better touch with his corps commanders, Lieutenant-Generals Barker (I Corps), Brooke (II Corps) and Adam (III Corps). The next day, 15 May, saw him just west of Brussels, with the BEF in action on the River Dyle from Louvain to Wavre, the Belgians on its left and the French 1st Army on its right.

There was more bad news. The Dutch surrendered that day after the *Luftwaffe* had bombed the undefended city of Rotterdam, and the Germans forced back part of the French 1st Army, compelling Gort to withdraw his right flank to conform. He was concerned that further withdrawal would leave his left flank forward of the main allied line at Louvain, and pressed Billotte for direction. The response was an order that the Allies would fall back on the River Senne that night, onto the River Dendre on 16 May and then onto the River Escaut on 17 May.

Things were worse elsewhere. Paul Reynaud, the French premier, had telephoned Churchill early on 15 May to announce: 'We are beaten: we have lost the battle.' Churchill flew to France and was shocked to hear Gamelin admit that there was no strategic reserve with which to counter the breakthrough. Pownall was equally aware of the danger. 'The news from the far south is very bad,' he wrote on 16 May. 'German mechanised columns are getting deep into France towards Laon and St Quentin. I hope to God the French have some means of stopping them and closing the gap or we are *bust*.'

Allied air power did its unavailing best. Battle and Blenheim bombers attacked German crossings at Sedan with extraordinary courage: in all, 45 out of 109 aircraft were lost. The Hurricanes of the Air Component were reduced to 50 serviceable aircraft after two days of fighting. Gort asked Anthony Eden, the newly appointed Secretary of State for War, for reinforcements, and promptly received another three squadrons which were sent to help the French.

On 17 May Gort cobbled together a force under Major-General Mason-MacFarlane, Director of Military Intelligence at General Headquarters (GHQ), to protect the right flank of the BEF: it was known as 'Macforce', and was the first of several improvised detachments. This was a wise precaution, although the French 1st Army, under heavier pressure than the BEF, held together better than Gort had expected. It had the disadvantage, however, of depriving Gort of the head of his intelligence staff. 'Had he remained in charge,' comments the official history, 'Lord Gort might not so often have been without adequate information.'

During the withdrawal to the River Escaut, Gort was visted by Billotte, who told him of the measures being taken to contain the breakthrough, 'though clearly,' wrote Gort, 'he had little hope that they would be effective.'

'I am completely done in,' admitted Billotte to a British liaison officer, 'and I can't do a thing against these panzers.'

If the gap could not be closed Gort had two alternatives. He could fall back southwards on his lines of communication, keeping in touch with the French but abandoning the Belgians. Alternatively he could retire to the coast for evacuation, a process that would result in the loss of equipment, and would abandon the French at a time when they needed all possible support.

Gort Considers Evacuation

Given that there were now no French troops between the Germans and the coast, the southern option seemed increasingly unrealistic; and Gort thought it prudent to consider what withdrawal to the coast might entail. Pownall discussed this on the telephone, in guarded language, with the Director of Military Operations at the War Office, whom he found 'singularly stupid and unhelpful'.

The Appointment of Ramsay

The War Office was actually more helpful than it seemed. That day, 19 May, a conference there discussed the temporary maintenance of the BEF through the Channel ports of Dunkirk, Calais and Boulogne, and the evacuation of personnel from them. At this juncture the army was considering only the evacuation of non-combatants and some key specialists, and announced that 'the hazardous evacuation of very large forces' was considered to be 'very unlikely'. The meeting decided that Vice-Admiral Dover would be responsible for the evacuation, and the available shipping would be placed at his disposal.

Vice-Admiral Bertram Ramsay was in command at Dover. He knew it well, for during the First World War he had served in the Dover patrol. After the war he commanded the battleship *Royal Sovereign* before becoming Chief of Staff, as a rear-admiral, to Admiral Sir Roger Backhouse, Commander-in-Chief Home Fleet. It was not a happy relationship. Backhouse was what we might term a workaholic, and personally controlled everything, whereas Ramsay believed in the proper delegation of staff duties. He quickly asked to be relieved of his appointment and went onto half pay. In 1938, after declining an appointment commanding the Yangtse gunboat squadron, he was placed on the retired list.

Ramsay was comfortably off and enjoyed a happy family life, so retirement was no burden, and in any event he was almost immediately commissioned to write a report on Dover. He revealed that it was in a

The perceptive and hard-working Vice-Admiral Bertram Ramsay was responsible for naval aspects of the evacuation. He served as Allied Naval Commander-in-Chief for the Normandy landings in 1944, but was later killed in an aircraft accident.

state of considerable neglect. Some money was made available to rectify the worst of its defects, and Ramsay was given the dormant appointment (to be taken up when war broke out) of Flag Officer in Charge, Dover. He was soon promoted and freed from the authority of the Nore Command becoming Vice-Admiral Dover, and reporting direct to the Admiralty.

Ramsay's headquarters were in tunnels beneath Dover Castle. These had been begun during the Napoleonic Wars, and were expanded as the Second World War went on. In 1940 the section known as Admiralty Casemates was divided into a number of offices, and Ramsay himself had a 'cabin' looking out onto Dover harbour. One of the chambers had previously contained dynamos and this room may have given the evacuation its codename, Operation Dynamo.

Large-scale Evacuation is Planned

As the situation worsened there were further conferences, and on 21 May the 'emergency evacuation across the Channel of very large forces' was considered. Several key decisions were made at this stage. All sea movement would be controlled by Ramsay, assisted by liaison officers from War Office Movement Control and the Ministry of Shipping. Air cover would be arranged direct with Fighter Command. Because the beaches around the Channel ports shelved very gently, Ramsay recognized that: 'It would be necessary to have a very large number of small boats to carry troops from the beaches to the off-shore ships.' However, only a limited number of troops could be lifted off the beaches and, if at all possible, the ports themselves would be used as well.

The Admiralty already had a Small Vessels Pool which maintained small craft at harbours and naval bases. On 14 May it had arranged for the BBC to broadcast an appeal for 'all owners of self-propelled pleasure craft between 30 and 100 feet [10-30 m] in length to send all particulars to the Admiralty within 14 days'. The call had been prompted by the fact that the danger of magnetic mines meant that boatyards were busy building wooden minesweepers, and the Small Vessels Pool needed more little ships.

Allied Uncertainty

While the staff of the Small Vessels Pool were cataloguing motor yachts and cabin cruisers the BEF's plight worsened. On 20 May it was on the Escaut line, with the Germans probing its defences and growing uncertainly about both flanks. Arras still held out but was almost surrounded, and Gort assembled 'Frankforce' with a view to attacking in order to gain more elbow-room around the town.

To the south, in what had once been the rear areas between the BEF and its base at Le Havre, were two under-equipped Territorial divisions, 12th and 23rd, which had been sent out to perform labour duties and were not fully trained as fighting infantry. They were ordered to hold several towns north of Amiens, but by nightfall on 20 May German armour had burst clean through and the divisions had practically ceased to exist.

That day Gort was visited by General Ironside, Chief of the Imperial General Staff, who brought with him a written order from the War Cabinet. Gort was to move south towards Amiens, attacking any Germans he met en route, and the Belgians were to be advised that their best hope was to move between the BEF and the coast. Gort demurred. Seven of his nine divisions were in action on the Escaut. How could he disengage and then swing southwards to attack an enemy of substantial if uncertain strength? He was still prepared to conduct the Arras operation, but convinced Ironside that any major attack from the north could succeed only if the French made a serious effort from the south.

That was precisely what the French proposed to do. Gamelin had been replaced by General Maxime Weygand, a trim 73-year-old then serving in the Lebanon. After an exhausting journey to Paris Weygand snatched some sleep and then, on 21 May, flew north to confer with Billotte, Gort and the Belgians in the Belgian town of Ypres. There were three meetings that day: Gort, who heard of the conference late, arrived for the third, by which time Weygand had already left.

Weygand's intentions were quite clear. The BEF and the French 1st Army would attack southwards while French forces, assembling south of the Somme, stuck north to meet them. The Belgians would withdraw to the River Yser to cover the Allies' left and rear. This scheme was not cordially received. At the first meeting the Belgians opposed withdrawal from the River Lys, arguing that successive retreats were 'the bane of discipline'. Billotte then arrived and pointed out that the 1st Army was already so hard-pressed that it could barely defend itself, let alone launch a counter-attack: this should be left to the BEF.

Only then, after Weygand had departed, did Gort appear. He observed that he was already counter-attacking at Arras, and that a further attack would only be possible if some of his divisions in the line could be relieved to form a reserve. It seems to have been agreed that the Belgians would hold the line of the Lys and relieve one British division, while the 1st Army would relieve another two. None of this could happen before the night of 23 May, and the earliest Gort could attack was 26 May. The confusion deepened when Billotte's car hit a truck on its way home. The General was mortally injured, and his successor, Blanchard of 1st Army, was not confirmed in his appointment until early on 25 May.

Gort left Ypres for a new command post in a modest château at Premesques, just west of Lille. Churchill, who had again visited Paris, where he had been favourably impressed by Weygand, sent Gort a telegram on the evening of 23 May, ordering him to attack southwards with about eight divisions, with the Belgian cavalry corps covering his right flank. Pownall was livid. 'Here are Winston's plans again,' he wrote the next day:

Can nobody prevent him trying to conduct operations himself as a super Commander-in-Chief? How does he think we are to collect eight divisions and attack as he suggests… He can have no conception of our sitiuation and condition. Where *are* the Belgian Cavalry Corps? How is an attack like this to be staged involving three nationalities at an hour's notice? The man's mad.

There were more misunderstandings the following day, and it was becoming clear to Gort that neither the Allied chain of command nor his own government really understood how serious the situation was. The 1st Army Group was encircled and outnumbered. The BEF was now on its old positions on the French frontier between Maulde and Halluin, with the Belgians on the Lys to its left; and, round to its right rear, a thinly held line along the canals to Gravelines and the sea. The *Lufwaffe*'s superiority grew more marked by the day, and the BEF's Air Component was now largely operating from England.

On 25 May Lieutenant-Colonel Gerald Templer – himself a future field marshal – had to go through Gort's room to reach Pownall's office. He saw the Commander-in-Chief standing:

in a very typical attitude – with his legs apart and his hands behind his back. He was staring – quite alone – at a series of maps of Northern France and the

Channel ports, pinned together and covering most of the wall of his small room...Though I had no precise idea of the problem which was then facing him, all my heart went out to him in his loneliness and tribulation.

By 6 p.m. Gort's mind was made up. He cancelled the British contribution to the planned offensive, and swung a division up to cover the area north-west of Menin, where the Belgians were in growing difficulties. He told Eden of his decision, and the Secretary of State's reply on 26 May acknowledged that his own information 'all goes to show that the French offensive from Somme cannot be made in sufficient strength... In such conditions the only course open to you may be to fight your way back to the West where all beaches and ports east of Gravelines will be used for embarkation'. Gort warned that even if all went well a great part of the BEF would be lost, but later that day the War Office authorized him 'to operate towards coast forthwith in conjunction with French and Belgian Armies.'

German tanks had reached the coast near Abbeville on 20 May, and on the following day began to thrust north-eastwards, placing the Channel ports in an increasingly perilous situation. Boulogne was belatedly garrisoned by 20th Guards Brigade, snatched from training in Surrey on 21 May. After a brave defence the brigade was embarked on destroyers on the night of 23/24 May.

The Defence of Calais
The defence of Calais, in contrast, featured what the official history calls 'some of the failings which have been matched too often in the conduct of our military excursions'. The garrison began to arrive on 22 May, and eventually consisted of 3rd Royal Tank Regiment, Queen Victoria's Rifles, a good Territorial motor-cycle battalion sent without its machines, transport or 3-inch mortars, and two regular battalions of 30th Brigade, 1st Rifle Brigade and 2nd King's Royal Rifle Corps, together with assorted gunners and base details.

Brigadier Claude Nicholson was given a series of conflicting instructions. First the tanks were to proceed south-westwards to Boulogne; then south-eastwards towards St Omer. Then they were to convoy rations for the BEF north-eastwards to Dunkirk. By this stage Calais was encircled and only three tanks got through. The remainder joined the infantry in defence of the town.

Nicholson was first told that evacuation was agreed in principle, but then informed that the garrison came under overall French command, so there could be no evacuation. The harbour was now 'of no importance to the BEF', and he should simply choose the best position from which to fight to the end. This did not appeal to Churchill, and on his instructions Eden sent a more inspirational message which concluded: 'HM Government are confident that you and your gallant regiments will perform an exploit worthy of the British name.'

Nicholson duly fought on, declining an invitation to surrender, and the Germans eventually over-ran Calais on 26 May. Both Churchill and Eden had found it a painful decision. 'I had served,' wrote Eden, 'with one of the regiments and knew personally many of those whose fate I now had to decide.'

Churchill was sure that, but for the defence of Calais, Dunkirk could not have been held, but historians have been less than convinced. 'For all the gallantry displayed by the defenders of Boulogne, Calais and the Canal line,' wrote Brian Bond, 'it is hard to escape the conclusion that there was no military solution to 1st Army Group's problem... Only remarkable blunders on the German side can explain why the total disaster...was averted.'

The German Armoured Advance

The German high command had never subscribed unequivocally to Guderian's view of war, and the sheer pace of the armoured advance after the Meuse crossing dismayed some generals, notably Kleist, commanding the panzer group of which Guderian's corps formed part, and Kluge of 4th Army. Hitler, too, had his doubts, and as early as 17 May General Halder, Chief of the General Staff, recorded how: 'He mistrusts his own success; he's afraid to take risks; he'd really likely to stop now.' Once he had reached the Channel coast Guderian planned to send a division apiece to Boulogne, Calais and Dunkirk, but one was temporarily taken from him and parts of the others had to hold the Somme bridgeheads until follow-up troops arrived. Nevertheless, by 24 May 1st Panzer Divison had secured crossings over the Aa Canal, only 15 miles (24 km) from Dunkirk.

After cautious braking came an emergency stop. Hitler and Rundstedt met at Charleville on the same day. Hitler first confirmed Rundstedt's earlier decision that the armour should halt on the canal line, a view based on the fact that the Flanders coast was poor tank country, and mopping up could be better undertaken by infantrymen of Bock's northern army group. The Arras battle of 21 May, when even the supremely confident Rommel supposed that he was being attacked by five divisions, rather than by less than one, also produced what the German historians, Jacobsen and Rohwer term 'a certain psychological effect'.

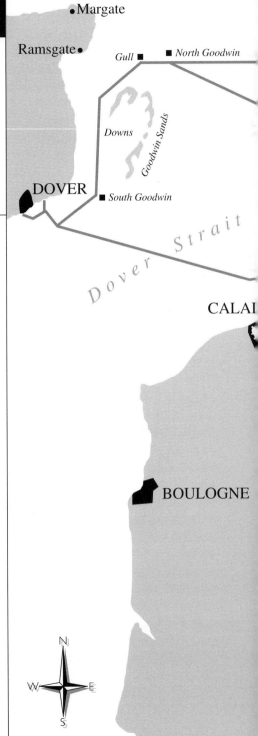

THE DUNKIRK SECTOR

 Canals or canalised rivers
(much simplified)

Sea routes

■ Lightships

0	10	20 Miles
0	10	20 Kms

Margate

Ramsgate

Gull ■   ■ North Goodwin

Downs

Goodwin Sands

DOVER

■ South Goodwin

Dover Strait

CALAI

BOULOGNE

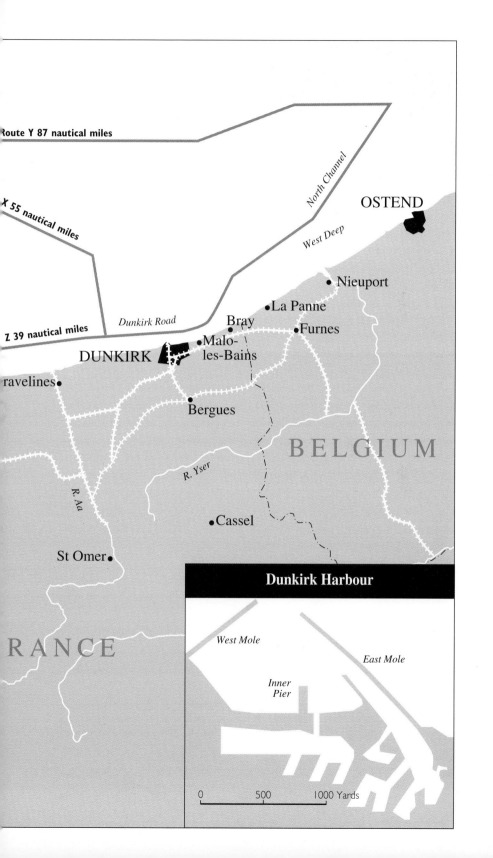

Route Y 87 nautical miles

X 55 nautical miles

Z 39 nautical miles

North Channel

West Deep

OSTEND

• Nieuport

Dunkirk Road

Bray

• La Panne

• Furnes

DUNKIRK

•Malo-
les-Bains

ravelines•

• Bergues

BELGIUM

R. Yser

R. Aa

•Cassel

St Omer•

RANCE

Dunkirk Harbour

West Mole

East Mole

*Inner
Pier*

0   500   1000 Yards

Hitler went further, announcing that he wished to preserve the panzer divisions for the next phase of the campaign, an attack on the French south of the Somme. He was also influenced by the views of Hermann Goering, head of the *Luftwaffe*, who was confident that air power could deal with the Allies in the Dunkirk perimeter. By midday on 26 May it was clear that the halt order could no longer stand. However, by this stage the advance had lost much of its momentum, and Operation Dynamo was well underway.

Operation Dynamo Begins
In 1940 Dunkirk was the third-largest port in France, with substantial harbour facilities and, to its south, a large complex of oil storage tanks. It had been fortified in the seventeenth century by the great military engineer Vauban, and the fortifications had been improved in the nineteenth century. Although Dunkirk had officially lost its fortress status, many of the old defence works still offered protection even against modern weapons, and the French maritime commander, Admiral Abrial, had established his headquarters in Bastion 32, just east of the harbour.

East of Dunkirk ran the beaches, broad stretches of gently sloping sand. At popular resorts, Malo les Bains and Bray Dunes in France and La Panne across the border in Belgium, there were sea walls, but elsewhere the beaches rose into sand dunes, held together by coarse grass. The low-lying meadowland behind the coastal strip was interesected by canals, the chief of which ran from the little town of Bergues to Furnes.

The Bergues–Furnes canal formed a convenient defensive perimeter. The sector from Bergues through Furnes and on to Nieuport, about 20 miles (32 km) in all, was to be held by the British, while the French defended the western flank. Gort ordered Lieutenant-General Sir Ronald Adam to organize the bridgehead. It was divided into three corps sectors – II Corps to the east, I Corps in the centre and III Corps to the west. There were ration and ammunition dumps in each sector, and as retreating troops arrived they were directed to a collecting area outside the perimeter and then sent to the appropriate corps area where they were allocated a sector to defend and an evacuation beach. Vehicles were to be disabled outside the perimeter, but this order was not always obeyed and the situation inside the perimeter was a good deal more chaotic than these arrangements might suggest.

Although the Admiralty ordered Ramsay to commence Dynamo at 6.57 p.m. on Sunday 26 May, he had already sent out vessels that afternoon. The first, the Isle of Man steam packet *Mona's Queen*, berthed in the harbour under air attack but took 1420 men aboard. On her way home

The accurate and reliable Bren light machine-gun had come into service just before the war. Each British infantry battalion had a platoon of Bren-gun carriers, open-topped light armoured vehicles, armed with Brens or other weapons. This Bren is firing in the anti-aircraft role. Although this was not enormously effective, it sometimes discouraged pilots from pressing home their attacks and gave men the feeling that they were able to hit back.

she was shelled by shore batteries around Gravelines and then machine-gunned from the air. Her experience suggested that the quickest route from Dover to Dunkirk, Route Z, only 39 nautical miles (72 km), was no longer practicable now that the Germans held the coast. A more northerly approach, Route X, was 55 nautical miles (102 km) long, but was known to cross minefields, and was not swept for several days. An even wider approach, Route Y, presented less risk of mines and could be used more quickly, but it lengthened the distance to 87 nautical miles (161 km).

To the Beaches
Heavy air attacks on Dunkirk did so much damage that the Senior Naval Officer ashore, Captain W.G. Tennant, concluded that it was no longer possible to use the harbour. He signalled Ramsay: 'Please send every available craft to beaches East of Dunkirk immediately. Evacuation tomorrow night problematical.' Soon the anti-aircraft cruiser *Calcutta*, nine destroyers, four minesweepers, 17 drifters and numerous *schuyts* (inevitably known as skoots) – Dutch coastal vessels with naval crews – were working the beaches with their boats.

As Ramsay was to report: 'A moderate surf on the beaches reduced the rate of embarkation, exhausted the boats' crews, the majority of whom were "hostilities only" ratings, rendering the whole operation slow and difficult.' Only 7669 men were landed in England on 27 May: unless there was radical improvement, most of the BEF would be captured while awaiting evacuation.

That was not the end of the day's miseries. At midnight the Belgians surrendered. Paul Reynaud, the French premier, railed bitterly against King Leopold, calling it 'an event without precedent in history'. However it is now clear that the Belgians had fought hard against overwhelming odds, and had given warning of the seriousness of their plight. The surrender opened a gap at the north-east end of the perimeter, but it was plugged by brilliant improvisation, some of it by Major-General Montgomery of 3rd Division, fast making his name as a man to watch.

The BEF fell back onto the Dunkirk perimeter like a collapsing balloon, leaving the River Lys on 28 May and the Yser, the last major obstacle south of the Bergues–Furnes Canal, on the following day. Devoted rearguards covered its withdrawal. The garrison of Cassel, on a lofty hill overlooking the Flanders plain at the junction of five major roads, held out until orders to retire reached it on 29 May. There were Germans all around, and most of the force was killed or captured in a series of bitter little fights on the way to Dunkirk. The orders never reached a handful of Gloucesters, under Second Lieutenant Roy Cresswell, holding a bunker on the road north from Cassel. They held out till the evening of 30 May. By that time there had been a fire in the bunker and there were Germans on its roof: it was only when a captured British officer was brought up to point out that everyone else had gone that they surrendered.

The Evacuation Begins

Gort's headquarters moved to La Panne on 28 May. Lieutenant-General Adam, his task now completed, was evacuated, and Gort laid down that the corps would be evacuated in reverse numerical order, I Corps leaving last. Late that day he received a personal message from Churchill telling him that if further evacuation became impossible he 'would become the sole judge of when it was impossible to inflict further damage upon the enemy' and could surrender.

By then the picture was less bleak. Two long moles or breakwaters ran out to sea at the entrance to Dunkirk harbour. The eastern mole was by far the longer. Although it could be used a a temporary mooring, it was made of timber latticework and had not been designed to bear the impact of

The eastern mole at Dunkirk, shown clearly on the left of the photograph, had not been designed as a mooring for large vessels. However, on 27 May a passenger steamer proved that the mole could be used, and thereafter it played a crucial part in the evacuation. These troops have boarded the destroyer HMS *Vanquisher* by ladder because of the low tide, though some soldiers, already tired, hungry and frightened, found the process difficult. Despite the remarkable contribution of the 'little ships', the majority of men evacuated from Dunkirk were taken off the mole by destroyers or passenger ships.

large vessels. Its top was 10 feet (3 m) wide, and there was a 15-foot (4.5 m) rise and fall in the tide beneath it. German pilots had not so far attacked it, and for the moment it was screened from their view by the pall of smoke drifting from burning oil storage tanks. Late on 27 May Captain Tennant ordered *Queen of the Channel* to go alongside. She got away with about 1000 men, and proved that the mole could be used. German bombers sank her in mid-Channel, but most of the men aboard her were rescued by *Dorrien Rose*.

Losses amongst shipping were heartbreaking. The destroyer *Wakeful*, with 650 troops on board, was hit by a torpedo and went down in seconds. *Grafton,* another destroyer, was torpedoed while picking up survivors and, though sinking, opened fire on a nearby vessel which she took to be an enemy torpedo boat. The drifter *Lydd* drew the same conclusion and rammed the ship, sinking her, only to discover that she was the drifter *Comfort:* only one of her crew and four of the soldiers she had rescued from *Wakeful* survived.

On 29 May the *Luftwaffe* struck hard at the mole. Of the 11 British ships alongside, *Grenade, Fenella, Crested Eagle, Polly Johnson* and *Calvi* eventually sank, and *Jaguar* and *Canterbury* returned home safely but could take no further part in the operation. The destroyer *Grenade*'s end was especially awesome. Captain John Horsfall of the Royal Irish Fusiliers was leaving the mole aboard a drifter and saw *Grenade* 'glowing white down her length in the darkness, with showers of sparks shooting up into the starry sky above her. She was barely afloat.' Ramsay was mistakenly informed that the mole was now unusable, and for a time all ships were directed to the beaches. But, despite the terrible losses, 47,310 men were landed in England that day.

Destroyer losses persuaded the Admiralty to withdraw modern destroyers from Dynamo, leaving Ramsay with only 15 old ones. It soon became clear that the remaining destroyers and all other available shipping had a daily lift capacity of only 43,000 men (well below the target of 55,000), and some of the modern destroyers were soon returned to Ramsay.

By now the navy's side of the operation was working smoothly. Naval officers, with small parties of sailors, served as beachmasters, supervising embarkation arrangements from the shore. Captain Tennant, sharing Admiral Abrial's headquarters in Bastion 32, was ably assisted by Commander John Clouston, pier master at the eastern mole, who set up a control post at the base of the mole. Clouston, a big, confident Canadian, was one of the heroes of the evacuation. He hastened the laggards, checked the panic-stricken, and regulated the incessant flow along the mole. John Horsfall wrote approvingly of the activities of the naval staff. 'They heeded nothing and simply got on with their job,' he declared, 'showing patience, courtesy and affability to all comers. They were sorely tried and I doubt that many of our own officers would have achieved those three marks of virtue consistently just then.' Senior naval officers offshore – Rear Admiral Wake-Walker for Dunkirk itself – controlled the shipping, using megaphones to marshal vessels around the mole or off the beaches.

The Waiting Troops

The army's arrangements were, of necessity, more haphazard. Some officers were issued with neat slips entitling them to embark a given number of officers and men from a specified beach. Unfortunately there were no routes signed to the beaches, and once there it became apparent that staff officers' logic did not apply to tens of thousands of waiting men. On 28 May the commanding officer of HMS *Gossamer* reported: 'There appeared to be a large wood close to the shore but on approaching nearer this was seen to be a mass of troops on the sand.'

Troops formed great lines stretching out into the water. Sometimes formal discipline prevailed, but more often it did not, and there was a powerful collective sense of natural justice which dealt harshly with queue-jumpers. A Royal Artillery officer who wrote under the pseudonym 'Gun-Buster' gives a graphic description of the apparently endless wait:

We tacked ourselves onto the rear of the smallest of the three queues, the head of it was already standing in water up to the waist. Half an hour passed. Suddenly a small rowing boat appeared. The head of the queue clambered in and were rowed away into the blackness. We moved forward, and the water rose to our waists.

Our only thoughts now were to get on a boat. Along the entire queue not a word was spoken. The men just stood there silently staring into the darkness, praying that a boat would appear and fearing that it would not. Heads and shoulders only showing above the water. Fixed, immovable, as though chained there…

When a boat appeared at last he was too exhausted and weighed down by sodden clothing to climb in, but powerful arms hauled him aboard. Then, he wrote: 'I felt that my job was over. Anything else that remained to be done was the Navy's business.'

The behaviour of troops during the evacuation varied dramatically. At one end of the scale there were sullen or drunken stragglers in the rubble of Dunkirk, terrified men cowering amongst the dunes, and instances of raw panic on the beaches themselves. At the other extreme, some foot guards impressed observers by swinging down to the mole in step. A surviving photograph shows a detachment of Grenadier Guards marching past the station on Dover docks after their return to England, rifles smartly at the slope.

It was easiest for soldiers in formed units, with the discipline and cohesion that spring from mutual regard, to remain steady in a world turned upside down. John Horsfall's men moved in single file along the mole under sporadic air attack:

chattering like monkeys. Sometimes [Company Sergeant Major] Good or one of the NCOs would bellow at them, but inevitably this drew repartee, probably [Fusilier] Given's, in the dark. There were variants as some warrior took a toss, and one heard the clatter of ironmongery or fragmented rock dropping into the water below…

In several places the mole was demolished, and it was a slow business dropping down into the void beneath, one by one, and swinging over the gap – or clambering in the black dark over unstable wreckage.

The commanding officer of a Territorial battalion of the King's Own Royal Regiment reminded his officers that they wore a distinguished cap-badge and urged them to 'set an example to that rabble on the beach', and the battalion marched down in good order.

Most of the waiting troops had long since run out of food and water, and on the night of 29/30 May some big lighters full of supplies were towed across the Channel and beached so that their contents could be unloaded as the tide receded. They then formed makeshift piers which made it easier for men to board the small craft which would ferry them to larger vessels. Commander Hector Richardson, Senior Naval Officer at Bray-les-Dunes, suggested that trucks could be manhandled out into the sea and then connected by planks to form improvised jetties – a military police officer had the same idea at La Panne – and these also helped.

The Little Ships
There were still too few small craft to get men off the beaches, and the ships' lifeboats, whalers and cutters were not ideal for the task: their keels dug deep into the sand as troops piled aboard, and sometimes they were overturned by the sheer weight of men clambering in. Allan Barrell, owner of *Shamrock*, one of the first civilian small craft to appear, was shocked to see 'what looked like thousands of sticks on the beach…turn into moving masses of humanity'. He went in as close as he dared to ferry soldiers, 80 at a time, to waiting destroyers. 'Navigation was extremely difficult,' he wrote:

owing to the various wreckage, upturned boats, floating torpedoes and soldiers in the water trying to be sailors for the first time, they paddled their collapsible little boats out to me with the butts of their rifles, and many shouted that they were sinking…

Eventually *Shamrock*'s propeller fouled what her skipper thought to be 'a human obstruction…I was too weak to dive under the thick black oil which surrounded us, so rather than be left sitting on our useless craft I asked to be taken on HM ship. This was the last straw, having to leave my vessel which constituted my life savings…'

Responding to the need to lift men off the beaches in greater numbers, Ramsay stepped up the flow of little ships. Many had started their journey at Tough Brothers' boatyard in Teddington where many Thames craft were collected, but the Small Vessels Pool had cast its net wide and boatyards from Cowes to Canvey Island played their part. Some owners were co-operative, and crewed their boats themselves; some never discovered that their vessels had been commandeered until long after they had gone, and a few raised bureaucratic objections. The small craft gathered at Sheerness, where their engines were checked over and they were given crews. Many of the latter were volunteers, shipwrights, marine engineers and yachtsmen, and there was a good leavening of Royal Naval Volunteer reserve officers and ratings. From Sheerness they went to Ramsgate, where they were given charts and water and sent off in convoys across the English Channel, usually escorted by an armed tug or skoot.

Some never completed the journey: they had been built for quieter times in the upper reaches of the Thames; and the Channel, even when miraculously calm, was too much for them. Others were hit by German guns (now ranging, with increasing accuracy, onto the beaches) or attacked from the air. Many of their crews found it a shocking experience, but most kept at their task. The skipper of the cockle-boat *Letitia* admitted that he turned back when a shell burst in front of his boat, but the young signaller 'who had only been "out" for about six weeks, and who had never been under fire, said "We've got to go in again" so we went in.' On 30 May 53,823 men were landed in England, almost 30,000 of them from the beaches. The author David Divine was right to hail this as 'the triumph of the little ships'.

The End of the British Evacuation

It was not only the crews of the little ships who felt the strain. There were difficulties in England when the crews of some steamers were reluctant to return to Dunkirk, and some were replaced by Royal Naval personnel or other volunteers from the Merchant Navy. There was even something approaching a collapse of morale aboard a destroyer which had been damaged and lost her captain, but Vice-Admiral Sir James Somerville, temporarily assigned to assist the tired Ramsay, spoke to her crew and gave them a night's rest: she went back to Dunkirk the next day.

As the evacuation reached its climax – 68,014 men, the highest daily total, were rescued on 31 May – the Germans pressed hard at the perimeter. In one of the many hard-fought battles that day Captain H. M. Ervine-Andrews of the East Lancashire Regiment was awarded the Victoria Cross, the only one won at Dunkirk. His company held a sector of the canal just east of Bergues quite literally to the last round, and he then brought the last of his men to safety, wading up to their necks down a side canal.

It was Gort's intention to stay till the end, but Eden, on Churchill's instructions, ordered him to hand over command to a selected corps commander and to leave for England. 'This is in accordance with the correct military procedure,' ran the order, 'and no personal discretion is left to you in the matter.' Gort considered appointing Barker of I Corps, but it became clear that the strain had told heavily upon him, and Major-General the Hon. Harold Alexander of 1st Division was selected. Gort told him:

to operate under the orders of Admiral Abrial, and to assist the French in the defence of Dunkirk. At the same time he was to occupy himself with arrangements for the evacuation of his command, and I stressed the importance of the French sharing equally in the facilities which were provided for evacuation.

Gort's headquarters closed at 6 p.m. on 31 May, and he was ferried out to the minesweeper HMS *Hebe*.

The French Evacuation

The instructions given to Alexander highlighted one of the dilemmas of the evacuation: the degree of French involvement. The message of 26 May which gave Gort permission to operate towards the Channel coast implied that the French premier had been informed of the change of policy, but it is clear that neither General Blanchard nor Admiral Abrial were told that evacuation was intended, an omission blamed by the British official history on the French High Command.

The following day, after a conference at Cassel, Gort asked Weygand's representative, General Klotz, what he knew of a plan to evacuate 30,000 men a day. 'I've never heard of it,' replied Klotz. It was only on the afternoon

This German photograph shows the base of Dunkirk's eastern mole after the evacuation, with abandoned British transport in the foreground. Commander Clouston's control post was in the centre right: this area is now a car park, and also houses a substantial German pill-box. Sunken ships can be seen near the mole.

of 29 May that Weygand authorized the evacuation of French troops, and by then much damage had been done.

'The French staff at Dunkirk feel strongly that they are defending Dunkirk for us to evacuate, which is largely true,' reported Captain Tennant.

Churchill had stressed, also on 29 May, that: 'It is essential that the French should share in such evacuations from Dunkirk as may be possible... Arrangements must be concerted at once, so that no reproaches, or as few as possible, may arise.' Yet when the Allied War Council met in Paris on 31 May he was nonplussed to hear that 150,000 British but only 15,000 French soldiers had so far been rescued. He refused to accept that the British should be evacuated first, and declared that the Allies should fight and then evacuate arm in arm – '*Bras dessus, bras dessous*!' A signal summarizing the meeting's conclusion was sent to Abrial. It decreed: 'The British troops will remain as a rearguard for as long as possible... The evacuation from Dunkirk will be carried out under your orders.'

In the event, Alexander, more concerned than Abrial about the tenability of the perimeter, withdrew his rearguard sooner than the Admiral wished, giving rise to further complaints that the British were saving themselves at the expense of the French. The last of the BEF got away late on 2 June. Tennant intended to signal Ramsay 'Operation completed. Returning to Dover,' but an enterprising signaller sent the more succinct: 'BEF evacuated.'

It was true of the BEF but not of the French. Confused instructions meant that many ships had sailed without being able to find French soldiers to fill them. When Weygand complained that the French were being sacrificed, Churchill replied that the navy would make one last try. Just after 10 a.m. on 3 June Ramsay signalled: 'We cannot leave our Allies in the lurch, and I call on all officers and men detailed for further evacuation tonight to let the world see that we never let down our Ally...'

The last foray was shot through with poignancy. Rear Admiral Wake-Walker sailed in MTB 102, flying an admiral's flag which had started life as a Southern Railways tea-cloth and had been suitably converted by one of her crew when she had acted as 'flagship' previously. HMS *Whitshed*'s harmonica band played as she drew out of port, and HMS *Malcolm*'s officers still sported their mess jackets for the end-of-evacuation party. The tug *Sun IV* – no less than 10 of her fellow *Suns* had taken part in the evacuation – set off towing 14 launches, skippered by the tugboat company's managing director.

Because the beach parties had been withdrawn – Commander Clouston, tragically, had been lost after the RAF crash boat taking him home was sunk – a berthing party had to be landed and it took longer than planned to get ships alongside. There were the usual linguistic difficulties, but over 26,000 men were rescued. There was no room for them all. As General Lucas of the French 32nd Division prepared to embark there were 1000 soldiers drawn up four deep, standing to attention with the flames flickering on their steel helmets. Lucas and his staff walked to the edge of the pier, turned, and gave a final salute. The last vessel out was MTB 107, commanded by Lieutenant John Cameron 'a settled barrister of 40' and future Scots law lord. He circled the outer harbour, littered with wrecked shipping, with French troops still standing on the mole. 'The whole scene,' he recalled, 'was filled with a sense of finality and death; the curtain was ringing down on a great tragedy.'

'A Miracle of Deliverance'
It did not seem a tragedy in England. The survivors were stunned by the warmth of their reception. Tom Collins of the Royal Artillery remembered:

Unwashed, unshaven, very prominent in our rags and tatters, we were welcomed it seemed by people from all walks of life; but those who were top of the league in my book were the crew who brought us back, the medical men who attended the sick and wounded – and the W(omen's) V(oluntary) S(ervice), who gave every man a mug of tea, a piece of cake and a cigarette. After we settled down in the waiting train…a soldier got to his feet and said, 'Boys, I'm thanking God I'm home. Now let's give a thought for the boys we left behind.' And we, all strangers from different units, held a minute's silence in that compartment; and as we travelled through the green fields, I thought that England wasn't such a bad place after all.

Churchill warned Parliament: 'We must be very careful not to assign to this deliverance the attributes of a victory. Wars are not won by evacuations.' Yet even he called it a 'miracle of deliverance', and somehow miracle seemed the right word. It was admittedly costly. Fighter Command lost 106 aircraft during the period of the evacuation. And, as David Divine put it, 'the price of admiralty was, as always, heavy.' Of the 693 British ships which took part in the operation, six destroyers, eight personnel ships, a sloop, five minesweepers, 17 trawlers, a hospital ship and 188 smaller vessels had been sunk and an equal number damaged.

Above all, Dunkirk was a sailor's triumph. During a difficult night's work off Dunkirk Coxswain H. Knight was hailed by a naval officer: 'I cannot see who you are: are you a naval party?'

'No, sir,' replied Knight, 'we are members of the crew of the Ramsgate lifeboat.'

'Thank you,' replied the officer. 'And thank God for such men as you have this night proved youselves to be.'

A View of the Field

Dover Castle
It is possible to get a good feel for Operation Dynamo without even leaving England. Dover is a giant among castles, with the longest recorded history of any in Britain. It is now in the care of English Heritage, and substantial parts of the tunnels beneath it are open to the public. These include the Admiralty Casemates, which housed Ramsay's heaquarters in 1940. A telephone exchange, similar to that which received so many of the crucial messages, retains all its equipment, and there is an anti-aircraft control room which postdates the battle. There is a good exhibition devoted to Hellfire Corner (as south-east Kent was known during the Second World War). The balcony outside Ramsay's cabin is

now unsafe, but the main entrance to the tunnels is on another balcony which, on a fine day, gives a good view of the French coast. During the evacuation Dunkirk was visible from here, marked by a pillar of smoke by day and fierce fires at night.

Ramsgate Maritime Museum

Several of the little ships have survived. Perhaps the most evocative is *Sundowner*, now the property of Ramsgate Maritime Museum. Built in 1912 as an Admiralty steam launch, in 1930 she was converted to a private motor yacht for her new owner Commander Charles Lightoller, senior surviving officer of the ill-fated *Titanic*.

On the evening of 30 May 1940 Lightoller was told that the Admiralty intended to requisition *Sundowner* for the evacuation, and was asked to take her to Ramsgate where a naval crew would take over. Lightoller demurred - 'they had another guess coming' - and decided to go to France himself, with his eldest son Roger and an 18-year old sea-scout Gerald Ashcroft as crew. They left Southend for Ramsgate at 3.15 a.m. on 1 June, paused there briefly, and set out across the Channel.

On their way they narrowly missed a mine, and then stopped to take on five men from the 25 foot (7 m) motor cruiser *Westerly*, broken down and on fire. Despite being bombed and machine-gunned, Lightoller reached the mole, where he went alongside a destroyer and took 122 soldiers aboard. Another of Lightoller's sons, an RAF pilot lost the day war broke out, had discussed tactics with his father, and Lightoller knew that an aircraft diving to attack must pull up out of its dive to make its guns bear. When attacked on the way home he waited until the aircraft was on the point of pulling up, and then turned the yacht sharply: 'This of course threw his aim off completely.' *Sundowner* returned home intact, but Lightoller discovered that many of his passengers had been unwell, and there was 'a nice clearing up job for the three of us'. Although *Sundowner* can only be visited by arrangement, she can be seen at her berth in front of the museum.

Lowestoft Yacht Harbour

Motor Torpedo Boats (MTBs) were high-speed craft armed with torpedoes. They were once judged to pose such a threat to battleships that destroyers – 'torpedo boat destoyers' in full – were initially designed to combat them. MTB 102 (believed to be the only surviving Royal Navy vessel which took part in the evacuation) was built as an experimental craft by Vosper Ltd and then bought into the service. She can now be seen in a heritage berth in Lowestoft yacht harbour. In 1940 she was commanded by Lieutenant Christopher Dreyer, made seven crossings to Dunkirk, and for the last two nights of the operation she acted as Rear Admiral Wake-Walker's flagship.

After the war she was sold off and converted to a private motor cruiser. In 1973 a Norfolk Scout Group found her in the process of being converted to a houseboat, and in 1976 she was refurbished to appear in the film *The Eagle Has Landed*. In 1985, 1990 and 1995 she participated in the Association of Little Ships' crossing to Dunkirk: on the last occasion Commander Dreyer took her into the harbour.

Dunkirk

Although Dunkirk was badly damaged by bombing it is not hard to trace the key events of 1940. The evacuation is commemorated by a war memorial on the Digue des Alliés on the north-east edge of the town. Bastion 32, Admiral Abrial's headquarters, lies beneath the modern art museum on the Canal Exutoire, just to its south. It is not open to the public, and its rather run-down exterior, approached via the Rue des Chantiers de France, gives little clue to its former importance. A small museum on the nearby Rue Militaire was open at weekends when this book went to press but has an uncertain future.

The Rue Militaire leads, past another bastion peppered with shrapnel, to a narrow bridge over the Canal Exutoire. A small car park and German bunker stand in the area of Commander Clouston's control post, and the eastern mole juts out to sea beyond it. Its landward end has been reinforced since 1940, and concrete tetrahedrons now protect it from the sea. At its far end, no longer approachable on foot, but easily seen from the Ramsgate ferry, the mole retains its distinctive 1940 latticed silhouette.

The beaches between Dunkirk and La Panne (now De Panne) have changed little, though there are several German concrete bunkers. There are still dunes behind them for much of their length. The Bergues–Furnes Canal (Canal de la Basse Colme) runs through low-lying meadows about 6 miles (10 km) inland: Captain Ervine-Andrews' VC-winning action was fought just north of Hoymille. Bergues itself is a pleasant little town, still girt about with Vauban's ravelins and bastions, redolent of an era when war moved at a slower pace.

CHAPTER 6

The Blitz
1940–41

Background

'When we got there,' wrote Alf Tyler of Civil Defence Rescue:

…one of the bombs had made a direct hit on an Anderson shelter situated at the end of a short garden belonging to one of the small terraced houses. A warden said that the family of six had been in the shelter, now blown to pieces with its occupants, parts of bodies were scattered over a large area, one large piece was on a slated roof…the dinner was still on the table in the back room, the family having left it to go down the garden into their shelter.

This 'incident', to use the official euphemism, from a single bombing raid on the northern suburbs of London on 15 September 1940, speaks volumes about the arbitrary brutality of the Blitz: it was indeed a people's war.

The German Occupation of France

After the evacuation from Dunkirk the campaign in France was soon over. Although there was some gallant fighting on the part of the French, the Germans rapidly crossed the Somme and pushed southwards. The 51st Highland Division, serving under French command, was trapped and forced to surrender at St Valéry-en-Caux, and a British force was evacuated from Normandy after a predictably confused campaign.

The French government left Paris on 12 June and established itself in Bordeaux. The premier, Paul Reynaud, was replaced by the aged Marshal Pétain, hero of the First World War battle of Verdun. And on 22 June French representatives concluded an armistice at Rethondes in the Forest of Compiègne, on the same spot, and in the same railway carriage, that the armistice of November 1918 had been signed.

This Anderson shelter was hit on the first raid on London on 24–25 August 1940: although buckled, it withstood the blast. Gallantry by members of fire, rescue and bomb-disposal teams could be rewarded by the George Medal *(right)* and George Cross.

Just as the 1918 armistice had been a national humiliation for Germany, so that of 1940 degraded France. It left the Germans in occupation of northern and south-western France, and the French government, now situated in the little spa town of Vichy, controlling only the unoccupied Zone of the Centre and South-East. The French army was reduced to 100,000 men, and French prisoners of war remained in German hands.

Charles de Gaulle, a temporary brigadier-general who had commanded an armoured division with some success, reached London after the fall of Reynaud and on 18 June broadcast an appeal urging Frenchmen to continue the fight. His Free French movement had a slow and painful start, but was to ensure that France never fully dropped out of the war, and was eventually able to assist in her own liberation.

The Planning of Operation Sealion

The French collapse left many British people feeling curiously stimulated. 'I feel happier now that we have no allies to be polite to & pamper,' wrote King George VI, and a reader assured the magazine *Picture Post* that: 'A nation without allies is a nation with no one to let them down.' Churchill had already made it clear that Britain would fight on alone. 'Even though large tracts of Europe and many old and famous states have fallen or may fall into the grip of the Gestapo and the odious apparatus of Nazi rule,' he proclaimed on 4 June, 'we shall not flag or fail. We shall go on to the end.' Two weeks later he was more specific, and warned the House of Commons that: 'Hitler knows that he will have to break us in this island or lose the war.'

At first Hitler was less convinced. He seemed indifferent to the notion of an invasion of England when it was mentioned at a conference on 20 June, but soon appeared to warm to the idea. On 2 July the German armed forces were informed that invasion would be considered under certain conditions, the most important being German acquisition of air superiority. Führer Directive No. 16 of 16 July 1940 laid down guidelines for the invasion, codenamed Operation Sealion. The navy set to work assembling barges and landing craft, and the army prepared plans for a landing between Brighton and Folkestone. It is one of history's strange coincidences that the 26th Infantry Division was to land near Pevensey, not far from the spot where Duke William's men had come ashore in 1066.

Sealion never looked easy. It hinged, as German planners were quick to recognize, upon command of the air. The German navy, far smaller than that of the British at the outset of the war, had suffered heavy losses during its campaign in Norway, and would have found it difficult to escort the invasion fleet and to keep a logistic lifeline open during the early stages of a campaign in southern England. 'The navy,' admits one German historian, 'unquestionably gave Sealion no chance of succeeding.'

However the land battle would have taxed the British most severely. Although the majority of the BEF had been evacuated from Dunkirk, its equipment had been left behind. Alan Brooke, now Commander-in-Chief of Home Forces, warned that Britain's exposed coastline was twice the length of the front the French had tried to hold with 80 divisions and the Maginot Line. He had 22 divisions, 'of which only half can be looked upon as in any way fit for any form of mobile operations'. It is hard to disagree with Ronald Wheatley, in his study of Sealion, that: 'Had Britain not been an island, she would have been overrun as surely as were Poland and France.'

The difficulties confronting Sealion have persuaded some historians that Hitler never took it seriously, and privately hoped that his preparations, and the air offensive which accompanied them, would persuade the British to sue for peace, thus making invasion unnecessary. We simply cannot be sure. Two things are, however, certain. The first is that the Germans strenuously attempted, in the Battle of Britain (mid-June to mid-September 1940), to gain the air superiority which was a prerequisite for Sealion. The second is that they then, from August 1940 to mid-May 1941, turned their attention to cities in an attack known, from abbreviation of the German word *Blitzkrieg* (meaning 'lightning war') as the Blitz.

In one respect the two campaigns were not distinct, for bombing attacks began in an attempt to reduce aircraft production and thus cripple the RAF, and became an assault on cities only when it became clear that the Battle of Britain had been lost. In another, though, their character was very different. It is no mere cliché to say that the Battle of Britain was fought by the few, the pilots of the RAF's Fighter Command. The Blitz was the business of the many: not only of the firemen, rescue workers, wardens, ambulance crews, policemen and anti-aircraft gunners, and the others, volunteer or professional, who played an active role; but also of the tens of thousands of civilians who had to tolerate blacked-out streets, air-raid warnings, the nightly terror of bombing raids and the bewilderment of seeing a familiar townscape changed for ever.

The German Air Attack Begins
Air attack on the United Kingdom came as no surprise, and Stanley Baldwin had glumly prophesied that 'the bomber will always get through'. In 1917 the Smuts report on the relatively modest German bombing of Britain in the First World War warned that: 'the day may not

be far off when aerial operations and their devastation of enemy lands and destruction of industrial and populous centres on a vast scale may become the principal operations of war…' Theorists like the Italian Giulio Douhet and the American Billy Mitchell had pointed to the value of air power, and Douhet specifically recommended the strategic use of bombing to shatter civilian morale.

Sir Hugh Trenchard, the RAF's Chief of Staff from 1919 to 1929, argued in favour of devoting most of the RAF's resources to Bomber Command for just this reason, and the National Government favoured the development of a bomber deterrent whose existence would dissuade potential adversaries from attacking Britain. This was an unwise policy. Not only did Bomber Command have little effect in deterring Hitler, but at the outbreak of war it was hard-pressed to reach well-defended targets in daylight or to find them at all in darkness. The *Luftwaffe*, whose leaders had been far less impressed by theories of strategic bombing, developed primarily as a ground support air force, a role it carried out brilliantly in the campaign in France. In 1940 it was not well-suited to launch a bomber offensive; and lack of clear direction, for which Hermann Goering, its commander-in-chief, must be held largely responsible, made matters worse.

Goering was born in Bavaria in 1893 and commissioned into the infantry on the eve of the First World War. In October 1914 he began flying, and by the war's end he had 22 kills to his credit, had been awarded Germany's highest decoration for bravery, the *Pour le Mérite*, and had commanded the crack Richthofen squadron. He joined the Nazi Party in 1922 and commanded Hitler's Bodyguard, but was wounded in the Munich putsch of 1923, became addicted to the morphine given to ease his pain, and spent some time in mental hospitals. Elected to the *Reichstag* in 1928, he became its president in 1932, and in the following year, when Hitler became chancellor, he began to enjoy a series of important posts, not least Minister of Aviation. As such he was one of the founding fathers of the *Luftwaffe*, and deserves some of the credit for its performance in 1939–40. His promotion to the unique rank of *Reichsmarschall* in July 1940 saw him at the apogee of his success. Thereafter, overweening personal vanity and an appetite for power which far exceeded his real abilities turned him into an overdressed buffoon, albeit a deadly one.

Goering's adversary in the summer of 1940 could scarcely have been a more different personality. Air Chief Marshal Sir Hugh Dowding, Commander-in-Chief of Fighter Command, was a lonely and aloof figure with the less than flattering nickname 'Stuffy'. Dowding had been an

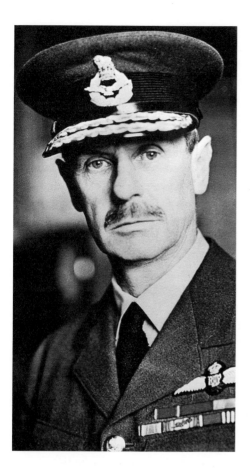

The rival commanders in the Battle of Britain could scarcely have been more different. Air Chief Marshal Sir Hugh ('Stuffy') Dowding *(above)* was chilly and austere, and had thought deeply about the air defence of Britain long before war broke out. *Reichsmarschall* Hermann Goering *(right)*, in contrast, was a flamboyant showman with a taste for self-designed uniforms. In fact Dowding fought the better battle, and Goering's failure to plan a coherent campaign contributed greatly to the German defeat.

artillery officer before joining the RAF, and from 1930 to 1936 he served as the Air Council's Member for Research and Development, encouraging the development of the Spitfire and Hurricane fighters. He was appointed to head Fighter Command in 1936, and at once set about remodelling Britain's air defences.

British Use of Radar

Dowding inherited an early warning system based on experience gained from the First World War: listening posts on the coast telephoned warnings to a control room, which ordered aircraft to take off and deal with the intruders. As aircraft became faster this scheme had obvious limitations, but the development of radar (in fact known as RDF, for Radio Direction Finding, during the Battle of Britain) changed this at a stroke. The first radar stations (known as Air Ministry Experimental Stations to preserve secrecy) came into service in 1937, and were expanded to form Chain Home, a network of 20 stations capable of detecting high-altitude long-range targets. The 12 sites of Chain Home Low, which picked up aircraft coming in beneath the coverage of Chain Home, became operational only in July 1940.

Dowding had consistently argued, often in the face of very heavy political pressure, against the diversion of key fighter resources to the campaigns in Norway and France. The fact that Fighter Command maintained a winning margin in 1940 is due, in no small measure, to his efforts. Dowding's aircraft, most of them Hurricanes and Spitfires, in a ratio of about 5:3, were deployed on RAF sector stations which had smaller satellites. Sectors were combined to form groups, and in August 1940 there were four of these. Air Vice-Marshal Park's No. 11 Group, with its headquarters at Uxbridge, was responsible for London and the South-East. From Watnall, near Nottingham, Air Vice-Marshal Leigh-Mallory commanded No. 12 Group, covering the Midlands and the Eastern Counties. Northern England, Scotland and Northern Ireland were the responsibility of Air Vice-Marshal Saul's No. 13 Group; and Wales and the West Country that of Air Vice-Marshal Brand's No.10 Group, activated only in June 1940.

Initially radar warnings of air raids were passed to Fighter Command Headquarters at Bentley Priory, near Harrow. Here the information was filtered and relayed to the appropriate group headquarters. Groups decided which of their sectors should deal with the raid and how many aircraft to allocate to it. Sectors sent orders to their aircraft to take off, and then directed them so as to put them in the best position to engage the enemy. Once raiders had crossed the coast their progress was relayed, not by radar, but by posts of the Royal Observer Corps.

The British Defence

The army's anti-aircraft command, under Lieutenant-General Sir Frederick Pile, had 1200 heavy and 580 light guns available when the Battle of Britain began. These formed seven anti-aircraft divisions, their

Top: It is hard to overstate the contribution made by radar to the British defence. These are the 300-foot masts of a typical 'Chain Home' radar station. Information from radar was relayed to sector control rooms by Headquarters Fighter Command at Bentley Priory *(above)*. Symbols representing hostile and friendly squadrons are moved across the map while officers in the gallery look on and consider the appropriate response.

guns deployed on sites across Britain. Royal Artillery liaison officers were stationed at RAF group headquarters, and telephoned gun operations rooms to warn them of the approach of hostile aircraft. Heavy 3.7-inch guns could aim at individual targets, but usually fired a barrage of shells, fused to burst at the estimated height of the aircraft, into the attackers' path. Finally, nearly 1500 gas-filled barrage balloons were flown on the expected flight path of intruders in the hope that aircraft would collide with their steel cables, or alternatively keep high in order to avoid them.

Although the government had not abandoned the notion of 'business as usual' (which decreed that rearmament must not be allowed to interfere with normal trade) until 1938, it had already begun to take key defensive steps. In 1937 Parliament passed the Air Raid Precautions (ARP) Act, which formed the basis for civil defence measures. There would be a warden post for every 500 people, manned by three volunteer wardens: chief wardens would supervise local groupings of warden posts. A Civil Defence Rescue Service was established, and steps were taken to form an Auxiliary Fire Service. In November 1939 the latter amalgamated with the London Fire Brigade to form a force whose more than 25,000 personnel – men, women and youths – crewed 3000 firefighting appliances.

In December 1938 the government announced that the Anderson air-raid shelter would be supplied free to low-income families living in likely target areas. Official booklets advised householders on how to protect their homes against bomb and gas attack, and gas masks were issued to adults and children alike. Many large public shelters were initially badly planned – some lacked seats and lavatories – but their design soon improved.

At first the London Underground was used as an unofficial shelter, and the authorities eventually bowed to the inevitable and provided bunk beds, medical cover and even libraries to entertain Londoners during the long nights below ground. The Women's Voluntary Service, whose soup-kitchens played such a vital part in sustaining civilian morale during the Blitz, furnished 7 tons (7 tonnes) of food and 2400 gallons (10,900 litres) of tea, coffee and cocoa each night. Few shelters were totally safe, and even the Underground had its share of misfortunes: on 14 October 1940 Balham Station suffered a direct hit and 68 people were killed; and on 12 January 1941 a bomb blew up the booking hall at Bank Station, killing at least 55 people.

The Balance of Forces
At the beginning of the Battle of Britain the balance of forces seemed to favour the Germans. Britain was within range of three *Luftflotten* (Air

Fleets): Field-Marshal Kesselring's *Luftflotte 2*, based in northern France and the Low Countries; Field-Marshal Sperrle's *Luftflotte 3*, in southern France; and General Stumpff's *Luftflotte 5* in Norway and Denmark. The fact that the bombers of *Luftflotte 5* were based too far from Britain to enjoy single-engine fighter cover meant that they made only a marginal contribution to the battle. Nevertheless the *Luftwaffe* had a daily fighting strength (two-thirds of the total strength of units engaged) of around 750 long-range bombers, 250 dive-bombers, more than 600 single-engined and 150 twin-engined fighters. Dowding could expect to fly perhaps 600 of his 900 fighters on any given day.

There was no clear technological edge. The Messerschmitt 109 was arguably the best fighter on either side, but its advantages were by no means decisive and its short range limited the time it could spend in British airspace. The twin-engined Messerschmitt 110 was too cumbersome to take on Spitfires and Hurricanes on equal terms, and the Junkers 87 *Stuka* dive-bomber, for all its formidable reputation, fared ill in air-to-air combat and bore only 1100 lb (500 kg) of bombs. Bombers like the Heinkel 111, Dornier 17 and Junkers 88 carried heavier loads. Even so, the 6600 lb (3000 kg) of bombs borne by the Junkers 88 was less than half the load carried by the Lancaster, workhorse of the RAF's subsequent bombing campaign against Germany.

Radar provided Fighter Command with an important advantage: indeed, it is hard to see how the battle could have been won without it. But in the summer of 1940 the system was in its infancy, operators were learning on the job and there was little margin for error. As Dr Malcolm Smith has shown, it took only six minutes for German aircraft to cross the Channel at Dover, and another 10 minutes to be over No. 11 Group's sector airfields. Radar could pick up bomber waves south of the French coast, but it took four minutes for the news to reach airfields and another 13 for Spitfires to reach 20,000 feet: even then there was a danger that they might find Me 109s, flying top cover for the bombers, immediately above them.

Campaign and Battle

The Battle of Britain began with a preliminary skirmish. There was, as we have seen, widespread recognition in the German high command that the success of Operation Sealion depended on winning air supremacy. Goering believed that this would take him about a month, and although his *Luftflotten* were prepared to launch the attack from mid-July it would take much longer for naval preparations to be complete. In the meantime

Atlantic Ocean

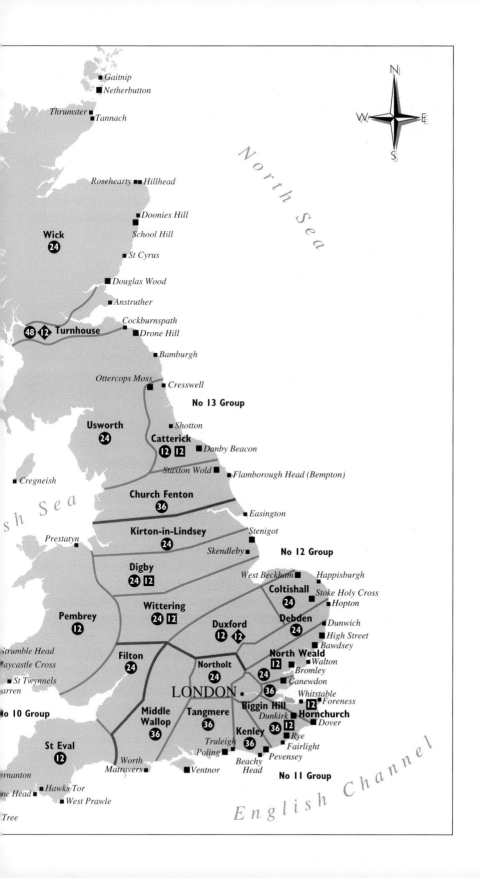

N

W · E

S

North Sea

Irish Sea

English Channel

LONDON

■ Gaitnip
■ Netherbutton
Thrumster ■ ■ Tannach
Rosehearty ■ ■ Hillhead
■ Doonies Hill
School Hill ■
Wick
24
■ St Cyrus
■ Douglas Wood
■ Anstruther
Cockburnspath
48 **12** Turnhouse ■
■ Drone Hill
■ Bamburgh
Ottercops Moss ■ ■ Cresswell
No 13 Group
Usworth ■ Shotton
24
Catterick
12 **12** ■ Danby Beacon
Staxton Wold ■
■ Cregneish ■ Flamborough Head (Bempton)
Church Fenton
36
■ Easington
Kirton-in-Lindsey Stenigot ■
Prestatyn **24**
■ Skendleby ■ **No 12 Group**
Digby West Beckham ■ ■ Happisburgh
24 **12** Coltishall ■ Stoke Holy Cross
24 ■ Hopton
Pembrey Wittering Debden ■ Dunwich
12 **24** **12** Duxford **24** ■ High Street
12 **12** ■ Bawdsey
Strumble Head Filton North Weald ■ Walton
aycastle Cross **24** Northolt **12** ■ Bromley
■ St Twynnels **24** **24** ■ Canewdon
arren **36** Whitstable
■ ■ Foreness
No 10 Group **12**
Middle Tangmere Biggin Hill
Wallop **36** **12** Hornchurch
36 Kenley Dunkirk ■ ■ Dover
St Eval Truleigh **36** **12** ■ Rye
12 Poling ■ ■ Fairlight
rnanton Worth Pevensey
ne Head ■ Hawks Tor Matravers ■ ■ Ventnor Beachy
■ West Prawle Head **No 11 Group**
Tree

there was much to be said for attacking ports and shipping, which would both weaken Britain (by depriving it of supplies) and begin to whittle away at Fighter Command.

However the attacks on shipping proved inconclusive. Several merchantmen and warships were sunk, and Channel traffic was temporarily interrupted. The *Luftwaffe* lost about 300 aircraft between 10 July and 12 August, but had more than made up this loss by 14 August. The RAF, in contrast, lost 150 aircraft, but another 500 fighters were produced during the same period, so that its relative strength actually improved.

'Eagle Day'

The air campaign proper was to begin with *Adler-Tag*, or 'Eagle Day'. Hitler had made it clear that the attack was to be 'directed primarily against the flying units, ground organisation and supply installations of the Royal Air Force, and against the air armaments industry'. Goering was less single-minded, and did much to confuse senior commanders by lecturing them on tactical detail rather than setting clear objectives. He was at first eager to free his high-performance fighters for independent sweeps over Britain and ordered the *Luftflotte* commanders to minimize the numbers allocated to bomber escort: this in turn induced them to weaken their strike forces so as to ensure the aircraft they sent were properly escorted.

Adler-Tag was eventually scheduled for 13 August. On the previous day there had been preliminary raids on No. 11 Group's forward airfields at Manston, Lympne and Hawkinge, attacks on south coast radar stations, on naval installations at Portsmouth and Gosport and shipping in the Thames Estuary. Although the airfields were damaged but usable, the radar station at Ventnor on the Isle of Wight was put out of action.

Unfortunately for Goering, the weather on 13 August was poor: low cloud cover meant that the high-level fighter sweeps would have been unable to intervene against British fighters attacking bombers and their immediate escorts. The morning's raids were to have been cancelled because of the weather but some were in fact launched, and more followed in the afternoon. A series of badly co-ordinated efforts resulted in the Germans losing 45 aircraft to the RAF's 14, only seven of whose pilots were lost.

The Fate of the Pilots

Pilots were often uninjured by the fire which hit their aircraft and could escape if they managed to bale out in time. This was not always straightforward, as Flying Officer Hugh 'Cocky' Dundas discovered when his Spitfire was hit above the Kent village of Elham, near Hawkinge:

White smoke filled the cockpit, thick and hot, and I could see neither the sky above nor the Channel coast 12,000 feet [3660 m] below… I stood up on the seat and pushed the top half of my body out of the cockpit. Pressed hard against the fuselage, half in, half out, I struggled in a nightmare of fear and confusion to drop clear, but could not do so… Try again; try the other side. Up, over – and out. I slithered along the fuselage and felt myself falling free. Seconds after my parachute opened, I saw the Spitfire hit and explode in a field below. A flock of sheep scattered outwards from the cloud of dust and flame.

Because most of the fighting took place over southern England or the Channel, RAF aircrew who baled out and landed safely were soon back at their bases. Some even found themselves back in action the same day. Michael Constable Maxwell, shot down for the third time on 30 August, crash-landed near Herne Bay. He had an unpleasant train journey, hatless and dishevelled, back to his base at North Weald in Essex, where he found that his brother had been shot down. The taxi-driver who drove him across London declined a tip, saying that he would be ashamed to take one from a man who had just risked his life for him. Baled-out German aircrew, in contrast, were captured. This meant that attrition of pilots was always higher for the Germans, no small matter at a time when it took far longer to train a pilot than to produce an aircraft.

German Miscalculation

Bad weather on 14 August forced the Germans to postpone attacks till the next day. This time *Luftflotte 5* was to play a leading part. The Germans believed that the fighting on 13 August had caused heavier losses in Nos. 10 and 11 Groups than was in fact the case, and that Dowding would accordingly shift squadrons from the Midlands and the North to defend the South. Both sides consistently over-estimated the number of aircraft they shot down: several pilots might claim the same kill, and anti-aircraft gunners lodged their own claims. Even now it is hard to be certain of combat losses, for accidents – to which battle damage was often a contributory cause – also eroded fighting strength.

The *Luftwaffe's* miscalculation was disastrous, and the defenders took full advantage of it. Air Vice-Marshal Saul's fighters intercepted German aircraft making for Yorkshire and Tyneside, shooting down eight bombers and seven of their escorts without loss. Further south, Air Vice-Marshal Leigh-Mallory's interception was less successful, but another eight bombers were shot down. The Germans did rather better against Nos. 10 and 11 Groups, hitting several airfields and Short's aircraft factory at Rochester. Nevertheless, although the Germans had flown almost 1800 sorties (the highest daily rate they were to achieve during the battle), they had lost 75 aircraft and destroyed only 34.

Goering remained confident: his intelligence staff believed that Dowding would be reduced to about 300 operational aircraft for 16 August. In fact they both over-estimated casualties inflicted and under-estimated aircraft production, for Dowding's 47 Hurricane and Spitfire squadrons had sufficient aircraft to fly at their normal tactical strength of 12 aircraft apiece. There were reserves in 'Group Pools', as well as aircraft in Operational Training Units and squadrons re-equipping or working up, and 230 more in the Aircraft Storage Units which topped up fighting squadrons.

However at this stage Dowding's victory was by no means assured. Over half Fighter Command's losses had occurred in the past 10 days, the supply of trained pilots was dwindling faster than the stock of aircraft, and a continuation of such attrition must eventually wear out the RAF. If they chose to do so the Germans could outnumber British fighters by about two to one, and much of Fighter Command's tactical advantage sprang from its system of early warning and control, which in turn hinged on the vulnerable radar stations. Goering never fully grasped their importance, and though Kesselring and Sperrle (commanders of *Luftflotten 2* and *3*) did attack them from time to time, there was no concerted plan for doing so.

Nor did Goering's decision to use more fighters to escort bombers improve matters. While visiting his aircrew he asked them just what they needed to beat the RAF. Major Adolf Galland, a fighter group commander who was to achieve 103 victories in combat, replied that re-equipping his squadrons with Spitfires would help. He was not being entirely facetious, for if the Me 109 had the edge in the 'free-hunting' fighter sweeps at which Galland excelled, the slower and more manoeuvrable Spitfire might have been better for escort duties.

On 16 August Kesselring and Sperrle pushed home more attacks, hitting the radar station at Ventnor yet again and inflicting severe damage on the airfield at Tangmere, near Chichester, where 14 aircraft were caught on the ground. Other airfields were also hit, and 48 training aircraft were destroyed at Brize Norton in Oxfordshire. After a day's respite the *Luftwaffe* struck again, hitting more airfields but losing 71 aircraft in the process. Goering's first attempt to achieve air superiority over southern England had conspicuously failed.

Night Bombing Begins
On 19 August Goering decided on a change of tactics. Targets like airfields, which the British would have no option but to defend, would be

attacked by smaller concentrations of bombers with powerful escorts. The remaining bombers would mount sporadic, unescorted raids at night or in bad weather to keep the defenders fully stretched. *Luftflotte* commanders were ordered to prepare for attacks on cities, but not to launch them without specific orders. In all, this was a much wiser policy, and had Fighter Command been as close to collapse as Goering believed it might very well have worked.

Bad weather delayed resumption of the fighting till 24 August, when Kesselring, now heavily reinforced, had some 1000 aircraft available against Air Vice-Marshal Park's 200 of No. 11 Group. The weight of numbers told, and Dowding's fighters found it hard to get at German bombers with their close escorts and top cover. Manston, defended by outclassed Defiant fighters, was so badly damaged that it had to be abandoned as a permanent base, and bombers also managed to reach Hornchurch and North Weald. Portsmouth was hard hit, though most of the bombs aimed at the dockyard fell on the city.

That night bombers ranged widely across England and Wales, and in the process several bomber crews, with little idea of their whereabouts, bombed London. Goering was furious, for attacks on London were strictly prohibited. 'An immediate report is required identifying those crews who dropped bombs within the perimeter of London,' he thundered. '*Luftwaffe* High Command will itself undertake the punishment of each aircraft captain involved. They will be posted to infantry regiments.' Damage was relatively light: nine people were killed, 58 injured, and 100 inhabitants of Bethnal Green were rendered homeless. Churchill had already declared that if London was hit 'it seems very important to be able to return the compliment the next day upon Berlin', and on the night of 25 August Bomber Command mounted its first attack on the German capital, paving the way for further escalation.

On 25/26 August the pattern of raids was much the same, with heavily escorted bombers attacking airfields. The pressure helped generate friction between Nos. 11 and 12 Groups. Leigh-Mallory's aircraft were often ordered south to guard 11 Group's airfields, and on 26 August their failure to intercept a raid on Debden caused resentment. There was also a dispute over tactics. While the basic *Luftwaffe* tactical unit was the *gruppe* of 30 aircraft, that of the RAF was the 12-aircraft squadron. In the early stages of the battle uncertainty over the strength of incoming raids and the short warning time meant that squadrons were sent off individually, and it took time for multi-squadron operations to be mounted. Eventually No. 12 Group created the 'Big Wing' of five fighter squadrons, based at Duxford, near Cambridge. The scheme remained controversial. Its

THE GERMAN NIGHT OFFENSIVE
September 1940–May 1941

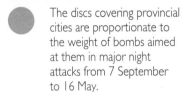 The discs covering provincial cities are proportionate to the weight of bombs aimed at them in major night attacks from 7 September to 16 May.

 The lighter circle around London shows the weight of bombs aimed at the capital in major night attacks during that period; the darker disc, the weight aimed from 14 November onwards.

0	50	100 Miles
0	50	100 Kms

Atlantic Ocean

Bel

N
W   E
S

North Sea

ock•   Glasgow•

R. Clyde

R. Tyne   •Newcastle-upon-Tyne

R. Tees

sh Sea

R. Humber   •Hull

Liverpool•   Manchester•

Birkenhead   •Sheffield

R. Dee

R. Severn   •Nottingham

Birmingham•

•Coventry

R. Thames   LONDON■

Cardiff•   •Bristol

Southampton•   •Portsmouth

Plymouth•
Devonport•

English Channel

advocates, like Squadron Leader Douglas Bader, who had returned to flying after losing both legs in an accident in 1931, argued that simultaneous attack by many aircraft was more effective, but opponents pointed out that it took a long time to get a 'Big Wing' into the air.

Goering's change of tactics had resulted in the *Luftwaffe* losing 99 aircraft to the RAF's 69 in three days of fighting, encouraging him to believe that he might yet achieve the 'specially favourable initial situation' upon which Sealion depended. On 29 August, after another satisfactory exchange on the previous day, Kesselring's fighter commander reported that he had achieved 'unlimited fighter superiority', and this note of confidence helped persuade Hitler to agree to postpone his decision on Sealion till 10 September with a view to mounting the invasion 11 days later.

In the meantime Sperrle was authorized to mount night attacks on Liverpool, and General Stumpff's *Luftflotte 5* joined in with raids on Tyneside and Hartlepool. The results were so derisory that it was never clear to the defenders what the attacks were trying to achieve. They did, however, show that Fighter Command could do little against night attack: indeed, Dowding had already warned that without special equipment he could hope for nothing more than 'the occasional fortunate encounter'.

The daylight battle followed the now-familiar pattern of well-escorted raids on airfields, with increasing damage to No. 11 Group's bases and a rate of exchange which reflected the difficulty of breaking through to reach the bombers. The key sector airfield of Biggin Hill was hard hit, its operations room destroyed and two of its three squadrons withdrawn, and a continuation of such attacks would have made it impossible for Park to defend London from airfields south of the capital. Although the rate of exchange between 30 August and 6 September, at 185 to 225, still favoured Fighter Command, Dowding knew that his tired pilots could not shoulder the burden much longer.

Thanks to Goering they did not have to. On 4 and 6 September some raids were directed, not against Park's crucial airfields, but against aircraft factories, a reflection of Goering's failure to grasp the essentials of the campaign. On 2 September he issued a new directive shifting the weight of the *Luftwaffe*'s attacks from airfields to cities. He was influenced by Hitler's desire to punish Britain for the RAF's raid on Berlin on 25 August, and also felt that, in order to meet attacks on London, Dowding would be forced to throw in what the Germans believed were his last reserves.

The Bombing of London Begins
London was to be bombed round the clock, *Luftflotte 2* attacking by day and *Luftflotte 3* by night. Although Hitler, in an address at the *Sportpalast*

in Berlin on 4 September, had announced that the *Luftwaffe* would now reply to British provocation – 'If they declare that they will attack our cities on a large scale, we will erase theirs!' – he was reluctant to order wholesale bombing of civilian targets. Goering's chief of staff argued in favour of striking residential areas in order to provoke mass panic, but Hitler believed that attacks on military and economic targets were more effective. In practice it mattered little, for at this stage in the war bombing was so inaccurate that attacks directed against military targets would inevitably cause damage across a wide area around them.

The Germans were doing their best to improve the accuracy of their bombing with radio navigation aids. *Knickebein* used narrow radio beams, originating in Occupied Europe, which were set to intersect over a

A Heinkel 111 over Wapping on the evening of 7 September 1940, 'Black Saturday'. This area, with the characteristic loop of the Thames, was known to the Germans as *Zielraum* (target area) G. Bomber crews were given specific targets like docks or gasworks and attacked them if visibility permitted: otherwise they simply bombed a designated target area.

target. The more sophisticated *X-Gerät,* first used in mid-November, also employed signals which crossed the bomber's path en route to the target, enabling bomb-aimers to work out the time at which their bombs should be released. A combination of deciphering at Bletchley Park, which produced ULTRA (above even Top Secret) intelligence from German high-level communications, the interrogation of captured aircrew, and painstaking work by Dr R. V. Jones, head of scientific intelligence in the Air Ministry, enabled the British to learn the secrets of these radio aids. *Knickebein* could be 'bent' or jammed, and the location of the beams gave advance warning of a raid, sometimes enabling fighters to be positioned to intercept it.

'Black Saturday', 7 September, was the first day of the offensive against London. There were minor attacks on Dover and Hawkinge in the morning. In the afternoon growing numbers of German aircraft formed up south of Cap Gris Nez, where Goering and a galaxy of senior *Luftwaffe* officers had assembled to watch the attack. Just after 4.15 almost 1,000 aircraft, stacked up at heights from 14,000 (4270 m) to 23,000 feet (7000 m), crossed the coast. Twenty British squadrons went up to meet them, bringing about the largest aerial battle yet seen.

There was no stopping the bombers, which pressed home their attack and dropped 300 tons (305 tonnes) of high explosive on London. About 2000 civilians were killed or seriously injured, and wide areas of warehouses and factories in the East End were soon ablaze. Sub-Officer Cyril Demarne's fire station was in West Ham, in the epicentre of the attack.

Flames erupted from the great factories and warehouses lining the River Thames from Woolwich to Tower Bridge. In the crowded dockland streets, massive warehouses and tiny dwellings alike came crashing down under the impact of high explosive, burying their occupants and any luckless passer-by...

Two hundred acres of tall timber stacks blazed out of control in the Surrey Commercial Docks. The rum quay buildings in West India Docks, alight from end to end, gushed flaming spirit from their doors. An army of rats ran from a burning Silvertown soap works...

When the bombers came back after dusk they needed no navigational aids: they were guided by the blazing East End and fires downstream at Thameshaven. They dropped another 300 tons (305 tonnes) of explosive and thousands of smaller incendiary bombs, and when the last of them left, before dawn on 8 September, London was still burning, with three of its main-line railway termini closed. 'Londoners emerged from their shelters to face scenes of devastation,' recalled fire officer Cyril

Thousands of Londoners spent the nights of the Blitz sleeping – or reading, chatting and playing cards – in the Underground The practice was not encouraged at first, but, recognizing that it was impossible to keep people out, the authorities did what they could to make things more comfortable. This crowded platform is at Elephant and Castle. Even the Underground was not totally safe: there were occasional accidents, and at least two stations, Bank and Balham, received direct hits.

Demarne. 'They were faced for the first time by problems that would confront them for fifty-seven mornings in succession.'

Thousands of London's children had been evacuated to the country-side on the outbreak of war. Despite official attempts to ensure that they remained in comparative safety, many had returned by the time the Blitz began. A study based on the Government's Mass Observation concluded:

Of those who stayed put with their parents, a few were continuously nervous, and a few constantly exhilarated. The greater part adjusted as well as their parents or mildly better. At no stage did they present a special problem as compared, say, with old ladies, or stray pets.

Fighter Command's failure to prevent the bombers from reaching London on 7 September placed Dowding under pressure to ensure that his most experienced squadrons were available for the capital's defence. When the Germans came again in strength, on the afternoon of 9 September, few of them were able to reach London, and they lost 28 aircraft to the RAF's 19. The battle swung in favour of the Germans again two days later. Bombs fell in the grounds of Buckingham Palace, and after another more dam-aging raid on the palace on 13 September the Queen remarked: 'I'm glad we've been bombed. It makes me feel I can look the East End in the face.' For the next two days losses were roughly equal and bombers were able to reach their targets. It seemed very much as though the *Luftwaffe* had the edge at last.

The Climax of the Battle of Britain
Sunday 15 September dawned fine, but soon became cloudy. Basil Collier catches the almost Agincourt-like mood of preparation:

At Park's sector stations and their forward aerodromes and satellites from the Sandlings to west Sussex, the pilots who would bear the burden of the daylight fighting were up early. At Debden and Martlesham on the borders of Suffolk and Essex, at North Weald in Epping Forest, at Hornchurch above Erith Reach, at Northolt and Hendon in the northern suburbs, at Croydon, Biggin Hill and Kenley, at Tangmere and Westhampnett below the hanging woods of Lavant Down, veterans of twenty-five began to move at dawn from messes and billets to dispersal huts.

Kesselring intended to hurl his full strength against London in two attacks, and the first of them reached the English coast at 11.30 that morning. Park already had 11 of his 21 Hurricane and Spitfire squadrons airborne to meet the bombers, which were mercilessly harried on their way to London. There the Duxford Wing joined in, though views on its effectiveness varied. After a brief pause the second wave rolled in, and it too was met as it approached. Squadron Leader Bob Stanford Tuck, newly promoted and given his own squadron, tells how:

We found a big bunch of mixed bombers, flying in formations of anything from thirty to sixty, with escorting fighters above them. As I led my new squadron in, I saw three of these parties nearing London. As the boys waded into the bombers, I went for some of the fighters. I picked off an Me 110 which I shot down over Barking, and one of his pals nearly got his own back when he put a bullet through my windscreen.

Twenty-six of Fighter Command's aircraft were shot down that day, but The *Luftwaffe* lost a total of 60 – not all to British guns and fighters – and others struggled back across the Channel with dead and wounded crewmen aboard. Few German bomber crews now believed bland assertions that it would never be possible to prevent the occasional fighter from appearing. The attainment of air superiority seemed as far away as ever, and on 17 September Hitler postponed Sealion until further notice: the Battle of Britain had been won.

The Blitz Goes On
The effective cancellation of Sealion changed the tempo of the fighting but did not end it. Goering ordered that the night bombing of London would continue, 'harassing attacks' would be launched in daylight, and pressure on aircraft factories would be stepped up. The Italian Air Force belatedly joined the battle on 25 October, when 16 of its bombers attacked Harwich. On 11 November 40 CR 42 biplanes escorted 10 bombers in another attack on Harwich, and although the fighters defended their charges bravely they were hopelessly outclassed: three bombers and three fighters were shot down without loss to the British, and daylight bombing raids were abandoned. A final daylight Italian fighter sweep on 23 November was also driven off with loss.

Two days later Dowding, who had remained on duty at the personal request of the Chief of the Air Staff despite being over the age limit for retirement, slipped into civilian life and was replaced by Air Marshal W. S. Douglas. The new Commander-in-Chief declared that 'it does not matter where the enemy is shot down provided he is shot down in large numbers', and made arrangements to set up more 'Big Wings'. However the Germans had suspended the daylight attacks which justified the use of large wings, and the task immediately facing Douglas was to deal with the night bomber offensive.

Steps were taken to form more night-fighter squadrons, to equip airfields with special equipment for night flying, and to produce more radar sets capable of permitting ground controllers to direct a night-fighter onto its target or, better still, to be fitted in aircraft. Other expedients were adopted, such as drifting balloons containing explosive charges; and a variety of deception measures were designed to encourage bombers to attack empty countryside.

Hardly any of General Pile's anti-aircraft guns were equipped with fire-control radar, and few had been able to fire during the first raids on London. By 11 September, though, there were some 200 guns defending the capital. They produced a vigorous barrage as soon as the raiders appeared, and searchlights lit up the sky. All this had little practical effect beyond forcing the attackers to remain high, but it was a fillip for civilian morale to feel that Britain was hitting back.

Britain was certainly being hit. London was bombed night after night, and during the second week in October there were almost 1400 killed in the capital. Terrible damage was caused by 2200 lb (1000 kg) parachute mines, provoking Churchill to order ministries that: 'No disclosure should be made of the severity of effect, in the public estimation, of these mines.'

One six-year-old girl described the weapon's effect with dreadful simplicity. 'There was a parachute and a landmine,' she said. 'The parachute was stuck on the school railings and a man pulled the parachute and the school blew up to pieces and so did the man.'

On the bright moonlit night of 15 October London was heavily bombed, while other raiders struck Birmingham and Bristol. Much of London's railway network was put out of action and both Becton Gas Works and Battersea Power Station were hit. There were more than 900 fires – firefighting was badly disrupted by ruptured mains – whose glare could be seen in mid-Channel by German aircrew. Although the RAF sent up 41 fighters, only one bomber was shot down.

In November London gained a brief respite, albeit at the expense of provincial cities like Birmingham, Bristol, Liverpool, Plymouth and Southampton. On the night of 13/14 November X-Gerät was used for the first time, against Coventry. Although Bletchley Park had deciphered messages announcing that a large operation was planned, it was not immediately clear what its targets were to be. The radio guidance beams were found to intersect over Coventry on the afternoon of 13 November, but attempts to jam them failed and, although Fighter Command was warned of the attack, 449 of the 509 bombers dispatched to Coventry reached it. Twelve armaments factories were destroyed: so too was the city's fourteenth-century cathedral. There is little real evidence for the assertion that Coventry was sacrificed to protect the security of ULTRA, though its ravaging probably did accelerate the planned replacement of Dowding.

On the night of 29/30 December London suffered the most spectacular attack of the Blitz. The square mile of the City was hit by a hail of incendiaries which caused six enormous fires, destroying the Guildhall and eight Wren churches. St Paul's Cathedral escaped by a miracle. One eyewitness found it 'a hauntingly beautiful picture' as buildings collapsed to reveal Wren's masterpiece rising in its glory amongst the smoke and flames. Because the Thames was low, fireboats could do little to help, and burst water mains impeded the work of their land-based colleagues. Casualties were lighter than might have been expected, possibly because it was a Sunday night, and the City was virtually empty, but 163 people were killed (16 firemen amongst them) and another 509 injured.

The survival of Sir Christopher Wren's masterpiece, St Paul's Cathedral, was little short of miraculous. On the night of 29/30 December, when much of the City of London burned, it was ringed by fires and hit by an incendiary bomb, but damage was slight. The image of the Cathedral's great dome rising proudly from the debris around it came to typify the spirit of London in the Blitz.

Anti-aircraft guns fired 4000 rounds that night and 29 aircraft took off to intercept the bombers, but none were shot down. Indeed, the night bombing raids of 1940–41 were cheap for the *Luftwaffe*. However the strain of operating in difficult weather and with tired crews, together with the need to repair and overhaul heavily used aircraft, helped reduce the combat strength of *Luftflotten 2* and *3* from about 800 bombers in September 1940 to 551 on 4 January 1941. In the first three months of 1941 night-fighters and anti-aircraft guns became somewhat more effective, leading the official history to suggest that 'while the menace of the night-offensive had not yet been overcome, at least its measure had been taken.'

The End of the Blitz
The campaign was already drawing to a close. On 6 February 1941, prompted by Grand Admiral Raeder, Commander-in-Chief of the Navy, Hitler gave attacks on ports the highest priority, and between February and May 46 raids were mounted on ports in England, Wales, Scotland and Northern Ireland, and only seven against the cities of London, Birmingham, Coventry and Nottingham. Some of these later raids were exceptionally heavy: Belfast, for example, was hit by 400 tons (406 tonnes) of high explosives and thousands of incendiaries in just two nights. But Hitler now had other priorities. His bomber squadrons were diverted to take part in the campaign in the Balkans and then shifted eastwards on a massive scale to prepare for Hitler's assault on the Soviet Union in June. The Blitz ended in mid-May, and Britain licked her wounds.

Materially these were serious. More than 43,000 civilians had been killed, 139,000 injured and tens of thousands made homeless. Great tracts of Britain's ancient cities and thriving industrial centres had been devastated. Port facilities and factories had been destroyed, transport severely interrupted and public utilities badly mauled. Resources of manpower and equipment, many of which could have been used elsewhere, had been diverted to military and civil defence. All this had been achieved for a cost of about 600 German bombers.

Yet the Blitz had not broken British will to resist. The American reporter Quentin Reynolds told his listeners:

I have watched the people of London live and die ever since death in its most ghastly garb began to come here as a nightly visitor… It is true that the Nazis will be over again tomorrow night and the night after that and every night. They will drop thousands of bombs and they'll destroy hundreds of buildings and they'll

kill thousands of people. But a bomb has its limitations. It can only destroy buildings and kill people. It cannot kill the unconquerable spirit and courage of the
people of London.

Of course it was not that simple. The government's own Mass Observation reports revealed that sometimes even the Londoners lost their
cheerfulness, and in smaller cities, where the concentration of bombing
was far greater, public morale became a matter of concern.

Quentin Reynolds lived through the London Blitz, but admitted:
'Nothing I had seen prepared me for the sight of Plymouth.' In April 1941
this West Country port was hit by over a hundred bombers a night for five
nights: 1000 of her citizens were killed and another 40,000 made homeless. Lady Astor, one of the local MPs, was furious that the official report
did so little justice to the city's sufferings: 'the raid did not last long, but
in one of the towns…a number of fires were started, some of them large.'

Following her complaint, a Regional Information Officer visited
Plymouth to compile a report. He admitted that 'the terrible strain and
steady casualties' had sapped the morale of the volunteer firemen. 'The
centre of both Plymouth and Devonport have been totally destroyed,' he
wrote, 'and the damage is in millions… It would be wrong to assume that
the people are broken. Equally it would be suicidal to ignore the implica-
tions and symptoms of the actual state of affairs…'

Herbert Morrison, the Minister for Home Security, recognized that
'people cannot stand this intensive bombing indefinitely and sooner or
later the morale of other towns will go even as Plymouth's has gone'.
Liverpool, too, was hard hit, and a Mass Observation report of May
noted: 'The general feeling – it is difficult exactly to express it, but the
residents spoken to felt it too – that there was no power or drive left in
Liverpool.' Britain was fortunate that the *Luftwaffe* was not better
equipped for strategic bombing, and that its commanders applied the
power they had in a less than focused way.

Air Chief Marshal Arthur Harris of Bomber Command was not slow
to learn the lessons of the Blitz. The raid on Coventry, he wrote, served to
'teach us the principle of concentration, the principle of starting so many
fires at the same time that no fire fighting services, however efficiently
and quickly they were reinforced by the fire brigades of other towns,
could get them under control.' One night (probably 29 December 1940)
he stood on the Air Ministry roof with Sir Charles Portal, Chief of the Air
Staff, and 'watched the old city in flames…with St Paul's standing out in
the midst of an ocean of fire'. As they turned to go, Harris said: 'Well,
they are sowing the wind'.

A View of the Field

As a boy I made frequent visits to a London which still had large, empty bomb sites, relics not only of the Blitz proper but also of the 'Little Blitz' of January-March 1944, a reprisal for the bombing of Germany, and of the V1 (flying bomb) and V2 (long-range rocket) campaign of 1944–45. These have all disappeared, and the buildings which have filled them are often dreary and soulless. The first bomb to fall on the City of London is commemorated by a plaque on St Giles' Church, off Wood Street, in the Barbican, an area badly damaged during the Blitz. St Clement Danes in the Strand was destroyed by fire on 10 May 1941, but restored and, in 1958, re-dedicated to the memory of the RAF, Commonwealth and Allied air forces. The ruins of St Michael's Cathedral in Coventry were preserved when the new cathedral was built in 1954-62, and a statue showing St Michael triumphing over the devil stands on the steps to the porch linking the old and new cathedrals.

Graves and Cemeteries
Some German aircrew killed during the Battle of Britain and the Blitz are buried in civilian cemeteries, but the majority now rest in the German military cemetery at Cannock Chase, Staffordshire. Of the civilians killed in the Blitz, some were buried in individual marked graves, and others, like Fred and Dorothy Gill, the first civilians killed on the mainland, who perished when a mine-laying Heinkel crashed onto their house in Clacton-on-Sea in May 1940, have unmarked graves in town cemeteries.

There are a number of mass graves, like that in Abney Park Cemetery, Stoke Newington, the result of a direct hit on a block of flats in Coronation Avenue. A bomb brought the building down onto the shelter beneath it, and those who survived the explosion and fall of debris were drowned by water and effluent which poured into the shelter from fractured pipes. It took rescue services a week to remove the bodies.

The dead of the Blitz are listed in a multi-volume Book of Remembrance in Westminster Abbey, in an alcove on the right just inside the west door: a page is turned each day. It underscores the sheer capriciousness of death from the sky. There are infants and grandparents, firemen and air raid wardens, dockers from the East End and the gilded youth of Mayfair. The RAF chapel, at the Abbey's east end, contains its own Book of Remembrance for the dead of the RAF, reminding us of the part played in the Battle of Britain by Czech and Polish pilots. A small hole, low down in the abbey wall at the far left-hand end of the chapel, is bomb-damage, deliberately glazed but not blocked up.

Museums

The Imperial War Museum's Blitz Experience, a reconstruction of a London street and air-raid shelter, captures the mood of the Blitz very well. The Royal Air Force Museum at Hendon has a Battle of Britain Hall which contains a series of tableaux whose life-size figures represent various aspects of the Blitz, amongst them an East End street scene, a 3.7inch gun site and a radar station. Upstairs, not far from figures of Dowding and Goering, is a reconstruction of No. 11 Group's operations room. The aircraft exhibited include most of the types that participated in the Battle of Britain and the Blitz. They include, most poignantly, the remains of a Hurricane shot down on 31 August but not recovered till 1973.

The Airfields of 1940

The airfields of 1940 have suffered a variety of fates. Duxford, near Cambridge, which housed the first of the 'Big Wings', is now a satellite of the Imperial War Museum. It is a unique combination: a historical airfield which houses Europe's largest and most popular aviation museum. History is quite literally in the air, for some 40 of its 140 or so aircraft, including Spitfires, Hurricanes and Messerschmitts, still fly from time to time. The sector operations room has been carefully restored to its September 1940 condition. Remove the parked cars and the airfield reverts to its Second World War appearance.

A few airfields, like Manston and Middle Wallop, are still used by the services. Some house civilian flying clubs, and others have disappeared altogether. The M11 has clipped the western edge off North Weald, but its hangars still remain. There is an aviation museum at Tangmere, just east of Chichester, open during the summer months. The front-line fighter base at Hawkinge, north of Folkestone, now houses the Kent Battle of Britain Museum, and both RAF and *Luftwaffe* aircrew are buried in Folkestone New Cemetery, on the edge of the airfield. Only 3 miles (5 km) to its south the Battle of Britain Memorial looks out across the Channel, that moat crossed by Duke William almost nine hundred years before Spitfires and Messerschmitts laced the skies above it with their vapour trails.

Further Reading

This is in no sense a comprehensive bibliography but is a short list intended as a guide for those who wish to read further.

HASTINGS
Christopher Gravett crams a scholarly appreciation into the well-illustrated Osprey Military Campaign Series booklet *Hastings 1066* (London 1992).Stephen Morillo *The Battle of Hastings* (Woodbridge, Suffolk 1996) not only contains major sources such as William of Poitiers, William of Jumièges and *The Anglo-Saxon Chronicle*, but also a number of scholarly interpretations including a good piece on William by John Gillingham. David C. Douglas *William the Conqueror* (London 1983) is essential reading. *The English Warrior: From the Earliest Times to 1066* by Stephen Pollington (London 1996) is a fine study of the men who fought for Harold, and Christopher Gravett *The Norman Knight* (London 1993) in the Osprey Warrior series has good colour plates by Christa Hook. Although Denis Butler *1066: The Story of a Year* (London 1966) was written without access to modern historiography, it cracks along in style and makes good use of primary sources including Snorri Sturlasson's *Heimskringla*.

BOSWORTH
For general surveys see John Gillingham *The Wars of the Roses: Peace and Conflict in Fifteenth-Century England* (London 1981), A. Goodman *The Wars of the Roses: Military Activity and English Society 1452–97*, and Charles Ross *The Wars of the Roses* (London 1976). Weapons and equipment are examined in the Osprey Men-at-Arms series booklet *The Wars of the Roses* by Terence Wise (London 1983). In *Battles in Britain 1066–1746* Glen Lyndon Dodds discusses rival sitings of the battlefield, concluding that Peter J. Foss *The Field of Redemore: The Battle of Bosworth 1485* (London 1990) is right to challenge the traditional location. Michael Bennett reaches a similar conclusion in a postscript to the second edition of *The Battle of Bosworth* (Stroud 1985, 1993), whose references are especially helpful. D. T. Williams' booklet *The Battle of Bosworth Field*, published by Leicestershire County Council, valiantly defends the traditional site. All these books on the battle made good use of contemporaries like Polydore Vergil and Jean Molinet. Much has been written about Richard: I have much time for Charles Ross *Richard III* (London 1981).

NASEBY
Glenn Foard *Naseby: The Decisive Campaign* (Whitstable 1995) outclasses all previous accounts by attention to topographical detail and incorporation of the results of metal-detector work: it is now the starting point for any serious study. Maurice Ashley *The Battle of Naseby and the Fall of King Charles* (London 1992) is an accessible, well-illustrated account. Christopher Hibbert *Cavaliers and Roundheads* (London 1993) is one of the best of the many general studies of the war. For the soldiers' view see Charles Carlton *Going to the Wars: The Experience of the British Civil Wars 1638–1651*(London 1992). Professor Carlton has also written a creditable biography of Charles I (London 1983). The opposing cavalry commanders are examined in Antonia Fraser *Cromwell: Our Chief of Men*

(London 1973) and F. Kitson *Prince Rupert: Portrait of a Soldier* (London 1994). Ian Gentles *The New Model Army* (London 1992) is the best study of the instrument of Parliamentarian victory.

THE BOYNE
J. G. Sims *Jacobite Ireland* (London 1969) remains the essential foundation, and John Childs *The British Army of William III* (Manchester 1987) provides the military background. The battle is covered succinctly in G. A. Hayes-McCoy *Irish Battles* (London 1969), and at greater length in Peter Berresford Ellis *The Boyne Water* (London 1976) and Robert Shepherd *Ireland's Fate: The Boyne and After* (London 1990). Some of the best work on the war is to be found in articles in *The Irish Sword*, Journal of the Military History Society of Ireland. Of particular value are Diarmuid and Harman Murtagh 'The Irish Jacobite Army 1689–91', Donal O'Carroll 'An indifferent good post: the Battlefield of the Boyne', Peter Harrington 'Images of the Boyne', Kenneth Ferguson 'The organisation of King William's army in Ireland' all in the Winter 1990 edition, together with J. G. Sims 'Eye-Witnesses of the Boyne' (Summer 1963) and Sheila Mulloy 'French Eye-Witnesses of the Boyne' (Winter 1982). The dashing Patrick Sarsfield has the biography he deserves in Piers Wauchope *Patrick Sarsfield and the Williamite War* (Dublin 1992).

DUNKIRK
The official history, L. F. Ellis *The War in France and Flanders 1939–40* (London 1953) is a good starting point and Brian Bond *France and Belgium 1939–40* (London 1975) is a succinct yet scholarly account. Of the many books on Dunkirk itself, David Divine *The Nine Days of Dunkirk* (London 1959) remains a classic, and Walter Lord *The Miracle of Dunkirk* (London 1982) is the best modern account. General Pownall's diaries were edited by Brian Bond as *Chief of Staff: The Diaries of Lieutenant-General Sir Henry Pownall* (2 vols, London 1972). J. R. Colville *Man of Valour: Field-Marshal Lord Gort VC* (London 1972) is a solid biography of the BEF's commander-in-chief. Of the many personal accounts of the campaign I particularly like John Horsfall *Say Not The Struggle* (Kineton 1977) and Airey Neave *The Flames of Calais* (London 1972).

THE BLITZ
The official history, Basil Collier *The Defence of the United Kingdom* (London 1957) puts the Blitz into its wider context, and the same author's *The Battle of Britain* (London 1962) remains useful. For Operation Sealion see Peter Schenck *The Invasion of England 1940* (London 1990) and Michael Glover *Invasion Scare 1940* (London 1990). The Blitz itself is the subject of Winston G. Ramsey (Ed) *The Blitz: Then and Now*, a comprehensive three-volume study which catalogues events day-by-day and includes copious research on crashed aircraft and their crews as well as specialist articles and eyewitness accounts. Volume II (London 1988) deals with the period September 1940–May 1941. Tom Harrison *Living Through the Blitz* (London 1976) is based on the government's mass observation reports, and Robert Westall *Children of the Blitz* (London 1985) is an illustrated compendium of children's accounts.

Index